5,000 AWESOME FACTS
(About Animals!)

NATIONAL GEOGRAPHIC

WASHINGTON, D.C.

»CONTENTS

A VEILED CHAMELEON CAN ACCELERATE ITS STICKY TONGUE AS FAST AS A JET PLANE TO CAPTURE PREY.

»15 HAIR-RAISING FACTS

1
Sea otters have **water-repellent** fur.

2
Domestic sheep's wool **never stops growing.**

3
Porcupine quills are actually **large, stiff hairs.**

4. Like other mammals, **whales have hair.** It's only visible in some species.

5
The musk ox has the **longest fur** in the world. It can reach nearly **40 inches** (100 cm) in length.

6. Cats can walk through a **completely dark room** by using their **whiskers to sense air currents** that bounce off objects around them.

7. A **skunk's stripes** warn potential attackers of its smelly spray.

8. Catfish can **taste with their "whiskers."**

9. Manatees use hairs on their bodies as **antennae to detect information** about what's around them in murky water.

10
One particular area of **a sea lion's brain** takes in information from **each individual whisker.**

11. Chinchilla fur is **30 times softer** than human hair.

12. "Skinny pigs" are a breed of mostly **hairless guinea pigs.**

13
The golden lion tamarin gets its **name from its mane,** which resembles the big cat's.

14
Cheetah cubs **follow their mother's striped tail** through the tall grass.

15
Honeybees have **three million hairs** on their bodies, each exactly spaced to fit one grain of pollen.

1. Corals are sometimes mistaken for **rocks or plants—** but **they're actually animals.**

2. Coral reefs cover **less than one percent of the ocean floor,** but are nicknamed the **"rainforests of the sea"** because they are home to about **25 percent of all marine species.**

3. **Male seahorses** give birth—sometimes to **2,000 babies** at once!

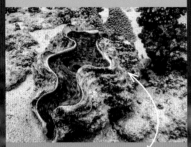

4. **Giant clams,** the largest mollusks on Earth, can weigh more than **440 pounds (200 kg),** about as much as a gorilla.

5. **Peacock mantis shrimps** are so unusual that experts call them the **"shrimp from Mars."**

6. Even though **pufferfish contain a deadly toxin,** their meat is considered a **delicacy in Japan.**

7. **Red lionfish** sting with **18 needlelike,** venom-filled fins.

8. **Green sea turtles** get their name from **a layer of green fat under their skin,** a result of their **marine plant diet.**

9. Scientists think that **pufferfish** get their **toxin from toxin-making bacteria** in their diet.

10. Some **sea sponges** can **filter an amount of water** that totals **100,000 times their size** in a single day.

11. **An anemone** keeps the **clownfish that live inside it safe from predators,** and the swimming clownfish **circulate oxygen-rich water** to their host.

12. **A frogfish lures prey** using a **spine on its forehead** that works like **bait on a fishing rod**—it's even **shaped like a worm,** small fish, or shrimp.

13. **Whitetip reef sharks** gather in **caves** and **pile on top of each other in huge groups.**

14. All **clownfish** are **born male.**

15. When an **anemone's tentacles** sense **passing prey,** they **fire a tiny, venomous "harpoon"** into their victim.

16. A species of **hermit crab** discovered in 2017 lives inside pieces of coral, **wearing them like a backpack.**

17. **The Great Barrier Reef** is about **500,000 years old.**

18. At night, **a butterflyfish's bright colors fade** to help it **hide from predators.**

19. The venom of the **stonefish, the world's most venomous fish,** can kill an adult human in less than an hour.

20. Some moray eels have two sets of jaws. The second set is hidden inside their throats.

21. **Parrotfish wrap their bodies in a cocoon** made of mucus to **protect** themselves from **parasites while they sleep.**

22. One species of **sea snake pulls oxygen** out of the water through a hole in the **top of its head.**

23. **Algae lives inside coral,** giving coral **oxygen** and its **bright colors** and removing its wastes.

24. **Seahorses** don't **have stomachs.**

25. **Sea snakes** are closely **related to cobras.**

26. **The hairy frogfish** is covered with thousands of **hairlike spines** that help the **fish blend in with coral and seaweed.**

27. **Peacock mantis shrimps** can **punch hard enough** to **split a human's fingers** to the bone.

28. **Seahorses** use their long snouts like vacuum cleaners to suck up food.

29. Some **coral reef fish** visit **"cleaning stations"** where **certain shrimps** and other creatures **eat parasites** off them.

30. **Male California mantis shrimps "growl"** to protect their territory.

31. **Fireworms** get their name from their **nasty sting.**

75 FACTS ABOUT CORAL REEF ANIMALS

32. Groupers are some of the **biggest fish** in coral reefs, weighing as much as **882 pounds (400 kg).**

33. Surgeonfish get their name from the **sharp spines** on the top and bottom of their bodies.

34. Parrotfish eat coral, which they poop out as sand. A single large fish can make 1,000 pounds (450 kg) of sand a year.

35. Many of the world's beautiful **white sand beaches** are made of **parrotfish poop.**

36. The spaghetti worm's long tentacles **look like pasta.**

37. The female psychedelic **frogfish** wraps her fins around her eggs, **fanning and carrying** them until they hatch.

38. A sea snake has **a flattened tail** that it uses like an **oar to help it swim.**

39. **Giant moray eels** can be at least **eight feet (2.5 m) long.**

40. When **toxic seaweed** touches coral, the coral sends a chemical signal to **goby fish, which come** and **eat the seaweed.**

41. **Seahorses use their tails** to **hold onto corals, seagrasses,** or other stable objects so that the current doesn't **wash them away.**

42. Sea snakes may be able to stay underwater for **eight hours** or more.

43. Mandarinfish don't have scales—they are **covered** in a **stinky, thick mucus** instead.

44. The blue dragon, a nudibranch, eats **deadly Portuguese man-of-wars** and stores their venom in its body to **use for protection.**

45. The green moray eel is actually **dark blue** in color, but gets its green appearance from **a layer of slime that covers its body.**

46. Groupers and **moray eels** sometimes **team up to hunt.**

47. Groupers shake their heads back and forth and wave their fins to entice the **eels to join them.**

48. Australia's Great Barrier Reef is the **largest living structure** in the world.

49. Brittle stars may help corals recover from **oil spills by eating debris** that collects on their branches.

50. Humphead wrasse can be so enormous they're sometimes called **"elephants of the coral reef."**

51. Saltwater crocodiles, which usually **stay by the shore,** have occasionally been sighted **swimming in coral reefs.**

52. Experts think **pufferfish** developed the ability to **inflate to avoid predators** because they are slow and clumsy swimmers.

53. The **smooth trunkfish** has a triangle-shaped body.

54. When threatened, **the flying gurnard fish** opens its **winglike fins** to scare off attackers.

55. Some corals are **fluorescent.**

56. Lionfish herd smaller fish into confined areas and then swallow them with one gulp.

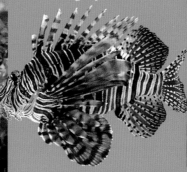

57. The lionfish is sometimes called the turkeyfish **because when viewed from the right angle,** its fins look like turkey feathers.

58. The dwarf seahorse is the **world's slowest-moving fish,** with a top speed of **five feet (1.5 m) an hour.**

59. Thirty species of dolphins and whales visit the **Great Barrier Reef.**

60. Sea cucumbers defend themselves by **shooting their internal organs** out their behinds. (They grow back later.)

61. Pygmy seahorses only grow to **0.8 inch (2 cm) long**—about the size of a fingernail.

62. Seahorse couples dance together every morning.

63. The mudskipper is a fish that **walks on land near reefs** and **breathes air.**

64. When threatened, **a pufferfish gulps down a huge amount of water,** inflating its elastic stomach and **turning into a spiny ball.**

65. Corals are related to **jellyfish.**

66. Just one pufferfish has **enough toxin to kill 30 adult humans.**

67. Before **clownfish** make their home in an anemone, they perform **a "dance," gently touching its tentacles** with their bodies.

68. Blacktip reef sharks sometimes come together to **hunt in packs.** But they don't share the prey—**the first shark to catch the fish eats it.**

69. Giant clams can live for more than **100 years.**

70. The tentacles of **a lion's mane jelly** can be **longer than a blue whale.**

71. Sea cucumbers are in the same family as **sea stars and sea urchins.**

72. Sea sponges have no **heads, eyes, or brains.**

73. The potato cod is named for the **potato-shaped markings** on its body.

74. Cleaner shrimps swim **inside a fish's mouth** to clean its teeth.

75. Some species of **unicornfish** have **a spine that sticks out between their eyes.**

1
Rhino **horns** are **made of keratin,** the same substance that forms **your hair and nails.**

2
A black rhino's horn can be up to **four feet** (1.2 m) long—about the size of **an eight-year-old child.**

3
Native to Africa, the **black rhino** and the **white rhino** are both actually **gray in color.**

4
Some species of rhino have **two horns.** Others have **one horn.**

5
Rhinos have been on Earth for **50 million years.**

6
One extinct rhino species that lived about **30 million years** ago weighed more than **four elephants.**

7
Rhinos' closest living relatives are horses and piglike animals called **tapirs.**

8
The greater one-horned rhino has **thick folds** in its skin that make it look like it's **wearing armor.**

9
The **Javan rhino** drags a hind foot to **scratch the dirt,** which is a way to **communicate with other rhinos.**

10
The **longest rhino horn** ever measured was **4 feet 9 inches** (145 cm).

11
Rhinos use their horns to **break down branches** and dig up roots for food.

12
Sumatran rhinos are covered with hair; they're related to extinct woolly rhinos, which lived about **10,000 years ago.**

13
Rhino horns are **pointy** from rubbing them on the ground and **using them as weapons.**

14
The **white rhino** is the **second largest land mammal.**

15
Rhinos were once **common** in **North America.**

16
Birds called **oxpeckers ride on rhinos' backs,** eating ticks, flies—and rhino blood.

17
Male rhinos are called **bulls,** and females are called **cows.**

18
The Javan rhino might be the **rarest land mammal** in the world.

19
Rhinos have **small feet** for their **body size.**

35 SHARP FACTS ABOUT RHINOS

20
The rhinoceros gets its name from the **Greek words** for **nose (*rhino*)** and **horn (*ceros*)**.

21
Despite their huge size, **black rhinos can run at 40 miles an hour** (64 km/h)—about as fast as a horse!

22
Rhinos are **hunted for their horns** because some people mistakenly believe they have **healing powers.**

23
Because of their **poor vision,** rhinos will sometimes mistakenly charge at trees or boulders.

24
If a rhino's horn is broken, **it can grow back.**

25
Rhinos **soak in mud** to help protect themselves from **insect bites and sunburn.**

26
Rhinos make **poop piles called middens** that they use to **send messages** to other rhinos.

27
A group of rhinos is called **a crash**.

28
Rhinos eat all day and night **except for during the hottest part of the day,** when they rest.

29
Calves may stay with their mothers until they're **four years old.**

30
The **Sumatran rhino** is the smallest of the five living rhino species, weighing in at **1,100 to 2,200 pounds** (500–1,000 kg).

31
Rhinos make a *mmwonk* **sound when they're happy.**

32
About **50 percent of male black rhinos** and **30 percent of females** die from fighting other rhinos.

33
When walking, rhinos put most of **their weight on their toenails.**

34
Rhinoceroses **rarely hang out with each other;** they're mostly solitary.

35
A century ago, there were **half a million** rhinos in the world. Today, there are **fewer than 30,000.**

100 EYE-POPPING FACTS ABOUT ANIMAL VISION

Lyle's flying fox

1. Sharks and cats both have a reflective layer in their eyes that helps them see in the dark. 2. Earthworms don't have eyes, but they have cells that can sense light or darkness. 3. Owls have "binocular" vision similar to humans'—it makes objects appear three-dimensional. 4. The box jellyfish has 24 eyes. 5. Camels' four-inch (10-cm)-long eyelashes protect their eyes from blowing sand. 6. All insects have compound eyes, thousands of tiny light detectors that work together. 7. Most hamsters can blink only one eye at a time. 8. Pit vipers have an extra sense organ that "sees" prey by detecting its heat. 9. The four-eyed fish has

just two eyes, but they're divided in half, one part to see above the water and one part to see below. 10. Scallops have up to 200 eyes that line the rim of their shells. 11. An eagle's vision is about five times sharper than a human's. 12. Owls can't move their eyeballs. 13. Scorpions can have up to 12 eyes. 14. Mantis shrimps have up to 16 types of sensory cells for seeing color. (Humans have three.) 15. A tiny crustacean called *Paraphromina* has eyes that take up nearly half its body. 16. A dragonfly's compound eyes have about 30,000 lenses. 17. Dolphins sleep with one eye open. 18. The giant squid has the largest eye in the world. 19. Geckos' eyes are about 350 times more sensitive to light than humans'. 20. An ostrich's eye is bigger than its brain. 21. Dogs can't see green or red. 22. Tarsiers have the largest eyes for their body size of any mammal. 23. Polar bears have an extra membrane that covers their eyes to protect them from the sun's ultraviolet rays—just like built-in sunglasses. 24. Sharks might see some colors, probably bright ones like yellow. 25. Some lizards have a third eye underneath the skin on top of their heads. 26. Moths' eyes are covered with a water-repellent coating. 27. Some butterflies have spots on their wings that look like eyes. Experts think these "eyespots" may scare off or confuse predators. 28. A horse has a blind spot directly in front of its nose. 29. The giant guitarfish can pull its eyes 1.6 inches (4 cm) back into its head. 30. Chameleons can see nearly 360 degrees around themselves. 31. Leaf-tailed geckos' pupils have tiny pinholes that widen at night to let in more light when the geckos are hunting. 32. The ogre-faced spider grows a new eye-covering membrane every night. 33. Spookfish eyes use mirrorlike structures instead of lenses to focus light. 34. Starfish have an eye on the end of each arm—and they can have up to 50 arms! 35. Fossils show that marine animals called trilobites had highly developed eyes, providing these more than 500-million-year-old creatures with 360-degree vision. 36. A dragonfly's eyes cover almost its entire head. 37. Geckos lick their eyeballs to keep them clean. 38. Reindeer eyes turn gold in summer and blue in winter. 39. The cockeyed squid's left eye can be twice as big as its right eye. 40. Sea urchins may use the whole surface of their bodies as one big eye. 41. Bacteria can see. 42. Most spiders have eight eyes. 43. Birds can see ultraviolet light that is invisible to humans. 44. Sharks may not be able to see color. 45. The first organisms to have what resembled an eye lived around 550 million years ago. They had eyespots that could only determine light from dark. 46. Bees have five eyes. 47. A wedge-tailed eagle can spot a rabbit from thousands of feet in the air. 48. Orb spiders weave patterns into their webs that may be undetectable to insects but warn birds to stay away. 49. The oldest known animal to have color vision is a 300-million-year-old fish called *Acanthodes bridgei*. 50. Dragonflies can see about 300 images per second. (Our eyes see about 50 images per second.)

tokay gecko

51. Birds of prey can see about four to five times better than humans can.   52. Birds have special molecules in their eyes that allow them to "see" Earth's magnetic field. This may help them find their way when migrating.   53. Snakes can't close their eyes.   54. Frogs squeeze their eyeballs backward to help push food down their throats.   55. Some snails can grow their eyes back if they lose them.   56. Cats express contentment by blinking slowly.   57. Unlike other animals, mantis shrimps process visual information in the eyes, not in their brains.   58. Small mollusks called chitons have eyes made of rock crystal.   59. A manatee's eyes close in a circular motion, like a camera lens.   60. Mantis shrimps have pigments in their eyes that act like natural sunglasses.   61. When disturbed, red-eyed tree frogs may flash their brilliant red eyes to startle predators.   62. Most predators that hunt during the day have circular pupils.   63. Some birds, including ducks and gulls, can sleep with one eye open.   64. Flowers have patterns that are visible only to honeybees and other pollinators.   65. Using infrared sensing, snakes can "see" prey in the dark up to three feet (1 m) away.   66. Giant squid can see glowing trails of light left behind when sperm whales—their main predator—swim through bioluminescent plankton.   67. Dolphins have crescent-shaped pupils.   68. If our eyes were the size of a tarsier's, relative to our body, they would be as big as grapefruits.   69. In addition to their two main eyes, dragonflies have three other eyes called ocelli that specialize in sensing movement.   70. A shark can see about 10 times better than a human.   71. Birds use their left and right eyes for different tasks.   72. Each of a colossal squid's eyes has a built-in "headlight" called a photophore. This helps them see in the darkness of the deep sea.   73. Stalk-eyed flies can pump air into their eye stalks to make them longer.   74. Each of a mantis shrimp's eyes is divided into three sections, which move independently.   75. Goats' rectangular pupils increase their field of vision, helping them watch for predators.   76. Owls' eyes are not shaped like balls as most animals' eyes are; they are tube-shaped.   77. Most web-building spiders have poor eyesight.   78. Eyelids help keep eyes moist. Fish don't need them because they live in water.   79. Some frogs have heart-shaped pupils.   80. Bulls don't really get angry when they see the color red— they're color-blind.   81. The strawberry squid has just one glowing, enormous eye.   82. Some moles have skin that covers their eyes.   83. A camel's third eyelid closes sideways, wiping away sand like a windshield wiper.   84. Some birds' eyes weigh more than their brains.   85. Worker honeybees have about 5,500 lenses in each eye. (Humans have one.)   86. Pigeons can see 340 degrees around themselves.   87. A frog focuses its eyes by moving the lens backward and forward, like a camera.   88. Crocodiles can't focus their eyes well while underwater.   89. A hammerhead shark has an eye on each end of its wide head, which allows it to precisely judge the depth and distance of its prey.   90. The pupils of ambush predators like cats and crocodiles are vertical slits.   91. A goldfish has more sensitive color vision than a human.   92. Cuttlefish can see polarized light—a type of

light humans can barely detect—better than any other animal.   93. A study found that painting large eyes on cows' rears can help keep predators from attacking them.   94. Many creatures that live in dark caves evolve—or change over many generations—to lose their eyesight.   95. Even though people say "blind as a bat," bats can see—some better than others.   96. Some bacteria can see by using their entire body as a miniature eyeball.   97. Toyota created night-vision cameras for its cars that were inspired by the eyes of animals that see well in darkness.   98. Japanese yellow swallowtail butterflies see with their rear ends.   99. Red-eyed tree frogs have see-through eyelids that are covered in a striped pattern.   100. Oysters have eyes all around the edge of their shells.

mantis shrimp

tarsier

1
Polar bear FUR isn't WHITE; it's TRANSPARENT.

2
A polar bear that wants to share another polar bear's food will ASK PERMISSION through A NOSE-TO-NOSE GREETING.

3
Polar bears have BLACK SKIN.

4
Polar bears could not survive without the ALGAE THAT GROWS ON SEA ICE. That's because the seals they eat feed on fish that eat algae.

5
To survive, polar bears need to eat about ONE RINGED SEAL, their main food source, every 11 DAYS.

6
Polar bears are so good at keeping warm that THEY CAN OVERHEAT EASILY—even in the ice and snow!

7
Polar bears WAG THEIR HEADS FROM SIDE TO SIDE when they want to play with each other.

8
Polar bears have no NATURAL PREDATORS.

9
Polar bears live about 20 YEARS ON AVERAGE.

10
A "GROLAR BEAR" is a cross between a polar bear and a grizzly bear.

11
Another name for these hybrids is "PIZZLY BEARS."

12
Male polar bears can WEIGH UP TO 1,600 POUNDS (726 kg)—that's nearly as heavy as two grand pianos!

13
While ONLY MOTHER POLAR BEARS BUILD DENS, other polar bears sometimes dig temporary shelters during bad weather.

14
Unlike other bear species, POLAR BEARS DO NOT HIBERNATE.

15
As sea ice melts, some polar bears are SHIFTING from EATING SEALS TO EATING BIRD EGGS.

16
To swim, polar bears use their FRONT PAWS to dog-paddle and their hind paws as rudders to steer.

17
A thick layer of fat, which can be more than FOUR INCHES (10 CM) THICK, helps polar bears float.

50
COOL FACTS ABOUT
POLAR BEARS

18

Polar bears CLOSE THEIR NOSTRILS when they're underwater.

19

International Polar Bear Day is FEBRUARY 27.

20

Polar bears are the LARGEST LAND CARNIVORES.

21

In 2015, a polar bear was recorded holding its breath for 3 MINUTES 10 SECONDS while diving. (The average human can last only two minutes.)

22

Polar bears need SEA ICE TO SURVIVE—and melting ice caused by climate change is their biggest threat.

23

NEWBORN POLAR BEARS only weigh about ONE POUND (0.5 kg), about as much as a basketball.

24

When polar bears hunt, they're successful LESS THAN 2 PERCENT of the time.

25

Polar bears are the TALLEST BEARS, with some males measuring more than 10 FEET (3 m) when standing on their hind legs.

26

In 2014, scientists collected polar bear DNA from skin cells LEFT BEHIND IN FOOTPRINTS.

27

Polar bears can SMELL A SEAL FROM more than 20 MILES (32 KM) AWAY.

28

Polar bears REMEMBER OTHER BEARS, even if they haven't seen each other for years.

29

Scientists fear that because of CLIMATE CHANGE, two-thirds of the polar bear population will disappear by 2050.

30

PREGNANT POLAR BEARS dig dens to keep their babies warm. It can be 40°F (22°C) warmer in there.

31

When mother bears are in their dens, THEY DON'T EAT, DRINK, or POOP for up to EIGHT MONTHS.

32

Polar bear females WEIGH HALF AS MUCH AS males.

33

When hunting, polar bears can wait HOURS WITHOUT MOVING above a seal's breathing hole for the seal to pop its head up.

34

Polar bears have an EXTRA EYELID that acts like GOGGLES, allowing them to see underwater.

35

Thick fur on a polar bear's feet HELPS IT GRIP THE ICE.

36

POLAR BEARS PLAY. Scientists have seen them sliding across the ice just for fun!

37

Polar bear fur REPELS WATER.

38

Polar bears sometimes use a BLOCK OF ICE AS A PILLOW.

39

Polar bears EVOLVED FROM BROWN BEARS when a group became isolated in a cold area about 150,000 YEARS AGO.

40

Sometimes, blowing snow covers a sleeping polar bear's body UNTIL JUST ITS NOSE POKES OUT.

41

A polar bear's stomach can hold 15 TO 20 PERCENT of its body weight in food.

42

Polar bears ROLL IN THE SNOW to clean their fur.

43

The polar bear's scientific name, *Ursus maritimus*, means "SEA BEAR."

44

Polar bears can EAT 100 POUNDS (45 kg) of seal blubber in a sitting.

45

Polar bears can SMELL A SEAL'S AIR HOLE IN THE ICE from half a mile (1 km) away.

46

Most polar bear CUBS ARE TWINS.

47

A polar bear's giant paw can be a foot (0.3 m) across.

48

Polar bears are often PICTURED WITH PENGUINS. But polar bears live near the NORTH POLE and penguins live near the SOUTH POLE.

49

The average polar bear might TRAVEL 100,000 MILES (160,000 km) in a lifetime.

50

Polar bear hairs are hollow; THEY TRAP HEAT to keep the animals warm.

1 An **oriental fire-bellied toad flips over** when it **feels threatened,** revealing its red and orange belly as a warning that it is **toxic if eaten.**

2 **Northern fulmars,** a type of seabird, **vomit on predators** from up to **five feet (1.5 m) away.**

3

California ground **squirrels chew on old rattlesnake skin** and apply the paste to their tail to **confuse the sense of smell of** their main predator— the rattlesnake.

4 When faced with a threat, **a blue tang fish** raises a pair of **sharp venomous spines** on either side of its tail, **whipping it back and forth.**

5 **Tawny frogmouth** birds make a **buzzing sound** similar to a bee **when startled.**

24 DARING FACTS ABOUT ANIMALS

6 When attacked in shallow water by land predators, **electric eels sometimes jump out of the water** and deliver a shock.

7 **La Plata three-banded armadillos** use their plates as **defense against both predators** and **thorny vegetation.**

8

White-cheeked gibbons, which live in Southeast Asia, defend their territory as a group, **calling to each other** from their home range boundaries with **updates on predators.**

9 When **goliath bird-eating tarantulas** need to defend themselves, they **rub the hairs on their legs** together to make a hissing sound.

10 **Pink-toed tarantulas** throw hairs from their body to **defend themselves.**

11 The **golden poison frog,** which lives in Colombia, gets its **deadly toxin from the tiny beetles it eats.**

12 Flying fish jump out of the water to escape predators in the sea, gliding up to **665 feet (200 m).**

13

When a meerkat **spots a predator,** it **alerts its family by barking** or whistling.

14 When disturbed, **leaf-tailed geckos** open **their bright red mouth** and **make a noise** that sounds like **a child's scream.**

15 **Hippos** don't use their long **canine teeth for eating,** but for defense against predators.

17 **The reticulated glass frog** earned the nickname **"ninja frog"** because it can **throw karate-style kicks** to **protect its eggs** from rainforest wasps.

16 To ward off an attack, millipedes release **a smelly, foul-tasting fluid.**

ON THE DEFENSE

18 **Bombardier beetles** release a stinky fluid from their rear ends **that can kill other insects** and startle bigger predators, like frogs.

19 When a tokay gecko is threatened, **it breaks off its tail,** which **shakes to distract the predator.**

20 An **elephant's tusks** are used for **digging, tearing bark off trees,** and **rescuing their calves,** and they're also used as a **weapon if attacked.**

21 To fight off wasps, **cockroaches karate-kick them in the head** with their spiky legs.

22 A tokay gecko **grows a new tail** in about **three weeks.**

23 Camels can **kick to the front, back,** and side to fend off predators.

24 To intimidate predators, **short-horned lizards inflate to twice their size,** looking like a spiky balloon.

15 CUTE FACTS ABOUT CREATURE COUPLES

1
Living near coral reefs in the western Atlantic Ocean, **French angelfish pairs guard their territory** together against other angelfish pairs.

2
Every year, Canada geese couples **raise their goslings together—** and they usually **stay together for life.**

3. When getting ready to mate, **shingleback lizards lick each other.**

4. While a **red fox mom** is taking care of her kits, **their dad brings back food,** and when they are old enough, **both parents teach their young** how to hunt and protect themselves.

6

Male bowerbirds create elaborate displays with objects they find in their forest homes, such as colorful flower petals, pieces of fruit, or even discarded human toys, to attract a mate.

5

About **one in five primates** (not including humans) **lives in a pair.**

9. **Blue-capped cordon-bleu** songbirds sing and dance for one another, **bobbing up** and **down** on a tree branch and even holding nesting materials to show their interest.

7. The alpha male and alpha female that **lead a wolf pack groom one another,** bump noses, and sleep together.

8. Seahorse couples **change colors** as they **dance together.**

11

Male blue-footed boobies **give females a stick** or **stone** before starting their **high-strutting courtship dance** that shows off their blue feet.

10. Beaver couples **live in a lodge, raising their young** and defending their territory together.

13

Prairie vole couples **bond for life.** If something happens to their partner, in about eight out of 10 pairs the single prairie vole **won't look for another mate.**

14. To impress his mate, a male crowned eagle **performs a series of swooping aerial dives** and **climbs.**

15. And if a female crowned eagle is interested in a male, she may **lock talons** with him as they both fly together, heading toward the ground.

12. Male mice **"sing"** to their mates using **ultrasonic sounds, which humans can't hear.**

1. There are at least **40 species of bats** that **eat nothing but insects.**

2. **Koalas** are one of only three animals that **eat eucalyptus** as a **staple of their diet.** (The other two are the greater glider and the ringtail possum.)

3. **Crocodiles** can go for **more than a year without eating.**

4. **Elephants** can eat about **400 pounds (180 kg) of food a day.**

5. **Red squirrels bite on sugar maple trees to get to the maple syrup inside.**

6. **Japanese house bats plan their flight paths according** to what **food they can eat along the way.**

7. **The pygmy shrew eats 125 percent of its body weight** every day.

8. The **panther chameleon** waits motionless **for insects** and **small birds** to get within reach of its **long tongue.**

9. **Orangutans** occasionally **eat soil.**

10. **Butterflies drink** turtle tears.

11. **Some caterpillars** can **eat 27,000 times their body weight.**

12. **Crocodiles swallow their prey whole.**

13. **Some leeches can swallow** several times **their body weight in blood.**

14. **A snake's upper and lower jaws are attached** with an **elastic ligament,** enabling them to **eat animals bigger than they are.**

15. The **great skua bird harasses other birds** until they drop their food. Then the **skua steals it.**

16. **A frogfish's jaws open so wide** that the frogfish can swallow prey almost twice its size.

17. **Rabbits, guinea pigs, gophers, lemmings, voles, and kangaroo rats all eat their own poop.**

18. The **wood tiger moth caterpillar** sometimes **eats toxic plants** to make itself **taste disgusting to predators.**

19. **Many birds eat stones,** which **help grind up and digest** their food.

20. Nearly **every Greenland shark lives with a small crustacean called *Ommatokoita elongata* permanently attached to its eye.** The crustacean **eats the shark's cornea.**

21. **Male nursery web spiders wrap up an insect in spider silk** and **present it to a female** for her to eat.

22. **The blue dragon sea slug eats toxic Portuguese man-of-wars,** and **stores their stinging cells in its skin** for its own self-defense.

23. Birds called **loggerhead shrikes impale their prey** on thorns, sometimes leaving it **hanging there to eat later.**

24. **Archerfish spit a jet of water** out of their mouths to **knock insects into the water.**

25. **Bees vomit flower nectar** and then **pass it from bee to bee until it becomes honey.**

26. **Mantis shrimps use their claws to punch with the force of a bullet to smash open their prey's shells.**

27. **A woodpecker uses its tongue**—which is so long that it wraps around the bird's brain—to **snag insects hidden deep** in tree bark.

28. **Dracula ants suck the blood** of their young.

29. **Carrion beetles hunt for dead mice and birds.** Then they **bury the carcasses** for their young to feed on later.

30. **Wild chimpanzees seek out** the **leaves** of certain plants **to treat ailments.**

31. **Flamingos eat with their heads turned upside down.**

32. **Flamingos have rows of plates inside their beaks** that they use to **filter food from water,** just like baleen whales do.

33. **Zombie worms eat** whale bones.

34. **Egg-eating snakes swallow eggs whole,** using bony plates in their throats to **crush the shells, which they then spit out.**

35. When a **sea star** is ready to eat, **its stomach comes out of its body through its mouth,** envelops the food, and then digests it.

36. **A bolas spider captures prey by flinging a length of silk** tipped in a **gluelike substance** at it. The "glue" sticks to the insect, which the spider then devours.

37. A **python can eat** a crocodile.

38. **Some mountain lions** like to eat porcupines.

39. **The blackpoll warbler doubles its body weight before** setting off on an **1,800-mile (2,897-km) nonstop flight over the Atlantic Ocean** in the fall.

40. **Wolverines weigh** no more than **40 pounds (18 kg),** but they're not afraid to fight a wolf or a bear for a meal.

41. **Ruminants—which include cattle, sheep, goats, deer, and giraffes—have four stomachs.**

75 FACTS ABOUT ANIMAL APPETITES

42. Giant pandas can eat 83 pounds (38 kg) of bamboo in a day.

43. Dung beetles are named for the food they eat—dung, or poop.

44. The carcass of a dead whale can feed an assortment of ocean creatures for two years.

45. Some chipmunks can carry an amount of food as large as their bodies in their cheek pouches.

46. ... of other birds.

47. Vultures can eat rotten food that is toxic to most other animals.

48. The blue whale eats four times more food in a day than a human eats in a year.

49. A species of clam discovered in 2019 eats rocks.

50. Monarch caterpillars only eat one thing: the leaves of the milkweed plant.

51. When stuffed full of food, a chipmunk's cheek pouches can be three times the size of its head.

52. A tiger can go two weeks without eating.

53. A black-footed ferret can eat 100 prairie dogs in a year.

54. According to x-rays of their stomachs, pet dogs have eaten a rubber duck, false teeth, a phone, a lightbulb, a fishing pole, and 43 socks.

55. Parasites called isopods eat a fish's tongue, then anchor themselves inside the fish's mouth where the tongue once was.

56. Green shore crabs can absorb some of their food directly from seawater.

57. An okapi uses its extremely long tongue to strip leaves off branches.

58. The sandgrouse uses its feathers like a sponge to soak up water and then brings it back to its chicks.

59. Before flies start eating, they vomit on their food.

60. The African penguin swims about 25 miles (40 km) every day in search of food.

61. Giant anteaters feed at each ant mound for just about a minute. This ensures that they leave some ants for next time!

62. Elephants use their trunks to suck up water, then squirt it into their mouths.

63. Only female mosquitoes feed on blood.

64. Crocodiles can't chew.

65. The sweeter a flower's nectar, the more bats like to drink it.

66. King snakes get their name from their habit of eating other snakes.

67. The world's fastest eater is the star-nosed mole. It can find and swallow an insect in a quarter of a second.

68. Some spiders eat bats.

69. A mosquito's mouth uses six different "needles" to pierce your skin and suck your blood.

70. A pygmy shrew can't survive a full hour without eating.

71. A swarm of desert locusts can number 80 million individual insects and eat 423 million pounds (192 million kg) of plants a day.

72. Leaf-cutter ants slice off pieces of leaves, carry them back to their nest, and use them as fertilizer to grow fungus, which they feed to their young.

73. A blind cave salamander called an olm can go 10 years without eating.

74. Frogs can change the stickiness of their spit to help them snag insects with their tongues.

75. Monkeys on Japan's Koshima Island like to dip sweet potatoes in salt water before eating them.

1
Squirrel nests are known as dreys.

2
Honeybees like to **nest either** in **trees** or in **bee boxes** built by humans.

3
As **wasp colonies grow** in number, they **expand** their **nests** to hold the **new members**.

4
When **scout bees** find a **new nest site** for their colony, they do a **special "dance"** to tell other bees its location.

5
It takes young **orangutans three to four years** to **learn** how to **build nests** in their **treetop homes**.

6
One species of male pufferfish **digs elaborate circular nests** in the ocean sand **to attract females**.

7
Atlantic puffins **use the same nest sites each year**, in burrows that they **dig in rocky crevices on cliffsides**.

8
Great **egrets** build **nests** that hang on **tree branches as high as 100 feet** (30 m) over the water.

35 FACTS ABOUT NESTS TO COZY INTO

9

Male jacanas, a type of water bird, **build nests** and **take care** of the **young** while the more aggressive **females act as protectors.**

10

Great crested grebes—water birds—**build floating nests** made of **reeds and water plants.**

11

Komodo dragon moms create **fake nests** to help keep the real nest safe.

12

The **malleefowl** uses its feet to scrape sand and leaves into a huge pile—the **world's largest ground nest.**

13

Sociable weaver nests can **hold hundreds of birds,** and different families **have their own "rooms."**

14

Squirrels will **build their nests on top of old bird nests and birds do the same,** so the site is exchanged over time.

15

A **lappet-faced vulture's nest** of sticks can be **as big as a king-size bed.**

16

An American **alligator** mom **makes a nest out of vegetation** that can be **10 feet** (3 m) **in diameter.**

17

The **nests of sociable weavers** can **weigh as much as a ton** (900 kg) and **stretch for 20 feet** (6 m).

18

Hooded orioles use part of the **fibers from a palm tree** to **sew their nests to palm fronds.**

19

Five species of **sea turtles** have been known to **nest** on **Florida's beaches.**

20

Squirrels build their **nests** in the **fork** of **tree branches** to **give them** more **stability.**

21

Blue-footed boobies **mark their nests** on the ground with **a ring of poop.**

22

Bonobos build their **stick-and-leaf nests near each other** for **protection** against predators.

23

Burrowing owls **line** the outside of **their nesting sites** with **poop**—it **attracts dung beetles** that the owls **eat.**

24

Paper wasps **chew plants and pieces of wood** and spit out **the soft pulp,** which is **used to make a paper nest.**

25

Male Siamese fighting fish **build floating nests out of air bubbles and guard them** until the **eggs** inside hatch.

26

Paper wasp **nests** are **water-resistant.**

27

Ruby-throated hummingbirds place **one to three eggs in nests** about the **size of a Ping-Pong ball.**

28

Emperor penguins are **unusual** among most **birds** because they **form nesting colonies** of **thousands of birds** on the cold Antarctic ice **during the winter.**

29

Sociable weaver birds use the **inner areas of their nests for warmth** at **night** and the **outer areas for shade** during the **day.**

30

Ostriches **lay their eggs in communal nests** that can **hold 60 eggs** from **different ostriches.**

31

A **group of wasps** in the United Kingdom **built their nest in a hat** they **found** in an outhouse.

32

Bonobos sometimes **share** the **same nest**—a **unique behavior** for primates.

33

The male pufferfish **never uses the same nest twice**—he always **creates a new one.**

34

In Tasmania, Australia, a **12-year-old boy found** a European **wasp nest** that was **so large** it took **four men to carry** it.

35

Squirrels build **winter and summer versions** of their nests—the **summer one** is more **open to the air.**

1
Tigers have a LARGE WHITE SPOT behind each ear, which scientists think may help cubs follow their moms.

2
Five subspecies of tigers—Bengal, Indochinese, Sumatran, Siberian, and Malayan—live in a wide variety of habitats, from SNOWY MOUNTAINS to TROPICAL RAINFORESTS.

3
Male Siberian tigers, which are also called Amur tigers, can grow to be LONGER THAN A SOFA.

4
In Indian mythology, TIGERS BATTLED DRAGONS and could bring rains during a drought.

5
Siberian tigers have the LARGEST HOME RANGE of any tiger because food is harder to find in the birch forests of Russia where they live.

6
Tigers SCRATCH TREE BARK to let other tigers know they are nearby.

7
Tigers are GOOD SWIMMERS: They have been recorded swimming across 18 miles (29 km) of open water.

8
Tigers have no natural predators (except for humans)—they even EAT BEARS and CROCODILES.

9
Tiger cubs quadruple in size in their FIRST MONTH of life.

10
A tiger can see about SIX TIMES BETTER at NIGHT than a human can.

11
Tiger paws have WEBBING between the toes.

12
A legend in Sumatra, an island in Southeast Asia, held that some PEOPLE TRANSFORMED into TIGERS AT NIGHT, and these "were-tigers" returned to human form in the morning.

13
Some people say tiger urine smells like BUTTERED POPCORN.

14
Tigers not only have striped fur but also have STRIPED SKIN.

15
In the Chinese zodiac, if you are born during the year of the tiger, you are COURAGEOUS and enjoy TAKING RISKS.

16
Tigers don't just roar; they also can HISS and GRUNT.

17
In 2013, one-year-old Amur tiger cubs at the Minnesota Zoo were treated to a BIRTHDAY "CAKE" made of fruit-juice-flavored ices (and a little meat).

50
TERRIFIC FACTS
ABOUT *TIGERS*

18
A RESCUED TIGER lives on the campus of Louisiana State University, U.S.A.— whose mascot is MIKE THE TIGER— and is cared for by people from the veterinary school.

19
Launched in 1973, INDIA'S PROJECT TIGER protects tiger habitat in 50 reserves throughout the country.

20
A FOUR-MILLION-YEAR-OLD FOSSIL found in Tibet—the oldest big cat fossil found to date—shows that big cats were living in Asia for millions of years.

21
A tiger's footprint is called a PUGMARK.

22
The Hindu goddess DURGA is sometimes shown riding a tiger.

23
Tiger cubs start following their mothers and begin to PRACTICE HUNTING with their siblings when they are about two months old.

24
SNOW LEOPARDS are tigers' CLOSEST RELATIVES.

25
Bengal tiger teeth can be FOUR INCHES (10 CM) LONG—the length of a toilet paper roll.

26
Prehistoric rock art from Inner Mongolia in China—some 10,000 YEARS OLD— includes carvings of deer, cattle, leopards, and tigers.

27
When a tiger flicks its tail, it can mean that the tiger is FEELING ANGRY and AGGRESSIVE.

28
Tigers sometimes communicate with LOW-PITCHED SOUNDS that humans can't hear.

29
"Tiger tail"— ORANGE-FLAVORED ICE CREAM with a swirl of black licorice—is a popular flavor in Canada.

30
Tigers are ambush hunters but can chase prey in short bursts of up to 35 MILES AN HOUR (56 km/h).

31
Players on the Detroit Tigers Major League Baseball team used to wear ORANGE-STRIPED SOCKS as part of their uniforms.

32
More tigers LIVE IN ZOOS than IN THE WILD.

33
The stripes of Sumatran tigers are CLOSER TOGETHER than those on other kinds of tigers.

34
Siberian tigers have A RUFF OF FUR around their necks and FURRY PAWS to keep them warm in their cold climate.

35
Tigers' hind legs are longer than their front legs, which gives them the POWER TO JUMP UP TO 30 FEET (10 m) in just one leap.

36
Kellogg's Tony the Tiger mascot began appearing on boxes of cereal in 1952, after winning a POPULARITY CONTEST against Elmo the Elephant, Katy the Kangaroo, and Newt the Gnu.

37
The Detroit Tigers' mascot, a "tiger" named PAWS, has dressed up in a SANTA SUIT and delivered presents to fans.

38
Bengal tigers' light orange or reddish coat blends in with the LONG GRASSES where they live. The animals they hunt are COLOR-BLIND, so the tigers' orange stripes appear to be a shade of green.

39
A tiger's tail is LONGER than a standard skateboard.

40
Tigers are ENDANGERED—only about 4,000 LIVE in the wild.

41
It's hard to tell the difference between the SKELETONS of tigers and lions.

42
Known as the "tiger cave," a cave by the Bay of Bengal in India has 11 TIGERLIKE HEADS carved into the rock around its opening.

43
Tigers can eat 50 pounds (23 kg) of MEAT AT ONE MEAL.

44
Tiger cubs are BORN BLIND—and they don't open their eyes for up to two weeks after birth.

45
Some tigers can appear to be almost COMPLETELY BLACK when their stripes are close together.

46
During floods in Bangladesh in 1969, TIGERS CLIMBED TREES to find refuge.

47
Tiger cubs stay with their moms for about TWO YEARS before leaving to find their own territory.

48
Tigers roar when they've MADE A KILL.

49
Tigers can haul animals about TWICE THEIR BODY WEIGHT up a tree.

50
Tigers can imitate the sound that SAMBAR DEER make to attract one of their FAVORITE PREY.

100 AWWW-WORTHY FACTS ABOUT BABY ANIMALS

duckling

giant panda

1. A mom duck will raise a group of ducklings that are not her own. 2. American alligators make high-pitched noises inside their eggs to alert their moms that they are ready to hatch. 3. Meerkats live in groups of as many as 40 animals, and all of the adults help babysit the babies. 4. Human caretakers at the Wolong Nature Reserve in China dress up as giant pandas to calm baby pandas during check-ups—they even add panda poop and pee to the costumes.

5. Bald eagle chicks weigh about two ounces (60 g) when they hatch but gain six ounces (180 g) of weight every day as both parents take turns feeding them. 6. Baby alpacas, llamas, vicuñas, and guanacos are called crias. 7. Sea lion moms gather their pups in pro-tected locations, such as a lagoon, so the pups can hang out together while their moms fish for food. 8. Sea otter pups have thick coats of baby fur that keep them from sinking in the water. 9. Kittens of the caracal, a wild cat that lives in parts of Asia and Africa, stay with their moms for about 10 months, cuddling with both her and their siblings. 10. Sea otter moms carry their infants on their chests for two months, until they are able to dive for food on their own. 11. When sea otter moms leave to dive for mussels, sea urchins, and sea stars, they anchor their babies with kelp fronds to keep them from floating away. 12. Born nearly blind, baby shrews follow their mom by forming a "conga line," where each baby holds on to the tail of the shrew in front of them. 13. Young female turkeys are known as jennies, and the males are called jakes. 14. When first born, coyote pups' ears are limp, but they perk up above their heads after about 10 days. 15. White-tailed deer leave their fawns in hiding spots for as long as four hours while they forage for food. 16. Some sharks give birth to live young while others release eggs that hatch by themselves. 17. Beluga whale calves nurse from both their moms and other females so that the babies get enough milk. 18. Young female white-tailed deer stay with their mothers for two years, but young males usually stay for only one year, growing small "buttons" on their heads where antlers will grow. 19. Some baby octopuses can double their weight in just one week. 20. When baby swans, or cygnets, are born, they weigh about as much as two sticks of butter.

21. About a day after cygnets hatch, their mom leads them to the water. 22. One type of funnel-web spider dies after her babies hatch, and her young eat her body. 23. A rhinoceros gives birth to a single baby every three to five years; both mom and calf wallow in muddy pools to keep cool. 24. Panda bear babies are pink at birth—their black-and-white markings don't appear for a month. 25. A mother orangutan carries her offspring on her back, side, or belly for about two years. 26. Panda moms cradle their babies, which are born unable to see or hear, in their large paws. 27. After developing in its mom's pouch for about six months, a baby koala rides on its mom's back for another six months, using the pouch to sleep and nurse. 28. Puppies perform what's called a "play bow" to show they are ready to play. 29. Baby sea turtles hatch on sandy beaches, but they quickly scurry to the ocean where they live for the rest of their lives. 30. Sea turtles hatch around the same time, turning the surrounding sand into what some people call "turtle boils," because the moving sand looks like a pot of boiling water. 31. Once baby sea turtles reach the ocean, they start a swimming frenzy to move away from the shore, where dangerous predators live, into the open ocean. 32. Scientists estimate that only about one out of 1,000 sea turtle hatchlings—or even as few as one in 10,000—will live to be an adult. 33. Elephant moms are pregnant for almost two years before giving birth. 34. It can take more than nine months before wandering albatross chicks fly for the first time. 35. When playing together, young chimpanzees clap hands, stomp their feet, hit the ground, and throw objects. 36. When an ele-phant's baby teeth start coming in, its mom eats plants that reduce inflammation. Scientists think this helps her produce milk that soothes teething pain. 37. For two weeks after it is born, a baby ring-tailed lemur travels by hanging on to its mom's belly. 38. For about 10 days after they hatch, wolf spiderlings hitch a ride on their mom's back—and if they fall off they climb right back on. 39. Inexperienced meerkat moms carry their infants however they can, but more experienced mothers pick up their young by the nape of their necks. 40. Cowbird moms lay their eggs in other birds' nests, forcing the adopted parents into raising the chicks. 41. A baby Eurasian pygmy shrew could fit into a teaspoon. 42. Beluga whale calves vocalize using clicks and whistles within hours of birth. 43. Green-rumped parrotlets use a specific "peep" to identify each of their chicks, just like human parents name their children. 44. Baby blue whales gain about 200 pounds (90 kg) every day for a year—that's the weight of some adult humans.

45. Great white shark mothers are pregnant for one year before giving birth to as many as 10 babies. 46. Great white shark babies are called pups. 47. Young ducklings bond to the first moving object they see after they hatch—usually their mothers—in a process known as imprinting. 48. Dogs can have identical twin puppies. 49. A crocodile has an "egg tooth" on its upper jaw to help it crack out of its eggshell in a process called "pipping." 50. The egg tooth is reabsorbed into its body after it hatches and disappears completely a few weeks later. 51. At birth, a baby giraffe weighs about 220 pounds (100 kg)—about as much as a large jaguar. 52. Crows live in family groups of parents, siblings and babies, and young crows have even been known to return and visit their parents once they've gone out on their own. 53. When born, sperm whale calves are about as long as a sports car. 54. Young Asian small-clawed otters sleep together in a big pile. 55. Some orangutans drink milk from their mothers until they are eight years old. 56. A baby opossum is about the size of a bumblebee. 57. In 2016 two St. Bernard dogs in Belgium helped raise a baby goat named Hans whose mother had died. 58. Wild turkey babies, or poults, start to peck at food within hours of hatching. 59. Small rodents called Norway lemmings are able to have babies when they are just three weeks old. 60. All kittens are born with blue eyes, but some change color as the kitten gets older. 61. Seahorse dads carry their babies in a special pouch and nourish them until they are ready to be born. 62. Less than one percent of seahorse babies will reach adulthood. 63. Baby seahorses are called fry. 64. After a mother hippopotamus gives birth, she isolates herself and her baby for as long as two weeks before rejoining the herd. 65. Hippo babies are able to nurse underwater by closing their noses and folding back their ears. 66. A litter of pigs is called a farrow. 67. A species of web-weaving spider plucks the threads of her web to warn her young ones of danger. 68. Tough, leathery egg cases, known as mermaid's purses, wash up on shore after the baby sharks or rays inside have hatched. 69. Pacific walruses give birth on thick patches of sea ice that are solid enough to hold up their huge bodies, which can weigh thousands of pounds (kg). 70. Baby walruses know how to swim as soon as they are born. 71. The hard-shelled clam begins its life as a free-swimming larva about the width of a human hair. 72. As the tiny clam larva grows, it starts to form a shell; the warmer the water the faster the shell forms. 73. Puppy dogs, especially larger breeds, don't reach their adult size until they are about two years old. 74. Adolescent females in an elephant herd protect newborns and help them stand, walk, and swim. 75. These young females seem to understand which mothers are more inexperienced, giving their calves more help than those of experienced mothers. 76. Horseshoe crabs, which are not really crabs but more closely related to spiders and scorpions, molt about 18 times before reaching maturity. 77. Baby horseshoe crabs swim upside down. 78. Scientists have observed the crabs—while still in their see-through eggs—already beginning to swim this way, using their legs to turn somersaults. 79. Birds known as least terns nest on beaches, and on warm days, the moms stand over their hatchlings to shade them from the sun. 80. Least tern moms also soak their chest feathers in the ocean, shaking the water over their chicks to cool them off.

81. A young wallaby jumps into its mother's pouch when scared. 82. Young chimps make different facial expressions when they play together, and when their mouths are relaxed and open, scientists think they are saying, "Let's keep playing." 83. Monkeys groom their babies, picking off dirt and insects to keep their fur clean. 84. By biting each other and wrestling together, wolf cubs learn how to hunt. 85. Meerkats teach their babies how to scratch for insects in the dirt in their arid African homelands. 86. "Baby" alpaca wool doesn't come from babies but from the softest part of an adult alpaca, which is usually its chest. 87. Alpaca babies are usually born in the middle of the day. 88. If a captive llama and an alpaca have a baby (this doesn't happen in the wild), it's called a huarizo. 89. Baby echidnas—rare Australian mammals that hatch from eggs—are called puggles. 90. Puggles hatch after 10 days and then spend time in their mom's pouch, just like a baby kangaroo. 91. Grizzly bear cubs are born without hair and can weigh less than two hamburgers. 92. A gray kangaroo joey stays in its mom's pouch for nearly a year. 93. Pigeon parents feed their chicks nutritious "crop milk" that comes from special cells in the parent's esophagus. 94. Many baby songbirds take short flights before their feathers are fully formed. 95. Female golden lion tamarins, small primates that live in South American forests, most often give birth to twins. 96. Golden lion tamarin babies are born with their eyes open. 97. Most octopus moms take care of just one set of eggs in a lifetime, and then die after the babies hatch. 98. Female common toads lay strands of eggs on water plants for male toads to fertilize. 99. National Puppy Day, celebrated every March 23 in the United States, focuses on adopting dogs in need of a home. 100. Scientists found the remnants of thousands of shark eggs 200 miles (320 km) off Ireland's west coast, evidence of a huge shark nursery where the newly hatched pups had congregated.

coyote pups

1 Teddy bear crabs are covered with a thick coat of **hairlike structures.**

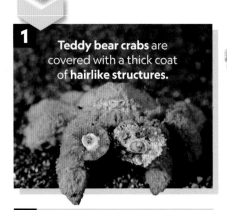

2 Japanese spider crabs have incredibly long legs—when extended, they **span 12 feet (3.7 m)** from the tip of one front claw to the other.

3 Horseshoe crabs have been around longer than the dinosaurs were.

4 Boxer crabs carry around stinging anemones for protection.

6 Soft-bodied hermit crabs don't have shells. Instead, they crawl into the empty shells of sea snails for protection.

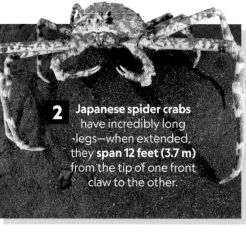

5 Crabs' skeletons are on the outside of their bodies, in the form of a shell.

7 Hermit crabs line up from biggest to smallest and exchange their old shell for a new one in the next size up.

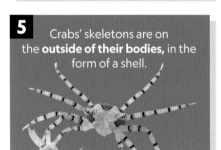

25 CRABBY FACTS

11 The coconut crab is the world's largest land-dwelling invertebrate. They can be three feet (1 m) wide and weigh 10 pounds (4.5 kg).

8 Halloween crabs have black bodies, orange legs, and purple claws.

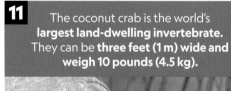

9 Crabs live in all the world's oceans, in freshwater, and even on land.

10 Crabs' shells don't grow, so when the crabs run out of room, they have to molt, or shed their shells, and grow new ones.

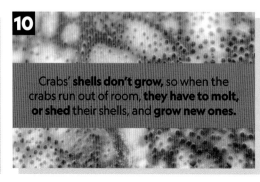

12 A coconut crab's claw can pinch with 10 times the force of a human's grip—enough pressure to break open coconuts.

13 Every year, about **50 million red crabs** leave their burrows on **Christmas Island, off the coast of Australia,** and scuttle to the ocean.

ROAD CLOSED
RED CRAB MIGRATION
NO ENTRY BY VEHICLES
BEYOND THIS POINT

14

Decorator crabs disguise themselves by covering their shells with **seaweeds, anemones, and sponges.**

15 **Horseshoe crabs** aren't technically crabs. They're more closely related to **spiders and scorpions.**

16

Pea crabs are tiny crabs that **live inside clams and mussels.**

17 In 2018, a scientist **saw a coconut crab ambush** and eat an **adult seabird**—the first time this behavior had been observed.

18 Female red crabs lay up to **100,000 eggs at a time.**

19

Crabs have **10 legs.**

20

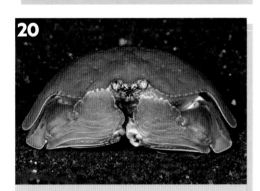

The **shame-faced crab** gets its name from the way it holds its **pincers in front of its face as though it's ashamed.**

21 An **arrow crab's legs** can be **three times the length** of its body.

22 **Ghost crabs have teeth in their stomachs.** They can vibrate them to "growl" at attackers.

23 The **orangutan crab's body** is covered with **orange-red hairs.**

24 A **fiddler crab** has one **oversize claw** that can be more than **half its body weight.**

25 The **masked crab** has a pattern on its shell that **resembles a human face.**

1 The **toadfish** sings a song that sounds like a **phone vibrating.**

2 The howl of the New Guinea singing dog sounds similar to **the song of a humpback whale.**

3 Male bottlenose dolphins gather in small groups and **vocalize in harmony**—just like members of human bands.

4 The cowbird can sing **40 notes.**

5 **Male superb lyrebirds** sing and dance to **attract mates.** They have different dances to go with each song.

6 **The nightjar bird** can sing **1,900 notes** in a single minute.

7 All male humpback whales in a population **sing the same song,** which changes every few years.

8 The album *Songs of the Humpback Whale,* a recording of whale sounds released in 1970, has sold 10 million copies.

9 Humpback whales can **sing for 20 minutes** straight.

10 Bees dance and **vibrate** to **communicate** the **location of flowers** to other bees.

11 The reason humpback whales sing is a **mystery.**

12 Some parrots can **dance to a beat.**

13 **Reef fish sing at dawn** and **dusk,** just like birds do.

35 LOUD FACTS ABOUT MUSICAL ANIMALS

14
The **club-winged manakin bird** knocks its special wing feathers together to create a **violinlike sound.**

15
Grasshoppers sing by rubbing their hind legs against their front wings— like a **bow playing a violin.**

16
When a frog "ribbits" in a movie, it's almost always a recording of a Pacific tree frog.

17
One study found that **cows make more milk** when they listen to slow songs.

18
Grasshoppers that live near busy roads **sing louder.**

19
Mockingbird males can sing for **24 hours a day** during the breeding season.

20
The **male kakapo** bird digs a shallow **"bowl"** in the ground, then **stands inside** and **sings.** The bowl amplifies its song.

21
Songbirds have **"accents"** that make their songs sound slightly different depending on where they live.

22
Nightingales know up to **300 love songs.**

23
Bats flying in a group take turns singing their **echolocation "songs"** so they can listen to each other.

24
Elephants can learn to **play the harmonica.**

25
The study of animal music is called **zoomusicology.**

26
Canaries can take **30 breaths a second** while singing, allowing them to **sing nonstop** for minutes.

27
Early sailors called beluga whales the **"canaries of the sea"** because they could hear the whales' songs from inside their ships.

28
Mexican free-tailed bats change their **tunes** to keep **females interested.**

29
Brown thrasher birds know as many as **2,000 songs.**

30
Mosquitoes "sing" with their **wingbeats,** and harmonize with potential mates.

31
Experts aren't sure **why birds sing early** in the morning.

32
Birds sing warning songs that can pass from bird to bird at more than **100 miles an hour** (161 km/h) through a forest.

33
Woodpeckers attract mates by **drumming on dead trees** and hollow logs.

34
Cats don't like **human music**— but they do like music written specifically for cats.

35
In their songs, mockingbirds mimic sounds around them— like the **squeaks of mice** and even **car alarms.**

»15 TERRIFIC FACTS ABOUT TAILS

1
When a male peacock **shakes his tail,** it makes a sound **as loud as a car passing by**—but it's too low-pitched for human ears to hear.

2
Some lizards have **detachable tails.**

3
When the **woolly monkey** walks on the ground, it uses its tail like a **tripod for balance.**

4. Using their tails, spider monkeys can **dangle from a branch to sip water** from a river.

5 Horses use their tails as **flyswatters.**

6. Giraffes have the **longest tails** of any land mammal. They can be up to **eight feet** (2.4 m) **long.**

7. Some monkeys' tails have a **hairless pad** on one side of the tip for **better sensing** and **gripping.**

8. Tree squirrels use their tails as **blankets when sleeping.**

9. The world's **fluffiest tail** belongs to the tufted ground squirrel. It's **130 percent** of the **squirrel's body volume.**

10 Thresher sharks **whip their tails** over their heads to smack **their prey into pieces.**

13 The ribbon-tailed astrapia bird has a tail nearly **four times the length** of its body.

11. When a **human fetus** is growing, it **develops**—and then **loses**—a tail.

12. The **Asian grass lizard** has a 10-inch (25-cm)-long tail—more than **three times as long as its body!**

15 The basilisk lizard uses its tail for **balance to run on water.**

14 Thanks to the balance that its tail provides, the long-eared jerboa, only **three-inches** (7.6-cm) in length, can **leap up to six feet** (1.8 m).

1. **Black mamba snakes** can slither faster than the average human runs.

2. The **Atlantic wolffish's** sharp pointed teeth are so large they stick out of its mouth.

3. The naked mole rat can survive for **18 minutes** without oxygen.

4. The **diving bell spider** hunts underwater by using a bubble of air like a scuba tank.

5. The bite of a **brown recluse spider** can cause skin to rot.

6. Hagfish release sticky goo to suffocate attackers.

7. Piranhas feed in **large groups** to eat large animals such as capybaras.

8. Vampire deer have long **"fangs"** that stick out past their lower jaws.

9. Six-inch (15-cm)-long camel spiders **sometimes beat the heat of their desert homes by lurking in a human's shadow.**

10. Goliath tiger fish **hunt in packs.**

11. Freshwater stingrays can measure **16.5 feet (5 m) long** and **weigh 1,320 pounds (600 kg).**

12. Needlefish **leap out of the water at high speeds,** sometimes spearing unwitting humans with their sharp beaks.

13. The nests of one species of ant, *Formica archboldi,* are littered with the skulls of its prey.

14. Basking sharks can be the **size of a bus.**

15. **Lionfish** spread their fins wide and **herd small fish** into tight spaces—**then swallow them.**

16. The crocodile monitor lizard can be **13 feet (4 m) long.**

17. The candiru fish attaches itself to the gills of larger fish and **drinks their blood.**

18. Cobras can **spit venom at their victim's eyes** with extreme accuracy.

19. The bearded vulture **eats mostly bones.**

20. Lampreys latch on to fish and **drain their blood.**

21. When threatened, the hairy frog **breaks its own bones** and shoots them through its toes to form claws.

22. More than **60 venomous snakes** in the cobra family can **swim in the ocean.**

23. A snapping turtle can **bite through bone.**

24. The matamata turtle **sucks its prey into its mouth** like a vacuum cleaner.

25. One expert estimates that mosquitoes have **killed about half of all people** ever born.

26. The frilled shark has 25 rows of backward-facing, trident-shaped teeth.

27. Whip spiders sense their environment by "whipping" their **superlong, modified front legs** back and forth in front of themselves.

28. Leaf-tailed geckos have silver, tan, or gold eyes **striped with red.**

29. One type of assassin bug **wears the corpses** of its ant victims on its body.

30. Gila monsters bite their victims and **chew to allow their venom** to flow into the wound.

31. The Goliath bird-eating spider is the **size of a puppy**—its leg span can measure 12 inches (30 cm).

32. The Budgett's frog screams.

33. Wrap-around spiders can curve their bodies around a tree branch and flatten themselves, **becoming nearly impossible to see.**

75
FACTS ABOUT
WEIRD
CREATURES

34. Some ants can **explode** when something **threatens their colony.**

35. Naked mole rats live in communities led by a dominant queen—like ants and bees do.

36. The cave robber spider has **hooks on its legs** that it likely uses to **snag flying insects out of the air.**

37. Botfly larvae can **burrow inside human skin** and feed on their flesh.

38. The tarantula hawk is a wasp that **captures tarantulas, paralyzes them,** and feeds them to its larvae.

39. Geese can have **toothlike serrations** on their tongues.

40. Asian giant hornets **kill up to 50 people** in Japan each year.

41. After a honey badger is bitten by a venomous snake, it can enter **a coma-like state—but** then **wake up and walk away.**

42. The marabou stork is nicknamed the **"undertaker bird"** because it eats dead animals.

43. The extremely rare **"cyclops"** shark has a condition that causes it to **have only one eye.**

44. Asian giant hornets **decapitate bees** and can wipe out a **whole hive in just hours.**

45. The goblin shark can **shoot its jaw forward** to grab its prey.

46. The golden-crowned flying fox, a type of bat, can have a **wingspan of 5.5 feet** (1.7 m)—about the same as a human's arm span!

47. The giant burrowing cockroach can **grow to be 3.5 inches (8.9 cm)** long and **live for 10 years.**

48. Fireflies can glow through a frog's body after being swallowed.

49. The squid *Promachoteuthis sulcus* looks like it has a set of human teeth—but they're actually **folded lips that cover its beak.**

50. Tapeworms **hatch inside human intestines,** where they can grow to more than 80 feet (25 m) long.

51. The deep-sea giant isopod is a cousin of the land-dwelling pillbug, but the giant isopod can grow to be **a foot (30 cm) long.**

52. A wolf eel is named for its **sharp front teeth.**

53. The lion's mane jellyfish has **tentacles** that can be **as long as a blue whale.**

54. Small, see-through sea creatures called **larvaceans use their own mucus to build homes** that capture floating bits of food.

55. The fangtooth moray eel has **rows of translucent teeth** that resemble shards of broken glass.

56. Some species of birds **poop on their own legs** to cool down.

57. Female black widow spiders eat their mates.

58. One cave in the **Yucatan jungle** is home to a group of snakes that dangle from the cave ceilings to gobble bats.

59. The olm, a **blind, cave-dwelling salamander,** is nicknamed the "human fish" for its pinkish skin.

60. The Peruvian giant yellowleg centipede can be 10 inches (26 cm) long.

61. Bird-dropping spiders **hide in plain sight** because they look just like bird poop.

62. When a pack of Asian giant hornets attacks a hive of honeybees, **the bees can fight back by forming a ball** around the hornets and vibrating their muscles until they "cook" the hornets alive.

63. Deer will gnaw on human remains.

64. Crocodiles can **climb trees.**

65. Tarantulas **inject their prey with chemicals** that liquefy it. Then, the spider slurps it up.

66. Certain snake species can **glide through the air** as far as **330 feet (100 m).**

67. The Australian mulga snake sometimes **bites people in their sleep.**

68. In France, a group of catfish have learned how to **lunge out of the water** to eat pigeons.

69. Vampire bats **can run.**

70. When disturbed, **ladybugs emit a nasty-smelling liquid** from their leg joints.

71. Some species of frogs make their homes in **elephant poop.**

72. A cockroach can **survive for weeks** without a head.

73. The bite of the slow loris is so toxic **it can kill a human.**

74. One species of moth **drinks the tears** of sleeping birds.

75. Cookie-cutter sharks have such a strong bite that they have **disabled nuclear submarines.**

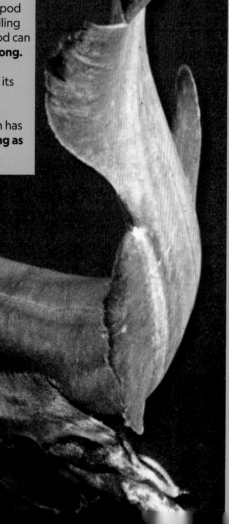

1 Like **helicopters,** hummingbirds can fly up, down, sideways, backward, and even upside down.

2 The bee hummingbird is the **world's smallest bird.** It weighs less than a dime.

3 A hummingbird's **heart can beat as fast as 1,260 times** per minute.

4 Hummingbirds **use spider silk** to build their nests.

5 Hummingbirds **can barely walk.**

6 Hummingbirds are the **only birds that can hover** for more than 30 seconds at a time.

7 A **bee hummingbird's nest** is about the **size of a quarter.**

8 A sword hummingbird's **beak is longer than its body.** It uses the beak to feed on the **nectar of tube-shaped flowers.**

9 A **ruby-throated hummingbird's wings** can beat more than **200 times per second** during a dive.

10 Hummingbirds beat their wings in a **figure-eight pattern** that gives them extra lift.

11 Hummingbirds **don't just drink nectar**—they spend much of their time **chasing down insects** to eat.

12 Hummingbirds need to eat about **half their body weight every day** and must snack every **10 to 15 minutes.**

13 Rufous hummingbirds **travel almost 4,000 miles** (6,437 km) to migrate **from Mexico to Alaska, U.S.A.**

14 A hummingbird's tongue can go **in and out of a flower 20 times** per second.

15 Hummingbirds **conserve energy by going into** a sleeplike state whenever **temperature and food conditions** require it.

16 The **ruby-throated hummingbird** has the **fewest feathers** of any bird—about 1,000.

17 There are **328 hummingbird species.** It is estimated that nearly 10 percent are **endangered or critically endangered.**

18 The green violet-ear hummingbird **can fly up to 93 miles an hour (150 km/h).**

19 **Black-chinned hummingbirds** build their **nests near hawks,** which keeps other birds called Mexican jays from eating their eggs.

20 Hummingbirds are named for the **sound that their beating wings make.**

35 FAST FACTS ABOUT HUMMINGBIRDS

Anna's hummingbird

21
Hummingbirds are the only birds that **can fly backward.**

22
Hummingbirds especially like **red flowers.**

23
When it rains, hummingbirds "shower" by **opening their wings and letting the drops fall on them.**

24
One hummingbird species **lives in the chilly Andes mountains of South America,** where it keeps warm by roosting in caves.

25
If a hummingbird were the **size of a human,** it would have to eat the equivalent of about **277 double burgers** a day!

26
Hummingbirds visit between **1,000 and 2,000 flowers in a single day.**

27
Hummingbirds can **completely digest a fruit fly** in 10 minutes.

28
Male broad-tailed hummingbirds **fly up to 100 feet (30 m)** in the air and then dive toward a **female to impress her.**

29
Hummingbirds are so small that **large insects such as praying mantises** sometimes hunt them.

30
A ruby-throated hummingbird's **eggs** are about **the size of peas.**

31
Usually, hummingbird **females lay two eggs.**

32
A hummingbird's **brain makes up 4.3 percent** of its weight—the **largest for its body size of any bird.**

33
Hummingbirds can keep track of **how long it takes each flower** in their territory **to refill with nectar.**

34
Hummingbirds can **snap their beaks shut** around an insect in **less than a hundredth of a second.**

35
The ancient Aztec worshipped a hummingbird **god of war named Huitzilopochtli.**

100 SWIMMINGLY FUN FACTS ABOUT MARINE MAMMALS

bottlenose dolphin

orca

1. Marine mammals live in the ocean, but they breathe air, are warm-blooded and feed their young with milk, and they don't lay eggs. 2. Dolphins are born with hair around their snouts, but they lose it shortly after birth. 3. Most marine mammals have a thick layer of fat called blubber that helps keep them warm. 4. Baby sea otter fur acts like a life jacket that keeps the little one afloat. 5. The ancient Greeks believed killing a dolphin was a crime punishable by death. 6. A blue whale can weigh as much as 40 elephants or 30 *Tyrannosaurus rex*. 7. Dolphins sleep with one eye open to watch out for danger. 8. The U.S. Navy trains marine mammals to find equipment lost at sea or buried in the seafloor. 9. Though they are nicknamed killer whales, orcas are actually dolphins. 10. Sea otters have the densest fur of any animal—up to one million hairs per square inch (155,000 hairs/sq cm). 11. Blue whales are the biggest animals on Earth, but they feed on some of the smallest animals in the sea: shrimplike critters called krill. 12. Queen Elizabeth I once paid £10,000—the cost of a castle at that time—for a jewel-encrusted narwhal tusk. 13. Some humpback whales trap fish by encircling them in a "net" made of bubbles. 14. Drone footage from 2017 shows that narwhals use their tusks to stun cod to make them easier to eat. 15. A humpback whale's songs consist of repeating patterns—just like human music. 16. Sea otters use rocks like hammers to crack open clams and mussels. 17. Greek scientist Aristotle figured out that whales are mammals, not fish, 2,400 years ago. 18. Bowhead whales can live for more than 200 years. 19. Long ago, sailors reported mermaid sightings—but experts think they were actually spotting manatees or dugongs. 20. Orcas live in groups of sons and daughters led by their mother. 21. The National Oceanic and Atmospheric Administration is developing a program to keep track of marine mammal populations with drones. 22. Sea otter moms float on their backs and hold their babies on their bellies. 23. Dolphin babies are born tail-first so they don't drown. 24. Unlike other marine mammals, sea otters don't have blubber. Their fur keeps them warm instead. 25. Every year, gray whales travel more than 10,000 miles (16,100 km) between their nursery lagoons in Mexico and their hunting grounds in the Arctic. 26. Manatees are sometimes called sea cows because of their large size, slow way of moving, and diet of grasses. 27. A walrus's layer of blubber can be six inches (15 cm) thick. 28. Seals can sleep while holding their breath underwater. 29. Sea otters float together in groups called rafts. 30. Walruses use their mouths to "vacuum" clams out of their shells. 31. "Thar she blows" is a traditional call whalers have shouted when spotting the spout of a whale exhaling. 32. Manatees are related to elephants. 33. Elephant seal pups gain about 10 pounds (4.5 kg) a day. 34. The brighter the pink color of a male Amazon river dolphin, the more attractive he is to females. 35. The Cuvier's beaked whale holds the record for deepest dive of any marine mammal: 1.9 miles (3.1 km). 36. Sea otters sometimes wrap themselves in kelp to keep from floating away while they snooze. 37. Manatees eat more than 10 percent of their body mass in a single day—that's 120 pounds (54 kg) of plants! 38. In 2000, an elephant seal named Homer wreaked havoc in Gisborne, New Zealand, crushing cars and boat trailers and knocking over trees. 39. Dolphins like to swim in boat wakes like surfers catching waves. 40. Manatees have roly-poly bodies because their stomachs and intestines must be large enough to digest their plant diet. 41. Like sharks, manatees constantly replace their teeth throughout their lifetimes. 42. Dolphins and porpoises have a special structure in their heads, called a melon, that produces sound waves. 43. A sea otter has loose skin under each front limb that it uses like a pocket to store food. 44. Manatees almost went extinct in Florida, but because of conservation efforts, thousands now swim in the waters once again. 45. Florida manatees have learned to use the warm water flowing from power plants to stay warm during the winter. 46. The extinct Steller's sea cow was a manatee relative more than 30 feet (10 m) long—three times the size of manatees today! 47. Scientists can learn details about a whale's life history from its earwax. 48. Harp seals are born on icebergs. 49. Dugongs like to relax by "standing" on their tails with their heads over the water's surface. 50. On Sable Island off Nova Scotia, Canada, the largest seal colony—100,000 gray seals— come every winter to breed. 51. Underwater noises such as ship sonar may damage whales' hearing. 52. Seals have 1,500 nerve endings in each whisker; cats have only about 200. 53. Baby dugongs will catch a ride on their mother's back. 54. In British Columbia, mountain lions hunt ocean-dwelling seals and sea lions. 55. Dolphins have unique whistles that they use to identify each other—the same way humans use names. 56. In 2009, a beluga whale saved a drowning diver by pushing her to the

surface. 57. A blue whale can be as long as a basketball court. 58. Seals are related to bears, raccoons, and skunks. 59. A narwhal's horn is actually one big tooth that grows through its upper lip. 60. Experts can tell how old a seal or a sea lion is by the growth rings in its teeth—just like a tree's. 61. Using echolocation, dolphins may be able to "see" a pregnant woman's growing baby. 62. Whales sing by moving air around inside their heads. 63. Dolphins have belly buttons. 64. Blue whales can eat half a million calories in a single mouthful. 65. Each humpback whale's tail is as unique as a human fingerprint. 66. Some whales stick their heads out of the water to see their surroundings in a move called a spyhop. 67. Walruses sometimes sleep by anchoring their tusks into the ice and letting their bodies hang in the water. 68. Humpback whales get their name from the way they arch their backs before they dive. 69. Supersocial bottlenose dolphins can gather in groups of more than 1,000. 70. *Gomphotaria pugnax* was a prehistoric walrus with four tusks. 71. Beluga whales can live in water at the freezing point, 32°F (0°C). 72. Humpback whales have bumps covering their heads, each with a stiff hair inside. Scientists don't know why. 73. Mother dolphins sing to their unborn babies. 74. Newborn dolphins and orcas—and their mothers—do not sleep for a month after they're born. 75. Walruses can puff up their necks to make a built-in neck pillow for comfortable sleeping. 76. Dolphins have no sense of smell. 77. Pinnipeds, the group that includes seals and sea lions, evolved from a land-dwelling carnivore. 78. Aside from primates such as apes and humans, sea otters are one of the only mammals known to use tools. 79. Elephant seals are the biggest of all seals. Males can weigh up to 8,800 pounds (4,000 kg)—about the same as the biggest hippopotamuses. 80. The walruses with the biggest tusks are usually the dominant ones. 81. Polar bears spend so much time on sea ice that they're technically marine, not land, mammals. 82. Spectacled porpoises get their name from the dark rings around their eyes. 83. Beluga whales can swim backward. 84. Orcas hunt as a team, and different groups in different areas have their own hunting strategies. 85. A humpback whale's tail can be 18 feet (5.5 m) wide. 86. Young humpback whales "whisper" to their mothers at low volume. Scientists think this may be so orcas don't overhear and attack them. 87. Bottlenose dolphins swallow fish head first, so the spines don't catch in their throats. 88. Sperm whales can dive deeper than 3,000 feet (1,000 m) and stay underwater for 90 minutes. 89. According to sailing superstition, spotting dolphins at sea brings good luck. 90. Whale bones were once used to make umbrella ribs. 91. A blue whale's calls are louder than a jet engine. 92. Beluga whales are born gray, and it takes years for them to turn completely white. 93. Since gray whales were protected from commercial hunting in 1947, their population in the eastern Pacific has bounced back to healthy levels. 94. Sea otters often have a favorite rock that they carry with them wherever they go. 95. Beluga whales

manatee

communicate with a wide range of sounds: They moo, chirp, whistle, and squeal, and even blow bubbles from their blowholes. 96. Blue whales live about as long as humans: 80 to 90 years. 97. Harp seals are born with white fur to help hide them against the ice and snow in their Arctic home. 98. Narwhals are sometimes called the unicorns of the sea because of their long tusks. 99. During breeding season, more than 75,000 northern fur seals can be found on the Pribilof Islands off the coast of Alaska. 100. The world's rarest marine mammal is the vaquita, a small porpoise that lives in the Gulf of Mexico.

humpback whale

1
Wolves are the LARGEST MEMBERS of the dog family.

2
Adult gray wolves can weigh up to 175 POUNDS (79 kg).

3
Wolves HUNT IN PACKS of about six to 10 animals—but a single wolf is powerful enough to kill a moose.

4
Wolves HOWL MORE TO THEIR "FRIENDS"—the wolves they spend the most time with.

5
A wolf can eat 20 POUNDS (9 kg) of meat in a single sitting—that's the same as 80 hamburgers.

6
Besides meat, wolves also like to EAT FRUITS and VEGETABLES.

7
A wolf pack is led by an ALPHA MALE and an ALPHA FEMALE. The alpha female makes most of the decisions for the pack.

8
ALL the ADULT WOLVES in a PACK work together to help TAKE CARE of the PUPS.

9
Wolf PUPS are BORN WITH BLUE EYES. They begin to turn yellow at about eight weeks.

10
Wolves RUN ON THEIR TOES.

11
A wolf can SMELL PREY more than ONE MILE (1.6 KM) AWAY.

12
Some people once believed WOLF POOP COULD TREAT STOMACHACHES and VISION PROBLEMS.

13
The gray wolf once RANGED ACROSS MORE AREA than any other land mammal, except for lions and humans—now they live in parts of North America, Europe, Asia, and North Africa.

14
Wolf puppies weigh only ONE POUND (0.5 kg) when they're born.

15
Wolves can hear something as far as 10 MILES (16 km) away.

16
A wolf can bite with 1,500 POUNDS of force per square inch (105 kg/sq cm). (Humans bite with 300 pounds of force per square inch.)

17
About 65,000 GRAY WOLVES live in the United States and Canada. (There were once about two million.)

18
In the Middle Ages, some people believed POWDERED WOLF LIVER could lessen the pain of childbirth.

19
Ireland was once called "WOLF-LAND" because so many wolves lived there.

20
Like humans, wolves use FACIAL EXPRESSIONS to communicate with each other.

21
DIRE WOLVES— bigger versions of modern wolves— were prehistoric wolves that went extinct about 10,000 YEARS AGO.

22
Wolves can run at a top speed of about 40 MILES AN HOUR (64 km/h) for a short time.

23
A wolf pack can travel 125 MILES (201 km) in one day.

24
Gray wolves' coats can actually be WHITE, BROWN, GRAY, CINNAMON, or BLACK.

25
Wolves howl to LET OTHER PACK MEMBERS KNOW where they are.

50 HOWLING FACTS ABOUT WOLVES

26
A wolf pack's TERRITORY can be as large as 1,200 SQUARE MILES (3,100 sq km).

27
Some scientists think wolves hunt in packs to help keep ravens from STEALING THEIR KILLS.

28
To ward off babies' teething pain, having them wear A NECKLACE WITH A WOLF TOOTH was once thought to be a MAGICAL CHARM.

29
When humans IMITATE A WOLF'S HOWL, wild wolves will sometimes howl back.

30
The Japanese word for wolf means "GREAT GOD."

31
Wolves were one of the first animals PROTECTED AS ENDANGERED species in the United States.

32
Wolves often MATE FOR LIFE.

33
Wolves can go more than a week WITHOUT EATING.

34
In the summer, when FOOD IS PLENTIFUL, wolves often HUNT ALONE.

35
Wolves mostly PREY ON LARGE ANIMALS such as deer, elk, and moose.

36
Wolves in Canada— sometimes called "SEA WOLVES"—fish for salmon.

37
Wolves can live up to 13 YEARS in the wild.

38
The red wolf may be a cross between a GRAY WOLF and a COYOTE.

39
Some Arabian wolves can weigh as little as 30 POUNDS (14 kg).

40
In Roman mythology, ROMULUS and REMUS are twin brothers who were RAISED BY WOLVES and founded the city of Rome.

41
One group of "sea wolves" on the Canadian coast is known to SWIM AS FAR AS EIGHT MILES (13 km) at one time.

42
Wolves don't howl at the MOON.

43
Usually, only the ALPHA FEMALE and ALPHA MALE in a pack have CUBS.

44
Wolves have WEBBED TOES that help them swim and walk over snow.

45
Wolves have about 200 MILLION SCENT CELLS in their noses. (Humans have about five million.)

46
Australia's DINGOES are a type of wolf.

47
When a pack of wolves howls, they purposefully HIT DIFFERENT NOTES to make the pack SOUND BIGGER.

48
One species of prehistoric wolf may have HUNTED WOOLLY MAMMOTHS.

49
A wolf howl can be heard up to SIX MILES (10 km) away in a forest.

50
Wolves hide EXTRA FOOD in under- ground caches. When the cache is empty, the wolf MARKS IT WITH PEE to note that the FOOD IS GONE.

1 Chameleons' skin changes color depending on the temperature, the environment, and their mood.

2 Peach-faced lovebirds have bright peach-colored heads and green bodies, which match the cactuses where they nest.

3 Sea stars, which range in color from orange to red to purple, can't see color themselves.

4 Light-reflecting crystals in chameleons' skin cells are what give them their different colors.

5 The gooty sapphire tarantula gets its name from the bright blue hairs that cover its body.

25 BRIGHT FACTS ABOUT COLORFUL

6 Researchers discovered that jewel bugs, which have bright, shiny colors and metallic spots, are better at hiding from bird predators than plain-colored insects are.

7 Rainbow parrotfish have parrot-like beaks that they use to scrape algae off rock and coral.

8 The scarlet macaw, one of the world's largest parrots, has an almost featherless face, but it has bright red, blue, and yellow feathers everywhere else.

9 The texture of bright red strawberry anemones resembles the fruit.

10 Sea anemones live in both warm and cold waters, but the most colorful ones thrive in warm water.

11 Stork-billed kingfishers use their large, scarlet-red beaks to hunt for crabs, fish, and frogs, chasing away eagles that try to steal their food.

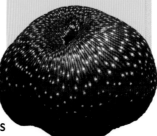

12

The **orchid mantis mimics the color and look of the flower** it is named after to **attract prey.**

13

The male ring-necked pheasant, which has an **iridescent green neck** and **bright red face,** has a roosterlike crow that can be heard a mile (1.6 km) away.

14

Colorful **wild betta fish can live in waters with low-oxygen levels,** like shallow rice paddies and small ponds.

15

A mandarin duck, which has **orange, blue, and purple feathers,** a pink bill, and is **native to East Asia,** was spotted in **Central Park, New York, U.S.A.**

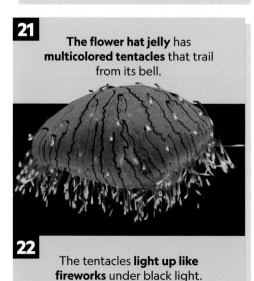

16

Blue poison dart frogs' bright color warns predators that **they are toxic—and capable of paralyzing** or **killing anything that attacks them.**

17

Christmas tree worms, marine worms that live on coral, **look like bright colorful Christmas trees.**

ANIMALS

18

Parrotfish can change their **shape, gender,** and **color.**

21

The flower hat jelly has **multicolored tentacles** that trail from its bell.

22

The tentacles **light up like fireworks** under black light.

19

When **prey is difficult to capture,** the lilac-breasted roller swoops over it, flutters its wings to confuse it, and then **grabs it.**

23

Parrotfish spend 90 percent of their day **picking algae off coral.**

24

Young, transparent bedbugs turn red after feasting on blood.

20

Adult blue tang fish are royal blue and canary yellow but when stressed turn a deeper blue and violet.

25

A **toucan's colorful beak is serrated** like a knife to cut into food.

»15 ANIMAL-INSPIRED INVENTIONS

1

Modeled on the design of a termite mound, a seven-story building in Harare, Zimbabwe, **stays cool in the summer** and **warm in the winter** without air-conditioning or heating.

2

Scientists built a **robot "wing"** modeled on **penguins' super swimming ability.** They hope it will allow ship propellers to make more precise movements.

3

Geckos use **millions of tiny hairs on their toes to climb walls,** and their gripping power has inspired the **design of tape** so strong that one small patch can hold **hundreds of pounds (kg) of weight.**

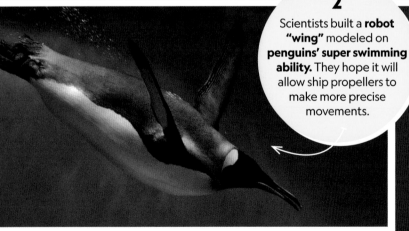

4. A Japanese engineer designed the **"nose," or front, of a high-speed train** based on the beak of a kingfisher, a bird that dives into the water without making a splash.

5

To **reduce the area that wind turbines take up,** researchers designed them to be **spaced like a school of swimming fish.**

6. To treat **human wounds and burns,** doctors created **a patch with tiny needles** that swells in water, adapting **a technique from a parasitic worm.**

7. Mimicking the **pattern of scales on a shark's** skin that keeps **barnacles and algae from sticking, scientists created** a coating that **repels germs.**

8. Scientists **etched a ball python's skin pattern** onto a **metal surface, creating a super-slippery surface** that could help reduce friction in a machine's moving parts.

9. A technology company's **computer screens** and e-readers mimic **how butterflies' wings reflect light.**

10

Scientists **copied the bumps on humpback whales' flippers** to create **wind turbine blades** that could capture more airflow and **produce more energy.**

11. Scientists are designing a **painless needle** for shots that **mimics a mosquito's stinger.**

12. Mussels use a **sticky, slimy substance** to adhere to rocks, and researchers copied it to help wounds stop bleeding in just 60 seconds, without scarring.

13

A desert beetle that uses the ridges on its back to **collect moisture** from the air has inspired scientists to **create devices that could collect water** on a larger scale.

14

In the 1930s, a British inventor looked at the **reflective nature of a cat's eyes** to design road reflectors for nighttime driving.

15

The **long tentacles of jellyfish** inspired scientists to make a device that **traps cancer cells** in the **blood.**

1. Newborn cubs are the same size and weight as an ice-cream sandwich.

2. You can **watch the pandas** at Smithsonian's National Zoo in Washington, D.C., eat and play any time of day on an online **"Giant Panda Cam."**

3. 99 percent of wild giant pandas' diet is **bamboo.**

4. One percent of giant pandas' diet is **meat,** including small rodents.

5. Pandas eat between **26 to 84 pounds** (12–38 kg) of bamboo **every day.**

6. Pandas eat more than **22,000 pounds** (9,979 kg) of bamboo in **a year.**

7. Pandas spend about **12 hours** a day eating.

8. They **poop** dozens of times a day.

9. Pandas often **eat in an upright sitting position** with their back legs stretched out in front of them.

10. Pandas' teeth are **self-repairing,** which allows them to eat tough stalks of bamboo.

11. Pandas' molars, or back teeth, are **flat,** which helps them crush hard bamboo shoots and its leaves and stems.

12. Pandas can snap a piece of bamboo, three inches (8 cm) in diameter, in half with their teeth.

13. Male pandas sometimes do a **"handstand"** to leave scent marks on trees.

14. Doing a handstand gets a panda bear's rear end higher on the tree—and the higher the **scent mark,** the more notice it gets from other pandas.

15. In China, pandas are called large **bear-cats.**

16. Each panda has its own unique markings.

17. A **rare genetic mutation** makes some pandas brown and white.

18. Scientists debated whether pandas were a type of raccoon or bear, but **DNA analysis** links them to bears.

19. Pandas are the **most vocal of all bear species.**

20. Pandas make a **"bleat"** that sounds similar to a lamb or a goat's.

75 GIGANTIC FACTS ABOUT PANDAS

21. A panda's **bite force** is almost as strong as an African lion's.

22. Zookeepers sometimes put pandas' **food in trees** to encourage them to climb.

23. A panda mother **cradles her newborn cub in one paw** and holds it close to her chest.

24. **Panda moms** don't leave their den for several days after giving birth, not even to eat or drink.

25. Panda cubs don't open their eyes until they're about two months old.

26. Pandas have thick and heavy bones relative to their size, but they are exceptionally **flexible animals** that love to do **somersaults.**

27. **China** gifted the United States **two pandas** as part of President Richard Nixon's historic visit to the country. (The U.S. gave China a pair of musk oxen.)

28. Today, almost all pandas living in zoos are **on loan** from China.

29. A **newborn** panda is about 1/900th the size of its mother.

30. Because fresh bamboo is difficult to keep on hand, zoos also feed pandas **biscuits, carrots, and apples.**

31. **Red pandas** are raccoon-size mammals that eat bamboo and live in Asia, but they aren't closely related to giant pandas.

32. March 16 is National Panda Day in the United States.

33. To keep pandas stimulated, zoos sometimes give them **tubs of bubbles** to pop.

34. When Tian Tian, a panda that lives at the Smithsonian National Zoo, turned 22, he got a **cake** made from his **favorite foods,** including juice, apples, pears, sweet potatoes, bananas, and sugarcane.

35. One of the **largest threats** to giant panda survival is **habitat destruction,** which causes groups of pandas to be isolated from each other.

36. Zookeepers in China **dress up in panda costumes** to prevent panda cubs—which one day may be released in the wild—from getting too attached to humans.

37. **Ten million years ago,** a bamboo-eating animal similar to a panda lived in what is now Hungary, suggesting pandas originated in Europe, not Asia.

38. Giant panda mothers give birth to **twins** about 50 percent of the time.

39. Because of their mostly plant-based diet, pandas only expend half the energy other large animals do.

40. Giant pandas' scientific name, *Ailuropoda melanoleuca,* means **"black and white cat foot."**

41. Pandas' white body markings help them **hide in snow,** while their black body markings help them **hide in shade.**

42. Pandas' **black eye patches** vary in size and shape, which may help pandas recognize each other.

43. Pandas **cover up their eyes** with their paws when they don't want to appear aggressive.

44. A **panda's tail is five inches** (13 cm) long—the second longest tail in the bear family after the sloth bear's.

45. Pandas have **catlike pupils** with vertical slits.

46. They have **five fingers** and an extra bony stump that serves as a **thumb.**

47. Pandas' fur is covered in an oily substance, which keeps it **waterproof.**

48. A panda's **esophagus** (the tube that carries food to its stomach) has a tough lining that might help protect it from bamboo splinters.

49. A panda's stomach has extra-strong muscles for mashing and digesting bamboo.

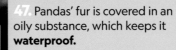

50. Pandas move only about **500 yards** (457 m) a day.

51. Pandas have **fur-padded paws** to help them walk on ice and snow.

52. Wild pandas eat more than **60 types** of bamboo.

53. Pandas may look soft, but their **fur feels scratchy,** like sheep wool.

54. On all four paws, a giant panda **can stand up to three feet** (0.9 m) tall—that's waist-high for the average sixth grader.

55. Pandas are the only bears that survive almost entirely on **vegetation.**

56. Panda moms can recognize the **scent of their cubs** after years apart.

57. Pandas use their tails to **smear odors** from the scent gland under their tails on anything they might pass.

58. Their scent can be smelled by other pandas up to **18 miles** (29 km) away.

59. A zoo in Denmark created an enclosure for its two pandas that resembles the **Chinese yin-yang symbol.**

60. Pandas appeared in **Chinese literature** more than 2,000 years ago.

61. A zoo in Thailand sold paper made from **panda poop.**

62. Bei Bei, a panda from Smithsonian's National Zoo, flew to China in 2019 on a **FedEx plane** with a decal on the side that featured him eating bamboo.

63. The plane was nicknamed the **"Panda Express."**

64. In 2014, 1,600 **giant papier-mâché pandas** toured cities around the world to promote conservation of pandas and their habitat.

65. In Germany, people set up a "hospital" to **repair any touring pandas** that might need a touch-up.

66. Snow leopards are a top **predator** of pandas, mostly attacking cubs.

67. **Pandas sometimes roll**—rather than walk—to move around.

68. Pandas are good tree climbers, capable of reaching heights of 75 feet (23 m).

69. Unlike many other types of bears, pandas **don't hibernate.**

70. About **1,800 pandas** live in the wild.

71. Pandas' **dark ears** can be a signal to potential predators that they are **fierce.**

72. **Panda dogs** are Chow Chow dogs groomed to look like pandas.

73. A panda cub **licks its mom's lips,** which helps boost the cub's immune system.

74. Pandas are usually born in **August.**

75. **Wild pandas** only live in the remote mountains of central China.

1
Some **5.4 million households** in the United States have a small animal **as a pet.**

2
Roborovski dwarf hamsters are only about two inches (5 cm) long—**the length of two quarters.**

3
A Roborovski dwarf hamster is **also called a robo.**

4
Guinea pigs are **social animals** and like to be around other guinea pigs.

5
The **National Mouse Club** of Great Britain was founded in 1895 for people who **breed and keep pet mice.**

6
Mice eat around **20 times a day.**

7
Common musk turtles only grow to be about **four inches (10 cm) long**—that's smaller than a cell phone.

8
In the wild, common **musk turtles burrow into the mud** to spend the winter.

9
Musk turtles **eat algae, and their shells** also can be striped with it.

10
Chinchillas, originally from the **Andes mountains in South America,** were kept as pets by the region's ancient Inca.

11
In the wild, chinchillas **make dens in holes or rock crevices** found in their mountain homes.

12
A scientist placed a **small exercise wheel outside** and found that wild mice, just like pet mice, **like to run on them, too.**

13
A male mouse **sings a high-pitched song** to a female mouse when trying to **attract her.**

14
Hamsters are typically **most active at night.**

pet rat

35
PINT-SIZE FACTS ABOUT POCKET PETS

15 The **Abyssinian breed of guinea pig** has facial hair around its nose that **looks like a mustache.**

16 The **whiskers** on a mouse's nose help it find its way in the dark.

17 The male **green anole** has a flap of pink skin called a dewlap that it uses to **communicate.**

18 Common **musk turtles** get their name from the smelly liquid they produce when startled.

19 In the wild, mice can **live in a lot of different environments,** from deserts to mountains and woodlands.

20 Guinea pigs are also known as **cavies,** a name that comes from their **scientific name,** *Cavia porcellus.*

21 **Chinchillas** have superdense fur but weigh less than **two pounds** (0.9 kg).

22 The Peruvian and Abyssinian breeds of guinea pigs have **rosettes,** areas where the fur looks as if it is growing in a circle.

23 Some mice have **tails** that are as long as their bodies.

24 Hamsters like to **sleep in small, enclosed spaces,** such as toilet paper tubes.

25 Male green anoles **defend their territories** by doing "push-ups" with their front legs.

26 Female green anoles **lay eggs in moist soil,** and when they hatch they look like **little adults.**

27 **Fat-tailed gerbils** are named for their **club-shaped tails,** which are used to **store fat and water.**

28 Hamsters have pouches in their cheeks **for storing food—** the pouches can extend about **half the length of their bodies.**

29 Guinea pigs make a variety of different sounds, including a purring or **chutting sound that can mean they're happy.**

30 There's **no need to give** a pet mouse a bath as mice will clean themselves.

31 In the wild, **fat-tailed gerbils** live in sand burrows in the deserts of northern Africa.

32 "Hamster" roughly translates to **"Mr. Saddlebags"** in Arabic, the language **spoken in Syria,** where it lives in the wild.

33 **Green anoles can change color,** from bright green to brown, in seconds.

34 The common hamster is **endangered in the wild.**

35 Mice have been found **living in** research stations in **Antarctica.**

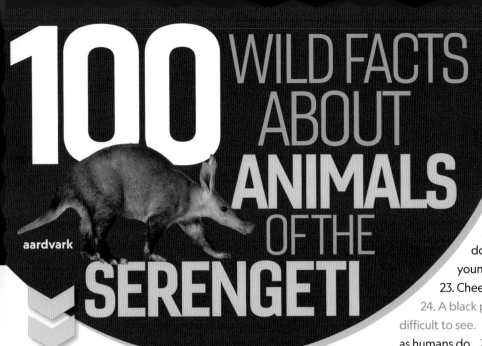

100 WILD FACTS ABOUT ANIMALS OF THE SERENGETI

aardvark

1. The Serengeti, an area of 12,000 square miles (30,000 sq km) in east-central Africa, is home to animals such as lions, leopards, buffalo, African elephants, and rhinoceroses. 2. African wild dogs often make their den in an abandoned aardvark hole. 3. The largest land migration on Earth takes place on the Serengeti. 4. About 1.2 million wildebeests, along with thousands of zebras and gazelles, travel 300 miles (483 km) in search of grass to eat. 5. When an elephant tries to eat leaves from a type of acacia tree in Kenya, ants run up the trunk, forcing the elephant to leave the tree alone. 6. Male topi antelope pretend there are predators nearby to scare females into staying close for protection. 7. Ostriches use their wings as rudders to help them make quick turns, stops, and zigzags. 8. Cape buffalo are known as the "black death" because of their aggressive nature. 9. Baby elephants suck their trunks, just as human babies suck their thumbs. 10. Cheetahs are so fast they usually overtake their prey in less than a minute. 11. Scientists used tools for detecting earthquakes to listen to vibrations in the ground when elephants walked, ran, snorted, and grunted. 12. Zebras, donkeys, and horses evolved from the same ancestor, but zebras can't be domesticated. 13. Ostriches can't fly, but they hold their wings out to help them balance when they run. 14. Elephants remember the location of watering holes, even if they're as far as 31 miles (50 km) away. 15. One elephant can hear another's low, rumbling calls from

African wild dog

five miles (8 km) away. 16. Elephants have a sixth "toe" beneath their skin that helps support their weight. 17. A leopard's spots—and a zebra's stripes—camouflage these animals by breaking up the outline of their bodies. 18. Adult male elands, the world's largest antelope, make a clicking sound when they walk that can be heard more than a mile (1.6 km) away. 19. A leopard can climb 50 feet (15 m) up a tree while holding prey heavier and larger than itself in its jaws. 20. "Aardvark" means "earth pig." 21. African wild dogs regurgitate, or vomit up, meat to feed their young. 22. Zebras have black skin under their white fur. 23. Cheetahs can't roar; they make a sound called a chirrup. 24. A black panther is a dark-colored leopard; its spots are just difficult to see. 25. Young elephants lose their first set of teeth, just as humans do. 26. Zebras, antelope, and even ostriches sometimes group together for safety. 27. Aardvarks eat their food whole and then "chew" it up with their muscular stomachs. 28. An aardvark is about the same size and weight as an adult human. 29. One elephant molar can weigh five pounds (2.3 kg). 30. Leopards can hear ultrasonic sounds, which are too high for humans to detect. 31. At up to 42 pounds (19 kg) and five feet (1.5 m) tall, the kori bustard is the world's largest flying bird, but it doesn't fly unless threatened. 32. Just as humans are right-handed or left-handed, elephants can be right-tusked or left-tusked. 33. A giraffe's neck is too short to reach the ground. 34. A male African elephant is nearly the same weight as a *Tyrannosaurus rex* was. 35. African wild dogs will care for sick pack members. 36. African elephants have ears shaped like the African continent. 37. Leopards and tigers are both good swimmers. 38. A zebra's stripes help keep biting flies away. 39. An elephant's trunk has 40,000 muscles. 40. A group of hyenas can eat an entire zebra—including the bones and fur—in less than half an hour. 41. An African elephant's ears act like an air conditioner to cool the animal down. 42. White spots on a leopard's ears and on the tip of its tail help the cats find each other in long grass. 43. An aardvark's burrow can be about as long as a semitrailer. 44. African wild dogs can outrun most of their prey, hitting speeds of 40 miles an hour (64 km/h). 45. An elephant's skin can be one inch (2.5 cm) thick in some places. 46. Leopards are the smallest of the big cats, but pound for pound, they are the strongest. 47. The tiny antelope called the dik-dik is named for the female's alarm call. 48. The name of the klipspringer, a type of antelope, gets its name from the Dutch word for "rock jumper." 49. The leader of an elephant herd is the oldest and most experienced female. 50. Female hyenas are larger, more aggressive, and more muscular than males. 51. Bison, which live in North America, are sometimes mistakenly called buffalo—even though they are not closely related to the African animal. 52. Elephant tusks are actually overgrown incisor teeth. 53. African buffalo can weigh up to 1,840 pounds (835 kg) and can live in herds of up to 500 individuals. 54. African elephants are the world's largest land animal. 55. Female cheetahs live alone, while males live in small groups. 56. To cool off and clean up, elephants suck water into their trunk and then spray it over their

bodies. 57. Zebras groom each other. 58. Impalas, gazelles, and wildebeests are all types of antelope. 59. Hyenas convey their social status with their laugh. 60. African elephants can live more than 50 years in the wild. 61. About the size of a rabbit, the royal antelope is the world's smallest antelope. 62. African wild dogs' hunting trips are successful about 80 percent of the time. (Lions are successful about 30 percent of the time.) 63. In one study, hyenas cooperated to solve problems better than chimpanzees did. 64. The Colobus monkey spends almost its entire life in the trees. 65. Each zebra's stripes are unique. 66. African wild dogs can swivel their big ears to pick up faraway sounds. 67. Vervet monkeys use facial expressions to communicate. 68. A black mamba's venom can kill in as few as 20 minutes. 69. In one leap, impalas can cover distances as far as 33 feet (10 m). 70. Vervet monkeys have a green tint to their fur that helps camouflage them in trees. 71. Elephants use dust as sunscreen. 72. About 500,000 baby wildebeests are born on the Serengeti each year. 73. Secretary birds prefer to hunt on foot rather than fly. 74. About 80 percent of wildebeests are born within the same two-week period. 75. Antelope are grazers, but some have been known to also kill and eat insects, small mammals, and birds. 76. African dung beetles use the Milky Way to help them navigate at night. 77. Elephants have the longest pregnancy of any known mammal—22 months. 78. Reebok sneakers are named after the rhebok antelope, a good runner, jumper, and climber. 79. Secretary birds

ostrich

kill venomous snakes by kicking them. 80. The three species of zebra—plains, Grevy's, and mountain—all live in Africa. 81. Nile crocodile fathers often roll their eggs gently in their mouths to help the babies hatch. 82. Gazelles sometimes jump up high into the air with all their feet off the ground, a behavior called "pronking." 83. African wild dogs are sometimes called "painted wolves" for their coats, which have splashes of brown, black, white, and yellow. 84. African wild dogs are neither dogs nor wolves, but their own species. 85. A group of giraffes is called a tower. 86. Cheetahs only need to drink water every three to four days. 87. Some gazelles can reach speeds of up to 60 miles an hour (97 km/h) for short bursts. 88. African wild dogs "vote" by sneezing. 89. Fischer's lovebirds mate for life. 90. An aardvark's sticky tongue can be 12 inches (30.5 cm) long. 91. The Nile crocodile can live for more than 100 years. 92. The elephant's closest relative is a small, furry mammal called a rock hyrax. 93. An aardvark's nostrils seal up when it's digging to keep out dust and insects. 94. Female gazelles hide their babies in tall grasses to protect them from predators. 95. Female giraffes often return to where they were born to give birth. 96. Ancient Egyptians mummified Nile crocodiles. 97. Antelope have horizontal pupils to help them spot predators from far away. 98. Baby giraffes inherit their spots from their mothers. 99. Some species of gazelle can shrink their hearts and livers to survive drought. 100. Colobus monkeys are able to eat toxic leaves that other monkeys cannot.

a herd of young male giraffes

1
FISH have FOUR NOSTRILS.

2
Instead of TEETH on their upper jaw, SPERM WHALES have a SERIES OF SOCKETS that their LOWER TEETH FIT INSIDE.

3
Some TICKS have EYES on their BACKS.

4
LIZARDS have a THIRD "EYE"—a patch of light-sensitive cells—on TOP OF THEIR HEADS that they use to NAVIGATE BY THE SUN.

5
A FROG'S TONGUE is ATTACHED at the FRONT OF ITS MOUTH instead of at the back like ours.

6
A BOX JELLYFISH has EYES but NO BRAIN.

7
Some SALAMANDERS have GLANDS on their CHINS that RELEASE CHEMICALS to ATTRACT MATES.

8
The PIT VIPER is named for the HEAT-SENSING HOLE on its FACE.

9
The snake *ERPETON TENTACULATUS* has TWO SHORT TENTACLES on its SNOUT—the only snake in the world with this feature.

10
ZOMBIE WORMS have NO MOUTHS. To eat whale bones, they OOZE AN ACID that DISSOLVES THE BONE, then absorb it through their skin.

11
One species of TURTLE PEES THROUGH ITS MOUTH.

12
About 10 PERCENT of a CAT'S BONES are in its TAIL.

13
A HAMSTER'S CHEEK POUCHES EXTEND from its MOUTH TO ITS HIPS.

14
PIGEONS produce a MILK-LIKE SUBSTANCE in their DIGESTIVE SYSTEM that they COUGH UP into their BABIES' MOUTHS.

15
MANY ANIMALS, including birds, cats, dogs, and camels, have a THIRD EYELID.

16
Some SPIDERS' BRAINS take up 80 PERCENT of their BODIES.

17
A DOG'S SHOULDER BLADES are NOT CONNECTED to its body by any BONES.

18
The PLATYPUS has NO STOMACH.

sagra buqueti beetle

50
FACTS ABOUT
ODD ANIMAL ANATOMY

19
CATS have the same throat ANATOMY AS DOGS—and THEY CAN BARK.

20
You can ESTIMATE a COW'S AGE by COUNTING the RINGS on its HORNS.

21
Some CAVE-DWELLING CREATURES have evolved to LOSE their EYES.

22
The GIRAFFE WEEVIL'S NECK can be about HALF the LENGTH OF ITS BODY.

23
Each of a TARSIER'S EYES is AS BIG AS its BRAIN.

24
A BLUE WHALE'S TONGUE can WEIGH as much as an ELEPHANT.

25
The GIANT SPHINX MOTH has a proboscis, or TUBULAR MOUTHPART, that's TWICE the LENGTH OF ITS BODY.

26
The MALE MAGNIFICENT FRIGATEBIRD has a red, BALLOONLIKE SAC on its THROAT that it INFLATES to ATTRACT FEMALES.

27
The BOOTLACE WORM is only a FEW MILLIMETERS WIDE, but it can reach 180 FEET (55 m) in LENGTH.

28
QUEEN WARRIOR TERMITES are about FOUR INCHES (10 cm) LONG.

29
The FROG-LEGGED LEAF BEETLE uses its oversize, FROGLIKE LEGS for WRESTLING other BEETLES.

30
A SHRIMP'S HEART is IN ITS HEAD.

31
ELEPHANTS CAN'T JUMP. That's likely because of their huge size, inflexible ankles, and weak leg muscles.

32
It can take a SLOTH about a MONTH to DIGEST A MEAL.

33
FROGS CAN'T VOMIT unless they EJECT their ENTIRE STOMACHS.

34
A GRIZZLY BEAR'S BITE is STRONG enough to CRUSH A BOWLING BALL.

35
PRAIRIE DOGS "KISS" HELLO by TOUCHING their FRONT TEETH together.

36
FLAMINGOS are BORN with WHITE FEATHERS, but they TURN PINK from EATING ALGAE and BRINE SHRIMP.

37
ANTEATERS have NO TEETH. HARDENED FOLDS in their STOM-ACHS DO THE CHEWING.

38
CATS are the only known mammals that DON'T have SWEET TASTE RECEPTORS.

39
WOMBAT POOP is CUBE-SHAPED.

40
A KOALA'S FINGERPRINTS are so SIMILAR to a HUMAN'S they could confuse investigators at a crime scene.

41
FEMALE BATS give BIRTH while HANGING UPSIDE DOWN. They catch the baby in their wings.

42
Even though PENGUINS DON'T HAVE VISIBLE EARS, they have EXCELLENT HEARING.

43
The AYE-AYE has SIX FINGERS.

44
HORSESHOE CRABS have BLUE BLOOD.

45
OTTER POOP can SMELL like VIOLETS.

46
KANGAROO RATS SURVIVE their desert environment by EXCRETING CRYSTAL-LIKE PEE, which reduces the amount of water that is lost.

47
MANATEES use DIGESTIVE GAS to FLOAT in the water.

48
BALD UAKARIS are MONKEYS with hairless, bright red faces.

49
A WALLACE'S FLYING FROG can leap from a branch and splay its four webbed feet to GLIDE more than 50 FEET (15 m).

50
KINKAJOUS can turn their FEET BACKWARD.

1

Antarctica is the only continent with **no scorpions.**

2

Scorpions can have up to **100 live babies** at a time.

3

Scorpion mothers carry their babies on their backs for **10 to 20 days,** until the babies' soft outside shell hardens.

4

Scorpions are arachnids, **like spiders.**

5

Most scorpions are solitary, but **Arizona bark scorpions** hibernate in **groups of up to 40** in the winter.

25 STINGING FACTS ABOUT SCORPIONS

6

In hot temperatures, **scorpions can stilt, or lift their bodies up** from the ground **to stay cool.**

7

Some scorpions can **survive** being **frozen.**

8

Some scorpions can survive a year **without eating.**

9

Whip scorpions, which can spray acid from a long appendage, **are not scorpions at all.**

10

The emperor scorpion can be **eight inches (20 cm) long,** about as long as a **dinner fork.**

11

The grasshopper mouse is **immune** to scorpion stings.

12

Scorpions glow under **ultraviolet light.**

13

Some scientists think **scorpions** may be able to **sense light with their entire bodies.**

14

While most arachnids have short life spans, at least **one species of scorpion** can **live 25 years.**

15

Some scorpions eat small mice and lizards.

16

In 2009, **Thailand's "Scorpion Queen"** stayed in a glass room for **33 days with 5,000 venomous scorpions.**

17

The deathstalker scorpion strikes its victims at a **speed of 51 inches per second (130 cm/s),** the fastest of any scorpion measured.

18

About **25 species of scorpion** have **venom deadly** enough to kill a human.

19

A prehistoric sea scorpion that lived 460 million years ago was about **the size of a human.**

20

After mating, the **female scorpion** sometimes **eats the male.**

21

Scorpions have **sensors in their legs** that help them **find their way around.**

22

Scorpions do a **mating dance** while holding each other's pincers.

23

Hairs on their pincers are so **sensitive** that scorpions can **locate and grab a flying insect to eat.**

24

If a **mother scorpion is hungry,** she'll **sometimes** eat her babies.

25

Some scorpion species **"sing"** by **rubbing their legs** together, **just as crickets do.**

»15 LEAFY FACTS
ABOUT ANIMALS
OF THE KELP FOREST

1
Cabezon fish can swallow abalone whole and **spit out the shells.**

2. Kelp can **grow 18 inches** (46 cm) a day.

3
The yellowline arrow crab tears and chews up pieces of seaweed, then sticks them to its shell for **camouflage.**

4
Garibaldi fish have a **heart-shaped tail.**

7 Bat rays flap their fins to **move sand off clams** and other **buried prey.**

5 The older the **leopard shark,** the **paler its spots.**

6. Many species of kelp have **gas-filled bladders** called **pneumatocysts that hold up the kelp in the water.**

8. Sea urchins can **"see" with their feet.**

9. Sea urchins can **mow down** kelp forests at a rate of **30 feet** (9 m) a month.

10. Some species of kelp are **edible.**

11. If a sea star tries to **eat an abalone,** the abalone twists its shell to **throw off the attacker.**

12 Sea urchins have **self-sharpening teeth** that can chew through **rock.**

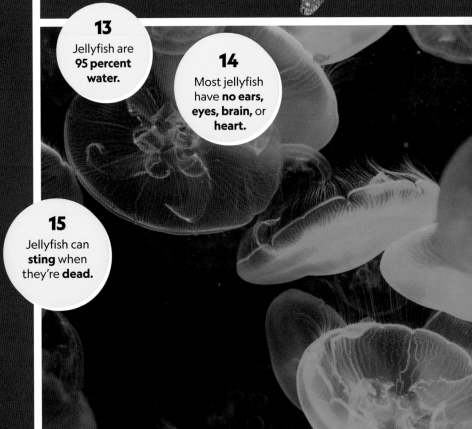

13 Jellyfish are **95 percent water.**

14 Most jellyfish have **no ears, eyes, brain,** or **heart.**

15 Jellyfish can **sting** when they're **dead.**

1. Many animals have stripes and spots **on their bodies to keep them camouflaged and safe from predators.**

2. No two Holstein cows have exactly the same pattern of spots on their black-and-white coats.

3. Adult Florida panthers have tan coats, but their **kittens are born with spots** on their **bodies and rings on their tails that fade** when they are about six months old.

4. The **patterns of spots** and **stripes on the coats** of **wild cats vary depending** on which **side of the cat you are viewing.**

5. Atlantic striped bass are also **known as "stripers"** for the **seven or eight stripes** they have on each of their sides.

6. Bumblebee species have more than **400 different color patterns.**

7. Making its home across North America, the **most common butterfly is the American copper,** which has orange wings with black dots.

8. Female lone star ticks, which most frequently bite humans, are **named for the one bright white spot, or "lone star,"** on their backs.

9. Calligraphy beetles come in many different colors—red, green, orange, and yellow—**but all have symmetrical patterns of dots and lines on their shells.**

10. The **large "eyespots" on the common buckeye butterfly**—whose range is the southern United States and Mexico—**make it easy to see.**

11. The **four-spotted velvet ant** is **actually a stinging wasp.**

12. The front of a Malayan tapir, a horselike mammal that lives in Southeast Asian rainforests, **is black with a white middle section, giving it the nickname "Oreo."**

13. With six to 10 white stripes on their tan coats, **male greater kudus,** a type of African antelope, **have more vibrant stripes than females do.**

14. Two-spotted stink bugs eat more than 100 different kinds of insect pests.

15. The tiger is the only cat species that is completely striped.

16. The **dark spots** on the Dalmatian's white coat vary in size from a **dime to a half-dollar.**

17. Some **foxes** have **one stripe down their back** and **another** one **across their shoulders,** forming **a cross.**

18. Researchers put striped coats on horses to learn how zebras' black-and-white stripes confuse insects, making it hard for them to bite and transmit deadly diseases.

19. If a British spotted pony has a dark coat with light spots, it's called a "snowflake" coat.

20. The jagged and irregular spots on leopards and jaguars are called rosettes because they look like rose flowers.

21. Leopard seals have spots all over their fur, just as their counterparts on land do.

22. Irregular yellow spots form two bands down the back of **spotted salamanders—and they even have spots on their feet.**

23. Tiger tails are ringed while **cheetah tails have spots at their base and stripes on the top third.**

24. The **Chinese character** for **"king" mimics** the horizontal **stripes on a tiger's forehead.**

25. When traveling through their forest homes, groups of **ring-tailed lemurs keep their tails raised high so that group members don't get lost.**

26. A small **system of blood vessels** underneath each one of the **spots on a giraffe's coat** can **release body heat** to help keep them cool.

27. Baby raccoons have **faint rings on their tails** that become **more pronounced** as they grow up.

28. The orange-and-black-striped wings of a monarch butterfly indicate whether they **are male or female**—males have a spot on each of their lower wings but females don't.

29. Male Wilson's birds of paradise have bright red and yellow feathers, blue legs, and a blue patch of skin with black lines on its head, all used to attract females.

30. The seven-spotted ladybug **was introduced** to North America more than **50 years ago to eat aphids that munch on crops.**

31. Jaguarundi kittens may **have spots on their coats,** but adults don't.

32. Some **skunk species** have **white stripes** on their fur to **warn animals of their smelly spray,** while others have **white spots that help keep them hidden.**

33. The **western diamond-backed rattlesnake shakes its rattles**—which are topped with a black-and-white ringed "tail"—**60 times per second to warn predators to stay away.**

34. Young zebras have brown stripes that darken to black as they grow up.

75 MARVELOUS FACTS ABOUT ANIMAL MARKINGS

35. Named for its markings that look like a clown costume, the **clown triggerfish uses its strong teeth and jaws to eat hard-shelled mollusks and sea urchins.**

36. **The large spotted genet,** a catlike mammal that lives in southern Africa, **has a spotted coat** and a **ringed tail, which it uses to help keep its balance when standing on two legs.**

37. The **color of a giraffe's coat** and the **shape of its spots vary depending** on what the **giraffe eats and where it lives.**

38. In the 1961 animated film *101 Dalmatians*, **the dogs in the movie sport a total of 6,469,952 spots.**

39. **Spotted moray eels poke just their heads out of their coral reef homes** to catch unsuspecting prey.

40. **Green anacondas have patterns** on the underside of their tails, **which are unique to each snake.**

41. Peacock males have about 165 to 170 eyespots on each of their colorful display feathers.

42. **Small black spots** form vertical lines on the **lemon butterflyfish's body,** and a black bar **extends** across **its eyes.**

43. In 2015, scientists found a **small giraffe in Uganda, just nine feet (2.7 m) tall, that had a long neck but short, stubby legs.**

44. The **bright yellow spots on a spotted turtle's shell can fade** as the turtle gets older.

45. To move quickly through the forest, **white-striped bongos tilt their chins upward so that their horns lie flat against their backs,** leaving bald spots where the horns' tips have rubbed away their fur.

46. **The Siberian chipmunk,** a small rodent known for its stripes, **is the only chipmunk species that doesn't live in North America.**

47. Unlike stingrays that hide along the sandy ocean bottom, **blue-spotted stingrays show off their vibrant blue spots and blue-striped tails to warn predators** of their **venomous spines.**

48. Rarely born in the wild, an all-white Bengal tiger lacks stripes on its coat.

49. With a skin pattern similar to a checkerboard, **whale sharks have spots and stripes** that are **unique to each individual shark.**

50. The **ten-lined June beetle,** named for the **10 white lines** on its back that are **visible when its wings are open, hisses when upset.**

51. **Venomous eastern coral snakes** and **nontoxic scarlet king snakes** both have red, black, and yellow bands, but the coral snake's red and yellow bands touch each other, while the scarlet king snake's don't.

52. **Five-lined skinks** have five lines on their bodies, and young skinks have **striking blue tails that they can break off to flee from a predator.**

53. **A black stripe down its back** is one way to **distinguish a gray fox from a coyote.**

54. **The spots on jaguars** (which live in the Americas) **are smaller and closer together than the spots on leopards** (which live in Africa).

55. Swarms of two-striped grasshoppers can destroy crops.

56. **Charles Darwin** had trouble understanding why male peacocks had elaborate feathers that females lacked, and **said the sight of the males "makes me sick!"**

57. His observations helped him develop the theory that **male animals can differ from females in ways that "show off" their fitness and make them more attractive as mates.**

58. The **bold white stripes** on a **badger's face warn predators** that it's dangerous.

59. After the movie *Finding Nemo* premiered, **sales of clown anemonefish tripled.**

60. Inspired by a line from the movie, **some children flushed their pet down the toilet to set it free.**

61. **Yellowtail wrasse fish are strong enough to push over rocks and coral** to find snails and crabs that live underneath.

62. **Clownfish** get their name from their striking coloration, which is **similar to the makeup clowns use on their faces.**

63. **Tropical zebrafish** get their common name from the **stripes on their bodies.**

64. Annamite striped rabbits, which live in the Annamite Mountains in Laos and Vietnam, get their common **name from the dark stripes on their backs.**

65. **The speckled Sussex,** a breed of backyard chicken, **gains more spots each time it molts**—the period when it loses and regrows its feathers.

66. **Chinstrap penguins,** named for the small black band around their white necks, are **also called bearded penguins.**

67. Two small **eyespots on the side of the two-spot octopus's head glow blue** and may **fool** other animals into **thinking they are its actual eyes.**

68. **Small marsupials** called numbats **develop white stripes across the length of their backs, which help them stay hidden on the forest floor** as they search for termites to eat.

69. Animals with colored flecks on their brown or gray coats are called "brindled."

70. The **saddleback caterpillar is named for the single brown spot on its back that's surrounded by a bright green "blanket,"** like a saddle on a horse.

71. **Raccoon butterflyfish** have a **black face mask and are active at night,** just like the land mammal.

72. **Plains zebras have wider stripes than Grevy's zebras,** a different species.

73. **Cave drawings in Europe show horses spotted like the Appaloosa,** leading experts to think they have been around since prehistoric times.

74. **About 70 percent of the genes found in zebrafish are also found in humans,** which makes the fish a popular animal to use in the study of human diseases.

75. Some **harmless snakes protect themselves** by mimicking the stripes and colors of venomous species.

1
E. B. White, who wrote *Charlotte's Web*, once HATCHED BARN SPIDERS in his apartment.

2
In the Lassie books, LASSIE is a FEMALE COLLIE, but the dogs that played the CHARACTER ON-SCREEN were ALWAYS MALE.

3
MRS. NORRIS, the cat in the Harry Potter movies, was a MAINE COON, a long-haired cat breed known for being a hardy barn cat.

4
Author Dav Pilkey based his Dog Man character on a comic he SKETCHED when he was in SECOND GRADE.

5
At about 25 feet (7.6 m) tall, Clifford the Big Red Dog is about 10 TIMES TALLER than the AVERAGE BLOODHOUND.

6
To make SVEN, the reindeer in the Frozen movies, seem lifelike, the animators studied the movements of REAL REINDEER.

7
The GERMAN SHEPHERD who starred in all 27 Rin Tin Tin movies was RESCUED from a FRENCH BATTLEFIELD by an American soldier during World War I.

8
Sweetpea in *The Secret Life of Pets* is a PARAKEET, a parrot that is around SEVEN INCHES (18 cm) from head to tail.

9
Sven's best friend, Kristoff, is based on the INDIGENOUS REINDEER HERDERS of Scandinavia.

10
Parakeets can understand that a BANANA HIDDEN UNDER a NAPKIN HASN'T DISAPPEARED but still exists.

11
In the movie *Pirates of the Caribbean*, TWO DIFFERENT BIRDS, one named Chips and the other Salsa, PLAYED the MACAW.

12
The PORGS in *Star Wars: The Last Jedi* were INSPIRED BY PUFFINS that live on an island off the Irish coast.

13
The porgs' antics are similar to PUFFINS', birds that are called "CLOWNS OF THE SEA" because of their clownlike faces.

14
A RARELY SPOTTED CRAB that hides in coral beds is named *Harryplax severus*, after the Harry Potter character SEVERUS SNAPE.

15
NAKED MOLE RATS HUDDLE to keep WARM, but Wilbur in Mo Willems' *Naked Mole Rat Gets Dressed* wears clothes.

16
To promote *March of the Penguins*, a CAR called "Ant-CARtica" was decked out to LOOK LIKE AN ICEBERG with penguins on top.

17
In *The Secret Life of Pets*, Mel is a purebred pug, one of the oldest dog breeds. Its history traces back more than 2,400 years.

18
ELEPHANTS and PIGS, featured in books by Mo Willems, are known for being SUPERSMART ANIMALS.

35 FACTS ABOUT ANIMALS IN BOOKS AND MOVIES

19
In *Blueberries for Sal,* a human child and a bear cub EAT WILD BLUEBERRIES— just LIKE REAL BEARS do to fatten up for the winter.

20
In the *Harry Potter* movie series, it took trainers three months to TEACH OWLS to CARRY LETTERS in their TALONS.

21
Snowy owls, like Hedwig in the Harry Potter series, have FEATHERS ON THEIR FEET to keep them WARM.

22
Hachi: A Dog's Tale is based on the TRUE STORY of a dog who, after his owner died, looked for him at a train station every day for many years.

23
In *Stellaluna,* a lost FRUIT BAT—a bat that lives in the tropics and eats nectar, pollen, and fruit—is REUNITED with her mother.

24
Scuttle in *The Little Mermaid* is a gull, a SEABIRD that follows ships to CATCH FISH thrown OVERBOARD.

25
In the *Wizard of Oz* movie, Dorothy's dog TOTO IS MALE, but the DOG ACTOR was FEMALE.

26
A bronze STATUE of Hachikō SITS OUTSIDE Tokyo's Shibuya station.

27
In *Moana,* Heihei is a bumbling rooster, but CHICKENS can understand that an OBJECT removed from sight STILL EXISTS.

28
In *The Lion King,* Pumbaa is a WART-HOG, an African mammal that lives in GROUPS of as many as 18 INDIVIDUALS.

29
Buddy, the dog in the *Air Bud* movies, was a STRAY who was RESCUED from the Sierra Nevada Mountains in California, U.S.A.

30
It took SIX MONTHS of training for Buddy to learn how to SHOOT a BASKETBALL through a hoop.

31
The movie *Oddball* tells the TRUE STORY of how a DOG PROTECTED little PENGUINS from foxes that almost wiped out the birds.

32
Only about a FOOT (0.3 m) TALL, little penguins are the SMALLEST SPECIES of PENGUINS.

33
Babar's mother was killed, and today AFRICAN ELEPHANTS are listed as a "VULNERABLE" SPECIES.

34
BABAR began as a story told by the author's mother, who called the elephant "BEBE," FRENCH FOR BABY.

THE STORY OF BABAR

35
The FIRST PET of Theodore Geisel, also known as DR. SEUSS, was a BROWN STUFFED DOG.

100 RAD FACTS ABOUT RODENTS

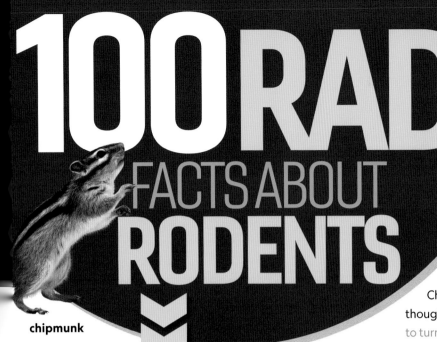

chipmunk

1. Rodents make up the largest group of mammals—there are more than 2,000 species. 2. The capybara, the largest rodent, can weigh as much as an adult human. 3. A "mouse potato" is someone who is always on the computer. 4. All rodents have two pairs of teeth, called incisors, in their upper and lower jaws, that grow continually throughout their lives. 5. Pygmy scaly-tailed flying squirrels, which live in trees in Central African forests, have scales on their tails to help them get a grip when climbing trees. 6. Hamsters can trace their history as pets to the 1930s, when a scientist from Jerusalem found a litter on an expedition and started raising them in his office. 7. Rodents can be found on every continent except Antarctica. 8. Syrian hamsters, the species of hamster commonly kept as pets, are considered vulnerable to extinction in the arid areas of Syria and Turkey where they live in the wild. 9. Great Britain's 7th Armored Division, which fought in the deserts of North Africa during World War II, uses a jerboa, a small rodent from the region, as its symbol. 10. Prairie dogs live in groups called towns; one town can have hundreds of prairie dogs in it.

11. A sculpture of a groundhog dressed as the Statue of Liberty stands in Punxsutawney, Pennsylvania, U.S.A., the town where a groundhog predicts every February 2 if winter will last for six more weeks. 12. Naked mole rats, rodents that live in underground colonies in East Africa, build tunnels that can stretch for 2.5 miles (4 km). 13. At birth, baby porcupines have soft quills that harden within a few days.

hamster

14. Alvin and the

Chipmunks have their own star on Hollywood's Walk of Fame. 15. Beavers in Canada's Wood Buffalo Park built a dam that stretched for about half a mile (850 m). 16. A two-million-year-old gigantic rodent called *Josephoartigasia monesi* weighed around 2,200 pounds (1,000 kg), and its head was nearly two feet (53 cm) long. 17. Chinchillas can have about 50 times more hair growing from one hair follicle than humans do. 18. Most hamsters have about five to seven babies at a time, but in 1974, a hamster in Louisiana, U.S.A., gave birth to 26 babies—the largest litter on record. 19. While hamsters are naturally solitary, gerbils are social animals and like to live in groups. 20. In the Chinese zodiac, people born during the year of the rat are thought to be funny, successful, and cunning. 21. The only rodent to turn white in the winter, collared lemmings turn from gray to white to camouflage in their snowy homes across the Northern Hemisphere. 22. The mouse-size long-eared jerboa has kangaroo-like legs long for its size and ears like a rabbit's. 23. Naked mole rats live in colonies of a few dozen led by a queen, the only naked mole rat to have babies. 24. Mickey Mouse was originally named Mortimer, but Walt Disney's wife didn't think it was quite right for the cartoon character. 25. The agouti, a rodent that lives in Central and South American rainforests, is the only animal that can crack open hard-shelled Brazil nuts with its teeth. 26. Agouti moms and dads mate for life. 27. Since beavers create ponds of freshwater when they dam a river, the animals are sacred to the Blackfeet Native Americans who live in the arid Great Plains.

28. Jerboas' hind legs are at least four times longer than their front limbs, and they use a zigzag motion to avoid predators. 29. A zoo in Japan began providing its capybaras with hot springs to soak in when a worker found them enjoying a puddle of hot water in their enclosure. 30. Meadow voles have to eat their weight in food every day. 31. Australia's spinifex hopping mouse doesn't drink water; it gets all the water it needs from the foods it eats in its desert home. 32. Kangaroo rats have pouches in their cheeks that they stuff with seeds to bring back to their burrows. 33. When Doug Engelbart invented a computer mouse in the 1960s, he called it a "mouse" because it looked just like one with a cord for its tail. 34. The large bamboo rat, which lives in Southeast Asia, can weigh about as much as a small cat. 35. Before the last ice age ended about 11,000 years ago, giant beavers the size of black bears lived in the wetlands and lakes of North America. 36. To make the movements of the rats in the movie *Ratatouille* as realistic as possible, animators kept pet rats in the studio hallway and studied them. 37. Gunnison's prairie dogs have different calls for different types of threats—for example, the call for seeing a hawk is different than that for a coyote. 38. To stay healthy, the sewellel or mountain beaver (it's not really a beaver) needs to drink about one-third of its weight in water every day. 39. Once considered extinct, the Santiago Galápagos mouse was rediscovered in 1997—it lives only on Santiago Island, one of the Galápagos Islands located off the coast of Ecuador. 40. Sonoma tree voles build nests in the

tops of fir and spruce trees in northwest California, U.S.A., and eat the trees' needles for food.   41. When hibernating, a groundhog's heart rate slows from about 80 beats a minute to five beats a minute.   42. Pacas, which live throughout Central and South America, build escape exits from their underground burrows, then cover them with leaves.   43. Tuco-tucos, small rodents that live in South America, are named after the *tuc-tuc* sound they make as they dig their underground burrows.   44. Chipmunks in northern North America may burrow three feet (1 m) under the snow to make a cozy spot to hibernate.   45. Some hamsters fill up their cheeks with air to become more buoyant when swimming.   46. World Rat Day began in 2002, when a group of rat lovers designated April 4 as a universal day to celebrate pet rats.   47. A painting from around 1580 shows a girl holding a brown-and-white guinea pig, and experts think it is likely the first ever portrait of a pet guinea pig.   48. A group of porcupines is called a prickle.   49. A squirrel will pretend to bury a nut to trick potential food thieves.   50. You can buy a sculpture of Stuart Little, the fictional mouse who lives with his human parents in New York City, U.S.A., for your garden.   51. The claws on the hind feet of tuco-tucos have hard hairs that they use to sweep dust from their underground burrows.   52. Just like dogs or cats, rats have distinct personalities.   53. To escape a predator, the African spiny mouse can shed the skin on its tail.   54. Rabbits and hares are not considered rodents but lagomorphs—they have different teeth and digestive systems from true rodents.   55. Mountain beavers are called "boomers" or "whistlers" even though they don't boom or whistle—they hiss and cough.   56. Flying squirrels don't use "wings" to fly; they have a special flap of skin between their front and back legs to glide between trees.   57. Woodland voles that live in the forests of the eastern United States weigh about one ounce (28 g).   58. Flying squirrels can glide through the air over distances of some 150 feet (46 m).   59. Mickey Mouse is known as Musse Pigg in Sweden and Mi Lao Shu in China.   60. Specially trained African giant pouched rats, which are about the size of a small cat, have saved thousands of lives by sniffing out buried land mines.   61. In about 20 minutes, a trained African giant pouched rat can check an area about half the size of a basketball court.   62. Pet rats can learn their own names.   63. To protect their young, some hamster moms carry their babies in their cheek pouches.   64. Locals in New York City call a giant, 450-million-year-old boulder in Central Park "rat rock" for the rats that like to nest and congregate nearby.   65. Most pet gerbils are Mongolian gerbils, which in the wild live in the dry plains of Mongolia, northern China, and southeastern Russia.   66. The Malabar giant squirrel has purple, orange, brown, and black fur.   67. Baby squirrels are only about an inch (2.5 cm) long.   68. An artist in Canada made a giant capybara sculpture entirely out of butter to honor two capybaras that escaped from a Toronto zoo. (They returned safely.)   69. Rats "giggle" when they are tickled, but the sound is at too high of a frequency for humans to hear.   70. A woman in Germany collected more than 47,000 items that related to either mice or rats.   71. Conservationists in New Zealand established sanctuaries for the Pacific rat, which holds deep cultural meaning for the indigenous Ngatiwai people.   72. When a prairie dog stands up on two feet,

raises its arms, and makes a high-pitched yip sound, other prairie dogs copy it. Scientists think these "jump-yips" let the colony know that everyone is keeping watch for predators.   73. The Hindu god Ganesha is often shown riding a rat or a mouse.   74. Muskrats have lips that close behind their front teeth, which lets them gnaw on objects underwater.   75. Beavers store fat in their leathery tails to help them survive the winter.   76. Chipmunks can gather 165 acorns in one day.   77. House mice can have as many as 14 litters of babies in a year.   78. More than a thousand years ago, when Polynesians were exploring the Pacific Ocean, they brought rats on board for food.   79. Adult squirrels eat two pounds (0.9 kg) of nuts a week.   80. Muskrats get their name for their resemblance to rats and their musky smell.   81. The first true rodents evolved in the Paleocene epoch, the time period right after the extinction of the dinosaurs.   82. In some Spanish-speaking countries, a "tooth mouse" gives gifts to kids who put a lost tooth

chinchilla

under their pillows.   83. In the wild, chinchillas roll around in dust made from volcanic pumice to keep their fur clean and healthy.   84. Beavers produce an oily substance from sacs on their rear end that some people think smells like vanilla—it has even been used to make perfumes.   85. Singing voles get their common name from their high-pitched alarm calls.   86. In Norse mythology, a mischievous red squirrel named Ratatoskr carried messages from the gods to create trouble between the eagle at the top of the mythical tree of life and the dragon at the bottom.   87. In Latin, "porcupine" means "quill pig."   88. Nutria, medium-size rodents from South America, live near rivers, lakes, and wetlands, and can stay underwater for five minutes at a time.   89. Nutria (also called coypu) have webbed feet, making them more agile in water than on land.   90. The African crested porcupine's quills are nearly one foot (0.3 m) long.   91. Squirrels are able to smell food buried under one foot (0.3 m) of snow.   92. Muskrats can swim backward.   93. In 2009, scientists discovered a giant rat species living in a crater inside an extinct volcano in Papua New Guinea.   94. Of the 25 species of chipmunks, all but Asia's Siberian chipmunk live in North America.   95. Rats can hold their breath for up to three minutes.   96. The beaver, Canada's national symbol, appears on the country's five-cent coin.   97. Rock art from some 25,000 years ago in what is today Brazil's Serra da Capivara National Park features capybaras.   98. Chinchillas can live to be 20 years old.   99. Groundhogs are also known as woodchucks or mouse bears.   100. Fear of mice is known as muriphobia or musophobia.

1

BIRDS are the only living ANIMALS with FEATHERS.

2

Scientists believe MOST DINOSAURS had FEATHERS.

3

DINOSAURS DIDN'T FLY; their feathers were likely used for insulation or ornamentation.

4

As some dinosaurs evolved into birds, the ROLE of FEATHERS EVOLVED to HELP THEM FLY.

5

The number of feathers that birds have varies—SONG-BIRDS have 1,500 to 3,000 FEATHERS and SWANS have 25,000.

6

HUMMINGBIRDS have the FEWEST feathers—about 1,000.

7

Scientists are STUDYING PENGUIN FEATHERS to make UNDERWATER SUITS—FOR PEOPLE—that retain heat and repel water.

8

DOWN FEATHERS, the tiny fluffy feathers closest to a bird's body, PROVIDE WARMTH and INSULATION.

9

MALE BIRDS often have MORE VIBRANTLY COLORED feathers to attract females.

10

Feathers are made of KERATIN, the same material as HUMAN HAIR and FINGERNAILS.

11

OSTRICHES LACK BARBICELS, tiny hooks that help connect feathers, which gives them their fluffy look.

12

Ostriches LOOSEN their FEATHERS to COOL OFF and TIGHTEN them to KEEP in HEAT.

13

The most VALUABLE cargo on the R.M.S. *TITANIC* included 12 CASES OF OSTRICH PLUMES valued at $2.3 million in today's money.

14

A MALE PEACOCK'S TRAIN, its tail feathers, is used to ATTRACT and COURT females.

15

The male sandgrouse fills its BELLY FEATHERS with WATER and carries it back to its NEST for its CHICKS.

16

The ribbon-tailed ASTRAPIA'S TAIL is THREE FEET (0.9 m) LONG, nearly QUADRUPLE its body length.

50
FABULOUS FACTS
ABOUT FEATHERS

17

A MALE PEACOCK'S TRAIN is 60 PERCENT of the bird's BODY LENGTH.

18

OSTRICH PLUMES, used in women's hats, fell out of fashion when OPEN-ROOFED CARS became POPULAR.

19

Most birds shed their feathers a few at a time, but PENGUINS LOSE THEIRS ALL AT ONCE.

20

CANARIES can TURN from YELLOW to DARK ORANGE if they regularly EAT SPICES such as paprika, cayenne, or red pepper.

21

Some birds, like pigeons, mourning doves, and egrets, have SPECIAL FEATHERS that DISINTEGRATE to a powder, providing a WATERPROOF COATING for their other feathers.

22

Studies have shown that MALE HOUSE FINCHES with the REDDEST FEATHERS attract the most females.

23

Snowy owls' REFLECTIVE white FEATHERS warn rivals to STAY AWAY.

24

Hummingbirds' shimmering, IRIDESCENT THROAT FEATHERS look colorful because the microscopic structure of the feathers creates a RAINBOW PRISM EFFECT.

25

Male BIRDS OF PARADISE'S long tail feathers don't help with flight: They are used in an ELABORATE DANCE to show off to females.

26

Male CLUB-WINGED MANAKINS rub their wings together, making a VIOLINLIKE SOUND that woos females.

27

Most BIRDS MOLT, or lose their feathers, and regrow new ones ONCE A YEAR.

28

The male WOOD DUCK'S HEAD CREST forms a COLORFUL FAN that changes the bird's HEAD SHAPE.

29

When Atlantic puffins MOLT, their CHEEKS turn from BRIGHT WHITE to GRAY, and they even SHED the outer sheath of their BILLS.

30

The common POTOO'S feathers mimic the COLORS of the TREE BRANCHES it PERCHES on.

31

Male ECLECTUS PARROTS have bright green feathers that they use as CAMOUFLAGE in the rainforest canopy.

32

WATER BIRDS, which have to swim alongside their parents immediately after they're born, usually HATCH with DOWN FEATHERS, which keep them warm.

33

Many SONGBIRDS are BORN WITHOUT FEATHERS.

34

The FEATHER TUFTS on the sides of a great horned owl's head are often MISTAKEN for EARS.

35

A bird's feathers usually WEIGH MORE than ITS SKELETON.

36

BLUE JAYS lower their head crests when resting or relaxed but RAISE THEM WHEN AGITATED.

37

Bald eagles don't get their signature WHITE HEAD FEATHERS until they are SEVERAL YEARS OLD.

38

OWLS FLY almost SILENTLY because the edge of the first feather on each of their WINGS is JAGGED.

39

Ducks MOLT most of their PRIMARY FLIGHT FEATHERS at once, which makes them UNABLE to FLY for up to 40 DAYS.

40

To SURVIVE the WINTER, goldfinches grow up to 50 PERCENT more feathers than their SUMMER PLUMAGE has.

41

AIRPLANE WINGS are MODELED after BIRD WINGS.

42

The DISKLIKE STRUCTURE of the feathers around an OWL'S FACE help it LOCATE PREY in the dark.

43

Many OWL species have FEATHERED FEET to help PROTECT them from being SCRATCHED or BITTEN BY the PREY they've captured.

44

Goose, swan, and crow FEATHERS were once used for QUILL-WRITING.

45

The DECLARATION OF INDEPENDENCE was SIGNED with a GOOSE FEATHER.

46

WOODPECKERS have STRONG TAIL FEATHERS that they use to prop themselves up when CLIMBING on trees.

47

A bird's TAIL FEATHERS are used for STEERING.

48

WATER BIRDS, like ducks, TRAP AIR in their DOWNY FEATHERS to FLOAT on water.

49

Grouse have FEATHER-COVERED FEET that work like SNOWSHOES to help them walk on snow without sinking.

50

A HERON sometimes uses its feathers to form an UMBRELLA over its HEAD, which might make it EASIER to SEE FISH as it HUNTS.

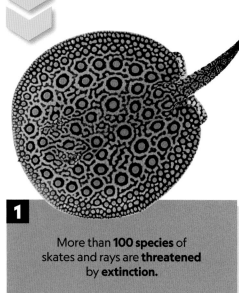

1 More than **100 species** of skates and rays are **threatened** by **extinction.**

2 Sawfish can **grow** to be **24 feet** (7.3 m) long.

3 **Relatives** of the **modern stingray** lived when **dinosaurs** roamed the Earth.

4 A **sawfish** is a type of ray that has a **long nose studded with sharp teeth,** just like a saw.

5 Like blue whales, **giant manta rays** use their huge **mouths** to **scoop up plankton.**

6 Giant mantas have the **largest brains of all fish** species ever studied.

25 SLICK FACTS
ABOUT SKATES AND RAYS

7 **Sawfish teeth** are actually **not teeth,** but modified scales.

8 A **skate's eggs** are enclosed in a **tough leathery pouch** nicknamed a "mermaid's purse."

9 Stingrays like to **live alone,** but will sometimes **come together** to **migrate** in groups **as large as 10,000.**

10 The 69 species of **electric rays** can produce **electric shocks** to **defend** themselves and **stun** prey.

11 **Skates lay** eggs, while **rays give birth** to live young.

12

The **giant manta ray** is the **largest** ray, reaching up to **29 feet** (9 m) wide.

13

Sawfish **use their saws** as **weapons** to split fish in half.

14

Some rays have **stinging barbs** on their **tails**.

15

The **clearnose skate** gets its name from its **see-through snout**.

16

The **smallest ray** is the **short-nosed electric ray.** It's only **four inches** (10 cm) wide.

17

Humans can **avoid stingray stings** by **shuffling their feet** when they enter the water, which scares away the rays.

18

Skates don't sting, but they can have **rows of spikes** for **self-defense**.

19

An **electric ray's shock** can be **220 volts**—strong enough to knock down or even kill a human.

DANGER

20

Skates and rays usually have **flat bodies**, a shape that helps them **hide under sand** on the seafloor.

21

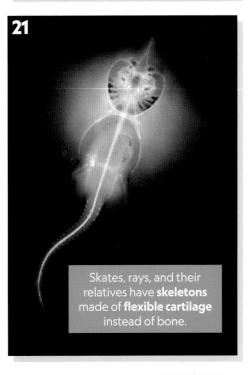

Skates, rays, and their relatives have **skeletons** made of **flexible cartilage** instead of bone.

22

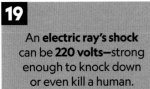

Skates and rays are closely **related to sharks**.

23

There are **more than 500 species of skates and rays,** including butterfly rays and guitarfish.

24

Scientists think a **sawfish's saw** may **act like an antenna,** detecting the electrical fields that passing prey emit.

25

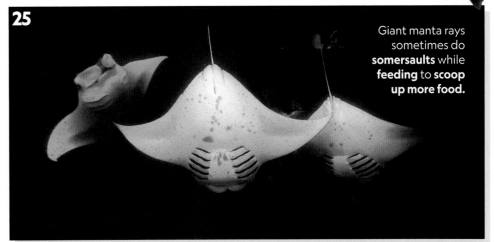

Giant manta rays sometimes do **somersaults** while **feeding** to **scoop up more food**.

.»15 HIGH-LIVING FACTS **ABOUT ANIMALS** OF THE HIMALAYA

1

A snow leopard can **leap six times** the length of its body.

2

In folklore, snow leopards are often depicted as **mountain spirits** that can **transform into other creatures.**

3

Takins, relatives of sheep, **stick their tongues out** when they call.

4

The Himalayan monal bird **bobs the metallic green feathers** on its head to **attract a mate.**

5. Himalayan marmots can hibernate for up to **eight months straight** to survive the winter.

6

Golden langurs live only on the **western side of the Manas River.** None are found across the water.

7. **The golden langur monkey** has long been **considered sacred** by the people of the Himalaya.

8. When predators come close, goatlike animals called **bharals run down nearby cliffs** to escape.

10

The Himalayan blue sheep is neither **blue nor a sheep.** (They're relatives of the goat, and they are **gray to pale brown** in color.)

9

Ganges River dolphins are **blind.** They use **ultrasonic sounds** to hunt their prey.

11. Goatlike **Himalayan tahrs** have hooves with **thin, sharp rims** surrounding a rubbery and flexible center—like a **hiking boot** that **helps them cling to steep rocks.**

12

Himalayan black bears **gorge on food** before **hibernating** during the long winter. They can reach up to **400 pounds** (182 kg).

13

Red pandas **once lived in North America.** Now, they live only in **small patches** of the Himalaya.

14

About **90 percent** of a red panda's diet is **bamboo.**

15

The Chinese name for the red panda translates to **"fire fox."**

1. When **tundra swans fly,** the **flapping** of their **wings** makes a **whistling sound.**

2. **Donald Duck** has a **star** on the Hollywood Walk of Fame.

3. **Tundra swans** have a **noisy, high-pitched call** that **sounds** like a **yodel.**

4. A **group of swans** on the **ground** is called a **bank.**

5. A **group of swans** in **flight** is called a **wedge.**

6. **Black swans are all black except for the tips of white on their wings, which are only visible in flight.**

7. **Ducks** can be **found** on **every continent except Antarctica.**

8. **Trumpeter swans** sometimes **nest** on **beaver dams.**

9. **Trumpeter swans** can **walk** for **more than a mile** (1.6 km) at a time.

10. **A trumpeter swan's wingspan is 10 feet (3 m)—that's the length of four skateboards.**

11. A **group of ducks** on the **water** is called **a paddling.**

12. The **constellation Cygnus** means "swan" in **Latin.**

13. In one interpretation of **Greek mythology,** the **Cygnus** constellation represents **Orpheus,** who **turns into a swan** after death.

14. When **mute swans** are **courting,** they face each other and their **curved necks** form a **heart.**

15. **Wood ducks** are one of **few ducks** that **nest** in **trees.**

16. In Britain, all **swans** without designated owners **belong** to **the queen.**

17. Up until the 18th century, **swans** were **eaten** as a **Christmas delicacy** in Britain.

18. The **mallard** is the **most abundant** and **wide-ranging duck** on **Earth.**

19. A **male** ruddy duck's **bill changes** from **gray** to bright **blue** during **mating season.**

20. When a **swan feels threatened,** it **flares** its **wings, hisses,** and **grunts**—a behavior **called busking.**

21. **All North American** mute **swans** are **descendants** of swans **imported** from **Europe** in the 19th century **for estates, city parks,** and **zoos.**

22. Because the **creamy white eggs** of **snow geese stain easily,** you can sometimes tell in what **order the eggs were laid** by the **color of the shells.** (The **dirtiest** shells **belong** to the **oldest** eggs.)

23. A **group of geese** on the **ground is called a gaggle** or a **flock.**

24. Within three weeks **after hatching,** snow geese **walk** with **their parents** up to **50 miles** (80 km) **from the nest** to **find food.**

25. Long-tailed ducks **dive as deep as 200 feet** (61 m) to **search for food.**

26. If a predator is near, a **mother mallard** may **pretend** to be **injured** to **distract** it from **her ducklings.**

27. **Female mallards quack; males are silent except when fighting with other males.**

28. **Snow geese** produce **six to 15 droppings** per **hour.**

29. Fifty **Canada geese** can make **two and a half tons** (2.3 t) of **droppings** in a **year.**

30. Tundra swans **travel in groups** of **up to 100.**

31. Ducks don't have **nerves** or **blood vessels** in their **webbed feet,** so they **can't feel** the **cold.**

32. **The American black duck isn't black—it is dark brown—but it looks black from a distance.**

33. **Mallards** have **few taste buds** on their **tongue—most** are **under** the **tip** of their **bill.**

75 SWIMMINGLY SENSATIONAL FACTS ABOUT DUCKS, GEESE, AND SWANS

34. Wood ducks sometimes share a nest with eastern screech owls.

35. A **female wood duck** sometimes **removes** the **screech owl's eggs** to **replace** them with **her own.** Then the screech **owl** helps them hatch.

36. When a **goose** in the **lead** of a **V-formation flight** gets **tired,** it falls back and **another goose** takes its position.

37. Researchers think that Canada geese **communicate** shifts in **flying position** by **honking.**

38. Flying in a V-pattern **reduces wind resistance** and **saves** the birds' **energy.**

39. The **American wigeon,** a type of duck, is known as a **baldpate** (a word used to **describe** a **bald person**) because the **white stripe on its head** makes it look bald.

40. Canada geese's **bills** have **serrated edges,** like a saw, which they use to **cut grass stems.**

41. The Canada **geese's** nickname is **"honkers."**

42. Canada geese can **see 12 times better** at night **than humans** can.

43. Canada geese can **travel up to 1,500 miles** (2,414 km) in **24 hours.**

44. Male ruddy ducks sometimes **run across the water,** making **flip-flop sounds** with their **webbed feet.**

45. The **emperor goose** is so **named** because the **bird's white head** and **neck reminded** early European **explorers** of the **white trim** on **royal cloaks.**

46. Before lifting off, trumpeter swans **sound** like **galloping horses** as they **run across the water's surface.**

47. Wood ducks have **claws** that can **grip** on to **branches.**

48. Harlequin ducks can **suffer broken bones** from **swimming** in **white-water rapids** in North America.

49. The harlequin duck's **nickname** is **sea mouse,** after the **squeaky sound** the ducks make when **interacting** with **each other.**

50. Mallards swim with their tail above water so that if threatened, they can spring into the air.

51. A **man** from Illinois, U.S.A., set a **world record** for making the **longest duck call**—a device used to imitate the sound of a duck. It was **as long as seven pencils** lined up end to end.

52. When **feeding,** flocks of **snow geese** have **lookouts** to watch for **predators,** alerting with a **call** if a **threat is sighted.**

53. The term **"goose"** refers **only** to a **female; a male** is a **gander.**

54. Muscovy ducks have **red warty faces** that **resemble** a turkey vulture's.

55. Male ruddy ducks **court females** by **thumping** their **bills against** their own **necks,** creating bubbles in the water.

56. Aztec rulers wore **cloaks** made from **Muscovy duck feathers.**

57. Rubber ducks are usually made of plastic, not rubber.

58. The world's largest rubber duck is six stories tall.

59. Some **airports** that have Canada **geese** hanging around the **runways** use **"goose herding" dogs** to **shoo them away.**

60. One way to tell adult **tundra** and **trumpeter** swans **apart: Tundra** swans have a **yellow spot** in **front** of their **eyes.**

61. When tundra swans are **70 days old,** they weigh **28 times more than** when they **hatched.**

62. Tundra swans **migrate up to 4,000 miles** (6,437 km) **round-trip** from the **Arctic** to the southeastern **United States.**

63. In New York City's **Central Park,** you can visit a **statue** of *The Ugly Duckling* author **Hans Christian Andersen,** who is shown **reading to** a bronze **duckling.**

64. A **pair of swans** named **Romeo and Juliet** began **living** in the **Boston Public Garden** in Massachusetts, U.S.A., in 2003.

65. As soon as a **baby** wood duck **hatches,** it has to **jump** from **its nest** in a tree to the ground.

66. Wood ducks **bob** their **head back** and **forth** like a **pigeon.**

67. Aggressive ruddy ducks sometimes **chase rabbits** on the shore.

68. In Iceland, people **attach boxes** to their **houses** to **attract Barrow's goldeneye ducks** to nest there.

69. Trumpeter swans are the **heaviest waterfowl** in North America—they **weigh as much as a beagle.**

70. Despite their name, **mute swans aren't silent**—they **grunt** and **make hissing sounds** but **don't call** like other swans do.

71. Because of their **weight,** trumpeter swans need a **100-yard** (91-m) **"runway"** to **build up speed** to **take off** for **flight.**

72. Instead of **sitting on their eggs,** trumpeter swans **cover them** with their **webbed feet.**

73. In the children's book *The Trumpet of the Swan,* a voiceless trumpeter swan **plays a trumpet** to catch the **attention** of a **female swan.**

74. At the **Public Garden** in **Boston** you can **ride a swan boat powered** by a driver who **pedals it like a bicycle.**

75. The idea for the boats comes from a medieval German story in which a knight crosses a river in a swan-pulled boat to help a princess.

1
Snakes **contract their muscles** to create a **slithering motion.**

2
Snake scales are made of **keratin, the same material as your hair** and fingernails.

3
Snakes have a thin coat of **a fatty, greaselike substance** on their skin that helps them slither.

4
About **100 million years ago,** ancestors of modern-day snakes had limbs.

5
Tree-dwelling snakes **slither vertically** up trunks to reach a branch.

6
There are more than **3,000 snake species** on the planet.

7
Snakes are found everywhere except Antarctica, Iceland, Ireland, Greenland, and New Zealand.

8
Flying snakes don't fly, but rather **free-fall** from a tree branch and contort their bodies to generate lift.

9
A few species of snakes are mostly **scaleless** but do have scales **on their underbellies.**

10
Snakes have **bones in their lower jaws** that pick up vibrations from rodents and other prey that scurry.

11
Corn snakes get their name from **markings on their bellies** that resemble **maize,** or Indian corn.

12
Tentacled snakes get their name from the two short and scaly tentacles that stick out of the **end of their heads.**

13
More people are **struck by lightning** than are bitten by venomous snakes.

14
A snake sheds its skin about **once a month,** which also helps get rid of parasites.

15
To shed, snakes **rub against a tree** or **branch** or other object and then slither out of their skin.

16
Mangrove snakes have **vertically slit pupils** like a cat, giving them their nickname, **yellow-ringed cat snake.**

35 SSSENSATIONAL FACTS ABOUT ANIMALS THAT SLITHER

17
A baby snake **sheds quickly** after it's born. Leaving its scent behind in shed skin helps **deter predators.**

18
About **70 species** of snakes **live in the ocean.**

19
Some venomous snakes deliver **"dry bites"** that don't release any venom.

20
Sea snakes and their cousins, **kraits,** are some of the **most venomous** of all snakes.

21
To hydrate, **yellow-bellied sea snakes** drink **rainwater** that collects on the ocean's surface.

22
Eyelash vipers have **big scales above their eyes,** which look like **eyelashes.**

23
Snakes that only **eat eggs** have a sharp bone in their throat that breaks the egg open as they swallow it.

24
The **many-horned adder snake** has hornlike scales **above each eye.**

25
The venom of a banded **sea krait is 10 times more toxic** than a rattlesnake's.

26
Snake scales help **trap moisture** in **arid climates.**

27
A snake **continues to grow its entire life** but its skin doesn't, which is why it has to molt.

28
About two weeks before a snake is ready to shed, **it stops eating.**

29
Snakes that lay eggs either **bury them** or **wrap their body** around them and shiver to generate heat.

30
Some snakes **give birth to live snakes,** and others lay eggs.

31
Flying snakes **flatten their body** and **spread out their ribs to glide.** They can even make turns.

32
Caecilians, legless amphibians, range in size from **3.5 inches** (9 cm) to **five feet** (1.5 m).

33
Legless lizards look like snakes, but most have ear openings and **moveable eyelids,** which snakes don't have.

34
If attacked or injured, legless lizards can **lose their tails** and **grow a new one.**

35
When **you find** a snake skin, it is **always inside out.**

100 PUP-ULAR FACTS ABOUT DOGS

1. A whippet named Toby popped 100 balloons in less than half a minute. 2. Dogs have unique "noseprints," which are similar to human fingerprints. 3. The basenji dog doesn't bark, it yodels. 4. About 40,000 years ago, gray wolves started hanging around human settlements, and scientists think that's how they likely became the first domesticated animal. 5. About half of all dogs in the United States sleep with their owners. 6. Bluetick coonhounds get their name for the pattern of small black-and-blue splotches on their coat, which is referred to as being "ticked." 7. The phrase "It's raining cats and dogs" to describe a downpour has existed since the 1600s, but nobody is exactly sure where it came from. 8. A "bagel" is a beagle and basset hound mix. 9. A dog's nose has as many as 300 million receptors for smells, while a human's nose only has about five million. 10. In the late 1800s, dogs competed while sitting on benches in what was called a "bench show." 11. Dogs with longer faces, such as Yorkshire terriers and toy poodles, tend to live longer. 12. An American Kennel Club study found that 17 percent of dogs in the United States sleep in a doggie bed. 13. The fluffy tails of Bernese mountain dogs help keep them warm in cold weather. 14. Every year, dogs dressed in costumes parade in Baton Rouge, Louisiana, U.S.A., during Mardi Gras to raise money for a local animal welfare society. 15. If they see a human yawning, dogs will yawn, too. 16. The character of Pongo, from *101 Dalmatians,* was based on a real-life Dalmatian whose owner wrote the 1956 novel that inspired the film. 17. *Cynodictis,* the earliest doglike creature on Earth, lived about 30 million years ago. 18. A veterinarian in California, U.S.A., created a bandage made of tilapia fish skin to help heal dogs that have suffered burns. 19. Dogs not only recognize their owner's faces but can interpret the meaning of different facial expressions. 20. Louis XI, who ruled France in the 1400s, had a greyhound whose velvet collar was decorated with 11 rubies and 20 pearls. 21. Some water-loving dog breeds, such as Newfoundlands and Chesapeake Bay retrievers, have webbed feet. 22. There are more than 340 different dog breeds. 23. In 2012, a service dog organization in Austin, Texas, U.S.A., created the world's heaviest ball of dog hair—201 pounds (91.2 kg). 24. Some fast-food restaurants offer "puppy lattes" or "puppuccinos," dog treats that are usually a version of whipped cream in a cup. 25. Mochi, a Saint Bernard, has a tongue that is 7.31 inches (18.6 cm) long—that's longer than a candy bar. 26. One company makes doghouses that are smaller replicas of a brick mansion, a Swiss chalet, and a Mediterranean villa. 27. On August 19, 1960, the Soviet Union sent two dogs named Strelka and Belka into space for several orbits to help pave the way for humans in space. (The dogs were returned safely to Earth.) 28. Soviet leader Nikita Khrushchev gifted one of Strelka's puppies, Pushinka, to U.S. president John F. Kennedy. 29. One passenger onboard the *Titanic* refused to leave her Great Dane, which was too large to be put in a lifeboat. 30. Dogs have blurry vision, so if given a human driving test, they would need glasses to drive a car. 31. Dogs with light-colored fur can sunburn, especially on their nose and eyelids. 32. There are about 90 million pet dogs in the United States, and about half the households have small dogs. 33. When a pet dog licks you, it's usually a sign of affection. 34. People have bred specific dogs to catch rats, guard sheep, pull heavy loads, help fishermen with their nets, or even warm people's laps. 35. Lucca, a mixed-breed dog that served with the U.S. Marines, was awarded the highest honor any animal can receive, for serving on more than 400 missions to sniff out and warn soldiers of explosives. 36. George Washington, an avid dog lover, had dogs named Sweetlips, Truelove, Mopsey, Madame Moose, and Ragman. 37. Dogs have three eyelids: two you can see and one in the corner of their eye that is not easily visible. 38. Smoky, a Yorkshire terrier, barked to warn soldiers of incoming shells during World War II. 39. Most dogs run at speeds of about 15 to 20 miles an hour (24–32 km/h). 40. Different languages have different words for dog barks—in Bulgarian, dogs say

"bau-bau" and in Hindi they say "bow-bow." 41. An Australian cattle-dog named Bluey lived to be 29 years and 5 months old—the oldest dog ever recorded. 42. Scientists think that while dogs can see yellow, blue, and gray, they can't see red or green. 43. The tiny Chihuahua is named after the state in Mexico where it was first bred. 44. A program in Washington State, U.S.A., trains dogs to locate the poop of endangered animals so that scientists can study how they are faring in the wild. 45. To welcome the Westminster Dog Show to New York City, U.S.A., the Empire State Building lights up in the show's colors—purple and yellow. 46. Every August 26 in the United States is National Dog Day, which honors pups and raises awareness for dogs that need a home. 47. Scientists studied the brain waves of sleeping dogs and think that dogs dream like humans do. 48. A pet store in Latvia created a 311-pound (141-kg) cake for dogs. 49. If a dog gets wet, it can shake off almost all the water in less than one second. 50. At a site called Saqqâra, near Cairo, Egypt, researchers found millions of mummified dogs. 51. Some people use dog-specific vacuum-cleaner attachments to suck up shedding hair from their dogs' coats. 52. Fear of dogs is known as cynophobia. 53. Sallie, a mixed-breed pup, became separated from her troop during the Battle of Gettysburg in the U.S. Civil War, but she was found three days later guarding her wounded soldiers. 54. Smaller dogs tend to live longer than larger ones. 55. Bulldogs, known for being both calm and courageous, are the official mascot of the U.S. Marine Corp. 56. Cocker spaniels are hunting dogs that were named for their skill at flushing birds called woodcocks out of the dense brush. 57. U.S. president Gerald Ford's daughter, Susan, surprised him in the Oval Office in 1974 with a golden retriever—he got on the floor and played with the puppy. 58. Chaser, a border collie, could identify more than 1,000 toy objects by their individual names—including about 800 different stuffed animals. 59. In September 2014 in Hong Kong, a record number of dogs—109 in total—each balanced a treat on their noses at the same time. 60. When a dog tilts its head, it could be trying to understand what its human is saying. 61. In the "Puppy Bowl"—the puppy equivalent of the NFL Super Bowl—two teams face off, and all the puppies can be adopted. 62. Some dogs howl when they hear music. 63. The Chihuahuas are a minor league baseball team in El Paso, Texas, U.S.A. 64. In 2018, Maria Harman from Australia walked 36 dogs at the same time. 65. A sculpture on a palace wall in Nineveh, the capital of Assyria in the Middle East more than 2,600 years ago, shows huntsmen walking with their hounds. 66. Dog drool is better at preventing cavities than human saliva. 67. Rin Tin Tin, a German shepherd that became a Hollywood movie star in the 1920s, had been rescued by an American soldier during World War I. 68. Great Danes were once thought to ward off ghosts. 69. Artwork from ancient Egypt shows dogs wearing collars. 70. The Scooby-Doo character was modeled after the Great Dane. 71. Zeus, the world's tallest dog at 44 inches (1.2 m), could drink water straight from the sink. 72. Dogs communicate their moods and social status with chemical signals in their pee, poop, and saliva. 73. Boxers were named "boxers" because of how they use their front paws to defend themselves—similar to a boxer in the ring. 74. During the 2019 Macy's Day Parade in New York City, a 49-foot (15-m)-tall Snoopy balloon wore a space suit to celebrate the 50th anniversary of landing a man on the moon. 75. In the 1800s, weavers in northern England bred Yorkshire terriers to chase rodents in textile factories. 76. Many colleges bring dogs on campus so that students can "pet your stress away" for a study break. 77. A mosaic found in the ruins of Pompeii included a picture of a dog and the Latin expression *cave canem,* which means "beware the dog." 78. Dingoes, wild dogs found in Southeast Asia and Australia, travel long distances in packs of about 10 and communicate with wolflike howls. 79. Research in Australia shows that dingoes help preserve populations of small marsupials by driving away or killing the rabbits and foxes that prey on them. 80. The Havanese, a small lapdog with a silky coat, was named for Havana, the capital of Cuba. 81. Archaeologists uncovered a 12,000-year-old burial site in Israel of a woman with her hand on a dog. 82. Dog Island, a seven-mile (11-km)-long barrier island located off the northwest coast of Florida, U.S.A., is only accessible by boat—cars are not allowed on it. 83. The Chinook breed was started after explorer Arthur Treadwell Walden traveled to Alaska, U.S.A., in the late 1890s during the Klondike Gold Rush and decided to breed his own sled dogs. 84. Spotty, an English springer spaniel, was the only pet to live in the White House during two presidential administrations: George H. W. Bush's and George W. Bush's. 85. Some dogs show that they're happy by swirling their tails around in a circle. 86. A recent survey found that 29 million Americans dress up their pets for Halloween. 87. In 2019, a pumpkin was the most popular Halloween costume for a pet. 88. The rounded tufts of fur found on the legs and tail of groomed poodles are known as pompons. 89. The ancient Greeks thought that the roots of a wild rose called the dog rose could cure someone bitten by a diseased dog. 90. Most dogs have about three to nine puppies in a litter. 91. The Labrador retriever has been the most popular dog breed in the United States since 1991. 92. Dogs shouldn't eat raisins, grapes, or chocolate. 93. In 2012, a dog named Baby Hope Diamond wore a $6,000 wedding dress at her "wedding" to a poodle in a New York City event to raise money for the Humane Society of New York. 94. Scientists think that dogs wave their tails more to the right when they feel happy and more to the left when they have negative feelings. 95. In 1984, the Department of Agriculture started using trained beagles to sniff luggage for forbidden plants or animals brought into the United States. 96. Bloodhounds can follow a two-day-old scent trail of an individual human. 97. Some dogs have dark noses that turn a lighter color during the winter months. 98. Puppies have 28 teeth, which fall out and are replaced with 42 permanent adult teeth—the same as an adult wolf. 99. Dogs have been able to sniff out some types of cancers in humans. 100. Sirius, or the Dog Star—part of the constellation Canis Major (the "Greater Dog")—is the brightest star in the sky.

1

NORTH AFRICAN OSTRICHES are the TALLEST LIVING BIRD: The tallest NBA basketball player would have to look up to the biggest ostriches.

2

WANDERING ALBATROSS have WINGSPANS that can be nearly as LONG AS TWO TWIN BEDS lying end to end.

3

Found in a small part of northeast Australia, the SMALLEST WALLABY species is the BURBRIDGE'S ROCK wallaby—it WEIGHS around TWO POUNDS (1 KG) and can easily climb steep, rocky cliffs.

4

A BLUE WHALE'S HEART can WEIGH as much as 1,600 HAMBURGERS.

5

In 2013, a DOG named Ozzy WALKED across a TIGHTROPE in less than 19 seconds—A WORLD RECORD.

6

OSTRICHES' EYES are TWO INCHES (5 CM) WIDE—the LARGEST of any land animal.

7

The PYGMY MOUSE LEMUR is the smallest lemur—and SMALLEST PRIMATE—on Earth.

8

THUMBELINA, a MINIATURE SORREL HORSE, stands only 17.5 INCHES (44.5 CM) at her withers.

9

Africa's SPECKLED TORTOISE is the SMALLEST tortoise species in the world—males are ONLY THREE INCHES (7.6 CM) LONG.

10

Weddell seal MILK has the MOST CALORIES of any mammal's milk.

11

The SMALLEST SHARK, the dwarf lantern shark, CAN FIT in an adult human's HAND.

12

One GRAY-HEADED ALBATROSS flew FASTER THAN CARS on a highway for more than eight hours.

13

NAKED MOLE RATS are the LONGEST-LIVING RODENT.

14

At 60 FEET (18 M) long, SPERM WHALES are the LARGEST animals on Earth WITH TEETH, which are all located on their lower jaw.

15

The giant anteater's TONGUE, at nearly TWO FEET (0.6 M) LONG, is the LONGEST in relation to its body size of any animal.

16

The LARGEST HIPPO canine TEETH are FOUR FEET (1.2 M) LONG.

17

HIPPOS also have the LARGEST MOUTHS of any land animal.

18

The ONLY FISH to have both gills and a lung, LUNGFISH can BREATHE AIR when the pools of water they live in dry up temporarily.

19

The BARBADOS THREADSNAKE is about AS WIDE AS a strand of SPAGHETTI.

20

BLUE WHALES— the LARGEST ANIMAL ever to have lived on Earth—WEIGH ALMOST HALF the weight of the INTERNATIONAL SPACE STATION.

50 STUPENDOUS FACTS ABOUT ANIMAL RECORD HOLDERS

21
LEATHERBACK SEA TURTLES can WEIGH as much as a TON (0.9 t)—and their diet is mostly jellyfish.

22
Measuring ONLY 0.4 INCH (1 CM) in length, a FEW species of FROGS are small enough to FIT ON A PENNY.

23
Living in caves in Thailand and Myanmar, the BUMBLEBEE BAT—the world's SMALLEST mammal—is about the size of a large bee.

24
The LARGEST OSTRICH EGG weighed nearly SIX POUNDS (2.7 KG).

25
The GREAT DANE towers over other dogs, with males reaching nearly THREE FEET (0.9 M) at their shoulders.

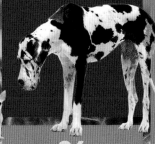

26
Feeding on plankton in the Arctic Ocean, BOWHEAD WHALES have the LARGEST MOUTHS of any animal and a TONGUE THAT CAN WEIGH 2,000 POUNDS (900 KG).

27
The world's SMALLEST bird, the BEE HUMMINGBIRD, lives only in Cuba and has a WINGSPAN of just TWO INCHES (5 CM).

28
Caught off the coast of Peru in 1953, a WORLD RECORD MARLIN stretched 14 FEET 6 INCHES (4.4 M) LONG.

29
Though the LARGEST of the four gorilla sub-species, the EASTERN LOWLAND GORILLA mainly eats plants.

30
Possibly the WORLD'S SMALLEST FLY, a species from Brazil has a body that is only .016 INCH (0.395 MM) long—BARELY VISIBLE to the human eye.

31
When migrating over the Himalaya mountains, BAR-HEADED GEESE FLY HIGHER than 21,000 FEET (6,400 M), which is higher than the tallest mountain in North America.

32
The northern JACANA uses its nearly THREE-INCH (7.6-cm)-long TOES—the LONGEST toes of ANY BIRD relative to body size—to balance on lily pads.

33
FENNEC FOXES' EARS can be ONE-THIRD the length of their bodies—the LARGEST ear-to-body ratio of ANY CANID (a family of meat-eating animals).

34
The SMALLEST SEA TURTLE, the KEMP'S RIDLEY, measures about TWO FEET (0.6 M) LONG and is the most endangered sea turtle in the world.

35
With a WINGSPAN of FOUR FEET (1.3 M), RAVENS are the LARGEST PERCHING BIRDS—birds with three toes facing forward and one backward—IN THE WORLD.

36
The INDRI is the LARGEST LEMUR, with a THREE-FOOT (0.9-M)-LONG BODY that it uses to leap from tree to tree in its forest home.

37
Curled up, the CARIBBEAN'S JARAGUA LIZARD—the world's SMALLEST lizard—could FIT ON A DIME.

38
KOMODO DRAGONS, the world's largest lizard at 10 FEET (3 M) LONG, are LARGE ENOUGH to EAT WATER BUFFALO and WILD BOAR.

39
The world's TALLEST horse is BIG JAKE, a Belgian who stands at 6.9 FEET (2.1 M) at his withers, the area between a horse's shoulder blades.

40
KING COBRAS, the LARGEST venomous snake in the world, can STRETCH for more than 18 FEET (5.6 M).

41
Stretching nearly TWO FEET (0.5 M) WIDE, the AUSTRALIAN PELICAN'S BILL, which the bird uses to scoop up fish, is the LONGEST IN THE WORLD.

42
One EMPEROR penguin DOVE to a depth of 1,854 FEET (565 M)—the DEEPEST dive for a bird that scientists have tracked.

43
Considered by many to be the SMALLEST breed of DOG, the CHIHUAHUA originally came from Chihuahua, Mexico, and is known as a "purse dog" for its small stature.

44
The LARGEST FLYING BIRD in North America, the CALIFORNIA CONDOR, has a wing-span of NINE FEET (3 M).

45
The NECK of a giraffe—the tallest mammal—WEIGHS MORE than the LARGEST GORILLA.

46
The SMALLEST member of the alligator family, CUVIER'S DWARF CAIMANS have heavily ARMORED SKIN that helps PROTECT them from being eaten by PREDATORS in the South American wet-lands where they live.

47
The CALLS of HOWLER MONKEYS, which live in Central and South America, are the LOUDEST monkey calls ON EARTH and can be HEARD THREE MILES (5 KM) AWAY.

48
Male southern ELEPHANT SEALS can tip the scales at 8,800 POUNDS (4,000 kg)—that's more than three large giraffes.

49
CUVIER'S BEAKED WHALES stay under-water longer than any other marine mammal, and CAN DIVE about TWO MILES (3 km) into the ocean depths.

50
The EUROPEAN CONGER, the LARGEST EEL in the world, can GROW to be nearly 10 FEET (3 M) LONG—longer than your sofa.

1 In 2018, scientists discovered that **puffins' beaks glow under UV light.**

2 One species of firefly can **synchronize its flashing;** the beetles light up together in short bursts.

3 The color of a firefly's glow can range from red to **yellow to green.**

4 Firefly males flash to **attract females.**

5 Firefly **larvae glow to warn potential predators** that they contain toxic or bad-tasting substances.

25 **BRILLIANT FACTS** ABOUT ANIMALS

6 Each species of **lanternfish lights up** with a **different pattern.**

7 **Vampire squid ink glows.**

8 Animals with the ability to glow are called **bioluminescent.**

9 Bioluminescent animals use **chemical reactions** to make light, or provide a home to bacteria that do.

10 **Brittle stars** can **detach a glowing arm** to distract a predator, then **escape by crawling away** in the darkness.

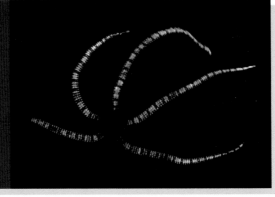

11 **Vampire squid** can turn their **glow on** and **off** to attract prey.

12 One type of **LED lightbulb** was inspired by the way fireflies light up.

13

About 76 percent of all ocean animals are bioluminescent.

14

The glow emitted by some fungi is nicknamed **"fairy fire."**

15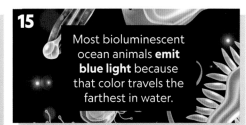

Most bioluminescent ocean animals **emit blue light** because that color travels the farthest in water.

18

Female *Photuris versicolor* fireflies mimic the glow of other species to lure males—then they eat them.

16

One of the few shallow-water species that can produce light, the **flashlight fish** uses a **skin flap** to show or hide the **light made** by an **organ under its eyes.**

17

Hatchetfish adjust their glow to match the **light from the sky.** That makes them nearly invisible to predators looking up from below.

19

Railroad worms get their name from the way the lights that run along the sides of their bodies look like a train lighted up at night.

20

Hawaiian bobtail squid use bioluminescence to **camouflage themselves against moonlight** on the ocean's surface.

THAT GLOW

21

Most bioluminescent creatures **live in the deep sea,** where there is no sunlight.

22

Most jellyfish glow.

23

Some **plankton can turn up their glow** when predators approach to scare them off.

24

Bioluminescence may be the **most common form of communication** on Earth.

25

Glowworm larvae spin glowing threads that cover the ceilings of the **Waitomo caves in New Zealand.**

»15 ZANY FACTS ABOUT ZOOS

1
Every year, San Francisco Zoo in California, U.S.A., holds a **"March of the Penguins"**: Chicks walk from the enclosure where they hatched to their new home on **"Penguin Island."**

2
Sarah, an 11-year-old cheetah at the Cincinnati Zoo, set a world record in 2009 when she covered **109 yards (100 m) in 6.13 seconds.**

3
Fiona, a hippo born at the Cincinnati Zoo in Ohio, U.S.A., was named after **Princess Fiona from the movie** *Shrek* because of the **shape of her ears.**

4. To **encourage the lions to sniff** and explore their enclosures, zookeepers at Smithsonian's National Zoo in Washington, D.C., U.S.A., **spray scents, including pumpkin spice.**

6. In 2011, **a peacock escaped** from Central Park Zoo in New York, U.S.A., **landed on an apartment windowsill, stayed there for 20 hours,** and then flew back to the zoo.

5
An aardvark born on the winter solstice at the Cincinnati Zoo was given the name **Winsol,** which is a blend of the words **"winter"** and **"solstice."**

7. During special nights, you can **pitch a tent** and **sleep next to the animals** in the children's section of the Oakland Zoo in California.

8
During **snowy weather** at Smithsonian's National Zoo, the cheetah enclosure has **heated termite mounds** to **keep the cats warm.**

9
More than **50 Caribbean flamingos** were placed in a men's bathroom at Zoo Miami in Florida, U.S.A., to take **shelter during Hurricane Georges in 1998.**

10. **The first animals** to arrive at Chicago's Lincoln Park Zoo, U.S.A., in 1868 were **two pairs of swans,** gifted by New York's Central Park.

11. The San Diego Zoo in California **has a frozen zoo:** Tissues and **cells of endangered animals** are stored to perhaps one day **bring back a species that has gone extinct.**

13. **Heads of lettuce bobbed** as treats in the pool of **Bubbles and Poppy, two hippos** at the Oregon Zoo in Portland, U.S.A., to **celebrate St. Patrick's Day.**

12. A teenage **male gorilla named Jim escaped** from a Los Angeles, California, zoo by **bending a faulty steel door.**

15
Louis, a 16-year-old western lowland gorilla at the Philadelphia Zoo in Pennsylvania, U.S.A., **prefers to walk upright,** rather than walking on all fours like most gorillas do.

14
For Christmas, elephants at the Tierpark Hagenbeck zoo in Hamburg, Germany, were **given wrapped boxes filled with fruit and nuts,** which they opened with their trunks.

1. All female marsupials have a **pouch, or marsupium,** where their newborns stay to nurse and grow.

2. The family name for marsupials, **Macropodidae,** means **"large-footed."**

3. There are more than **300 species of marsupials** worldwide, and more than **200** of those species live in Australia.

4. Koala bears aren't bears—they're marsupials.

5. Baby marsupials are called **joeys.**

6. Rock wallabies don't move their back legs independently of each other **except when swimming.**

7. In 1951, a female red kangaroo **leaped 42 feet** (12.8 m) in one hop—that's nearly half the length of an NBA basketball court!

8. The **Virginia opossum,** the only marsupial native to the **United States** and **Canada,** has been around **since the age of the dinosaurs.**

9. Koalas have **two fused toes on each foot** that they use to groom themselves.

10. The greater bilby **slurps seeds from the ground** with its long tongue, licking up a lot of sand in the process.

11. Opossums are **omnivores,** which means they eat nearly everything from **fruits** and **veggies to eggs, worms, small rodents,** and even **human trash.**

12. The water opossum, which lives in South America, is the only marsupial that is partly **aquatic—it has webbed toes,** and females can **close their pouches** so their **babies won't get wet.**

13. Kangaroos **can't walk backward.**

14. Baby Tasmanian devils are called **imps.**

15. There are about **two times as many kangaroos** in Australia as there are people.

16. Koalas sometimes **eat a little dirt** to **help them digest the tough eucalyptus** leaves that make up their diet.

17. Eucalyptus leaves can be **toxic** to other animals.

18. Quokkas, marsupials that are about the size of a house cat,

can **climb trees** to reach leaves or fruit, which kangaroos and wallabies can't do.

19. Many Australians call female red kangaroos **"blue fliers"** because their fur can look bluish.

20. In the late 1600s, when explorers first **spotted quokkas,** they thought they were **large rats.**

21. *Thylacosmilus,* a **saber-toothed ancestor** of modern-day marsupials, lived in South America **three to seven million years ago.**

22. Four-eyed opossums get their name for the spots over their eyes, which make them look as if they have **four eyes.**

23. A male kangaroo is called a **boomer or a jack,** and a female is called a **flyer or a jill.**

24. The **tiny long-tailed planigale** weighs about as much as a **teaspoon of sugar.**

25. A group of opossums is called **a passel.**

26. When a predator is near, Virginia opossums close their **eyes or stare into space,** stick out their tongues, and foam at the mouth—a protective behavior nicknamed "playing possum."

27. Kangaroos **regurgitate plants to chew** them some more before swallowing again **for final digestion.**

kangaroo

75 FACTS ABOUT ANIMALS WITH POCKETS

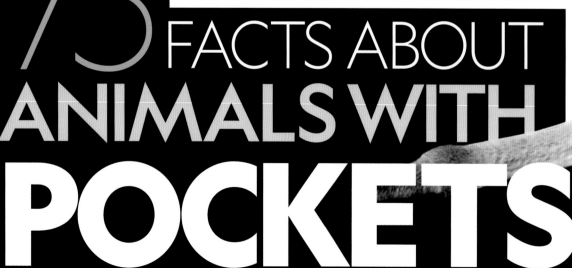

28. **Tree kangaroos** spend most of their time in the forest canopy and can jump **30 feet** (9 m) to get from tree to tree.

29. William the Wombat, a **6.5-foot** (2-m)-**tall sculpture** of a northern hairy-nosed wombat, was built in Thallon, Australia, to **raise awareness** of the critically **endangered marsupial.**

30. A baby koala **leaves** its mom's pouch about **six months** after it's **born,** but it hops back in when scared.

31. The word "kangaroo" comes from *gangurru*—the **Australian Aboriginal word** for the **gray kangaroo.**

32. To help keep them **camouflaged,** Virginia opossums have **gray-white fur** in the **northern areas** of North America and **darker fur** in **southern areas** of the continent.

33. The San Diego Zoo in California, which has the **largest koala colony** outside of Australia, received its first **koala pair—Snugglepot** and **Cuddlepie—** in 1925.

34. While many land mammals use their tails for balance, **kangaroos** use theirs as a **fifth "leg"** that helps support their weight when they **hop.**

35. The **largest marsupial ever,** *Diprotodon optatum*, which went extinct about 25,000 years ago, weighed as much as **three tons** (2.8 t).

36. Because of their diet of eucalyptus leaves, some people think that koalas **smell** like **minty cough drops**.

37. When **sleeping in trees,** the common spotted cuscus **camouflages** itself with **leaves** and **branches** to keep it safe from predators such as Kapul eagles and sea eagles.

38. To prepare for a newborn, **female marsupials lick** their **pouch clean,** including pee and poop left over from previous babies.

39. Australia minted a **gigantic gold coin** with a picture of a **hopping kangaroo**—it was worth one million Australian dollars and weighed more than 2,200 pounds (1,000 kg).

40. Marsupial moms have a **special muscle** that they use to **open** and **close** the **pouch** where their joeys live.

41. Most Australian marsupials live in dry or desert habitats, but the **mountain pygmy-possum,** found in the Australian Alps, is the **only marsupial** that **lives** in a **snowy area.**

42. Kangaroos are the **only large animal** that get around mostly by **hopping.**

43. When the **molar teeth** of kangaroos become **worn down** by the tough plants and shrubs they eat, the **teeth fall out** and are replaced.

44. **Tasmanian devils sneeze** before they get into a fight with another Tasmanian devil.

45. The **Lone Pine Koala Sanctuary** in Queensland has been rescuing koalas for almost **100 years**—it's the **world's oldest** koala sanctuary.

46. To hide from predators, numbats take **refuge** in a **hollow log.**

47. Wombats, the **world's largest burrowing** animals, can **weigh** about as much as a **10-year-old kid.**

48. Kangaroos can hop at speeds of more than **35 miles an hour** (56 km/h).

49. Tasmanian devils are the world's largest **carnivorous marsupial.**

50. **Opossums** use their **tails to grasp**—and even carry—bundles of grass or other materials.

51. **Red kangaroos**—the world's largest marsupial—can **weigh more** than an adult man and grow to more than five feet (1.5 m) tall.

52. Koalas spend about **80 percent** of a 24-hour period either **sleeping** or **resting.**

53. Kangaroos live in groups called a **mob,** and some mobs can have more than **100 kangaroos.**

54. In 2001 the **oldest known fossil** of a marsupial, *Sinodelphys szalayi,* was found in China; it's about **125 million years old.**

55. After 2020 brushfires damaged lands where brush-tailed rock wallabies live in Australia, government **helicopters dropped thousands of pounds** (kg) of **carrots** and **sweet potatoes** to feed them.

56. Young koalas get **piggyback rides** from their moms.

57. Australian marsupials known as **phalangers** are **called possums** because they look like the Virginia opossum, except their tail is covered in fur and the Virginia opossum's is hairless.

58. George, an **orphaned wombat** that was raised at Australian Reptile Park, was voted **Australia's most adorable animal.**

59. Scientists think that large *Diprotodon*, an extinct marsupial from Australia, **ate** as much as **330 pounds** (150 kg) of **plants a day.**

60. *Antechinus* look like mice, but they are actually **small carnivorous marsupials.**

61. **Folklore** held that Virginia opossums gave birth through their noses—they **"sneezed" their babies into their pouch.**

62. The **yellow-bellied glider** can glide through the air for more than **330 feet** (100 m)— that's longer than three NBA-size basketball courts.

63. Common spotted cuscuses spend most of their time lounging in trees, but they are able to gallop on the ground.

64. The Royal Botanic Garden in Sydney, Australia, has a "Hello Koalas" trail featuring more than **70 colorfully painted** koala **sculptures,** each with its own name.

65. Numbats' main food is **termites,** and they can **eat 20,000** in one day.

66. The female wombat's pouch opens toward her rear end so that she doesn't get her **joey dirty** when she digs.

67. Bandicoots, small marsupials with long noses, leave **"snout pokes"** in the **soil** as they look for insects and grubs.

68. Numbats, which live in eucalyptus woodlands, are the only marsupials that are active during the day.

69. The name **bandicoot** comes from the word *pandi-kokku,* which means **"pig rat"** in Telugu, a language spoken in India.

70. The greater bilby lives in **spiral-shaped burrows** that it digs underground to avoid predators and to cool off—some burrows are more than 100 years old.

71. Some people have tried to **replace** the **Easter Bunny** with the **"Easter Bilby"** in Australia to raise awareness of the endangered marsupial.

72. Fat-tailed mouse opossums get their name from the way they **store fat** in their **tails.**

73. Fossils of **prehistoric koalas** from 100,000 years ago suggest they might have grown to be about as **big as a bull** is today.

74. When first born, the Julia Creek dunnart, a tiny species of marsupial mouse, has muscles that are too small to inflate its lungs, so it **breathes through its skin.**

75. An **artist** created a **giant 16-foot** (5-m)-**tall kangaroo** out of **recycled wooden pallets** in Carrara, Australia—six people can fit in its pouch.

1
A snow leopard's ability to blend into its surroundings helped give it the nickname "ghost of the mountain."

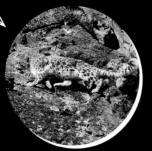

2
Praying mantises have a **flat, triangular shape,** like the leaves they sit on while waiting for prey.

3
Buff-tipped moths have **mottled gray wings** that **match the bark of birch trees,** where they rest during the day.

4
Leafy sea dragons have leaf-shaped appendages all over their bodies that make them **look like seaweed.**

5
Weedy sea dragons camouflage like leafy sea dragons, but their appendages are simpler.

6
Cuttlefish can match the color and texture of their surroundings—like that of a spiny piece of coral.

7
The **dead leaf butterfly** gets its name because its wings look like a **dry leaf.**

8
Buff-tipped moths have mottled gray wings that **match the bark of birch trees,** where they rest during the day.

35 FACTS ABOUT CAMOUFLAGED ANIMALS
THAT MAKE YOU *LOOK TWICE*

9
When **flounder** swim near the water's surface, their **skin color becomes almost clear.**

10
Flatfish, like flounder, **bury themselves in the sand on the ocean** floor with only their eyes peeking out.

11
A **leaf-tailed gecko** has **fringed flaps** on its sides that help it flatten against a surface and camouflage its body's outline.

12
Arctic foxes' white coats allow them to **roam undetected** in the **tundra's** snow and ice.

13
Nightjar birds have feathers that resemble bark, which allows them to camouflage on low branches during the day.

14
Adder snakes' skin matches the Namib Desert sand, where they **hide to wait for prey.**

15
Orcas have white bellies and black backs that help them blend in when viewed from below or above the water.

16
Spotted scorpionfish, whose color and texture match ocean reefs, **hide motionless** until they strike their prey.

17
Reef stonefish match their environment so well that they **look like a stone** on the ocean floor.

18
A **Congolese giant toad's coloring resembles the Gaboon viper's,** which wards off potential predators.

19
A **walking leaf insect** rocks back and forth when it walks to mimic **a leaf blowing in the wind.**

20
Pygmy seahorses, smaller than a paper clip, **take on the color of the coral** that they cling to.

21
The **lichen-colored katydid** matches the lichen that it eats from trees.

22
The **pattern** of a giraffe's coat helps it **camouflage** with **shadows and leaves.**

23
Gray tree frogs sometimes have mottled patterns on their skin that resemble lichen.

24
Baby tapirs have brown and beige stripes and spots, helping them blend in with the dappled light of the forest.

25
A **three-toed sloth** tucks its head to its chest in the trees, making itself look like a **clump of leaves.**

26
Axolotls, a type of salamander, can change their coloring a few shades **lighter** or **darker** for **camouflage.**

27
Red pandas' **raccoon-like face mask** helps it camouflage in red and white lichen.

28
Common baron caterpillars evolved to blend in perfectly with mango leaves to **avoid predators.**

29
The **bird-dropping spider** curls up and resembles a **pile of bird poop** to avoid predators.

30
Over the course of a few days, **a crab spider** can **switch colors to match the flower** that it is sitting on.

31
Wolf spiders mostly hunt on the ground—their dark color helps them **blend in with decaying plant matter.**

32
Willow ptarmigans' feathers are **snow white in winter** and **red** and **brown in the summer.**

33
When **red bats fold their wings** around their body, they look like **dead leaves.**

34
The **eyes** of crocodile fish **match the seafloor** to help disguise themselves while hunting there and in reefs.

35
Trumpetfish sometimes **swim vertically** to better blend in with coral.

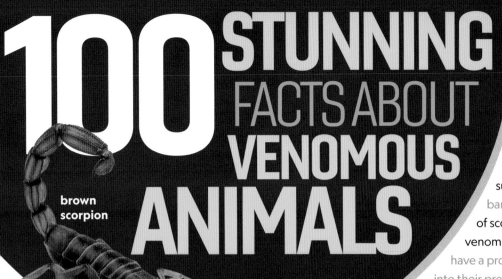

100 STUNNING FACTS ABOUT VENOMOUS ANIMALS

brown scorpion

1. Of the 3,000 snake species, only about 600 are venomous. 2. Most venomous snakes channel toxic saliva, or venom, through narrow grooves in their fangs. 3. A bullet ant's sting is said to be so painful it feels like getting hit by a bullet, which is how it got its name. 4. Snakes use venom as self-defense and to kill their prey. 5. Black mambas are considered the world's deadliest snake. 6. Only two drops of a black mamba's venom can kill a human; its fangs hold 20 drops. 7. A black mamba's head is coffin-shaped. 8. Drop for drop, a king cobra's venom is not as potent as other snakes', but it produces a lot with each strike—enough to kill an elephant. 9. King cobras can spit venom up to eight feet (2.4 m). 10. The venomous Gaboon viper has the world's longest snake fangs—they're up to two inches (5 cm) long. 11. Snake venom is made by special glands located behind a snake's eyes. 12. Venomous snakes live on every continent except Antarctica. 13. Sea snakes and kraits rarely come to shore. 14. Eastern diamondback rattlesnakes are the largest venomous snake in North America. 15. The eastern diamondback's distinct rattle sound comes from hollow bony segments that shake inside the end of its tail. 16. Rattles can break off, but a new one appears each time the rattlesnake sheds its skin. 17. Venomous copperhead snakes are the only snake with hourglass-shaped markings. 18. Inland taipans are one of the most venomous snakes, but they mostly hang out in deep cracks in the dirt in remote Australia. 19. Sydney funnel-web spiders have large, rearward-facing fangs that can pierce through fingernails. 20. A bite from a Sydney funnel-web spider can kill within 15 minutes. 21. Since an

antivenom was developed in the 1980s, there haven't been any fatalities from a Sydney funnel-web spider bite. 22. Black widow spiders, the most venomous spider in North America, are known for the red hourglass marking on the female's abdomen. 23. Black widows bite insects that they've caught in their web, and their venom liquefies their prey's body, which they then suck up. 24. Scorpions deliver venom through a barb in their tails. 25. Of the nearly 2,000 species of scorpions, only about one percent have enough venom capable of killing a person. 26. Mosquitoes have a proboscis—a long, hollow tube—to inject saliva into their prey. 27. Like bees, some mosquitoes are pollinators. 28. A bite from a goliath bird-eating tarantula's venomous fangs can kill a frog or a bird. 29. The goliath bird-eating tarantula has a leg span as wide as a basketball. 30. The assassin fly's venom kills its prey almost instantly, then liquifies the prey so the fly can slurp it up. 31. Box jellyfish have 15 tentacles and are covered in 5,000 stinging cells. 32. A box jellyfish's venom is one of the world's deadliest—it attacks its prey's heart, nervous system, and skin cells. 33. Box jellyfish stun their prey instantly, which prevents it from trying to escape and damaging the jellyfish's tentacles. 34. Sea turtles regularly eat box jellyfish—their shells help protect them from stings. 35. Stingrays carry their venom in a sharp, serrated spine at the end of their tails. 36. Although cone snails are only six inches (15 cm) long, they are some of the deadliest animals on Earth. 37. Geography cone snails attract prey by waving their tube-shaped proboscis. 38. Once prey is close, a geography cone snail launches a harpoonlike tooth that delivers a toxin, killing instantly. 39. The blue-ringed octopus is the size of a golf ball, but it has a parrotlike beak that releases a venomous bite. 40. When threatened, a blue-ringed octopus lights up 25 rings that cover its body. 41. Stonefish have bumpy skin that blends in with rocks on the ocean floor, camouflaging them. 42. Stonefish have 18 dorsal fin spines, 13 of which are venomous. 43. Stonefish don't use venom to catch prey but to defend themselves, jabbing predators with their spines if they get too close. 44. Sea anemones look like plants, but they are venomous meat-eaters, stunning prey with their tentacles. 45. Taylor's cantil, a type of venomous snake, has a yellow-tipped tail when it is a juvenile that it uses to lure prey, but loses the color when it becomes an adult. 46. Poisonous animals transfer their poison to predators, often secreting it through their skin; most venomous animals inject their poison with a stinger or fangs. 47. Venomous scorpionfish camouflage themselves on the seafloor with feathery fins that blend in with the surrounding coral. 48. Scorpionfish are called "sit and wait" predators—they attack when an unsuspecting fish swims by. 49. The Greening's frog uses small spines to headbutt predators, jabbing them and releasing a venom. 50. Yellow-bellied sea snakes live in the open ocean, attacking fish at the water's surface. 51. Male duck-billed platypuses have venomous spurs on their ankles. 52. Male duck-billed platypuses poke other male platypuses with their spurs in fights, injecting them with their painful venom. 53. While duck-billed platypus venom is painful to humans, it is not known to be lethal. 54. Venom in a vampire bat's saliva allows the blood of its prey to keep flowing, so the bat can eat more. 55. Slow lorises are the only venomous primate. 56. Slow lorises have glands under their inner arms that makes toxins, which they spread over their bodies during grooming, discouraging predators from attacking. 57. They also have toxins in their saliva that can be lethal to predators if the slow loris bites in an attack. 58. A shrew's venom doesn't instantly kill its prey—it paralyzes it. 59. Shrews stash their paralyzed prey and eat it when they're hungry. 60. A Komodo dragon's venom causes slow but constant bleeding in its victims. 61. Komodo dragons use their advanced sense of smell to track down their wounded prey—which can bleed for days—and then eat it. 62. Komodo dragons have been observed tracking down wounded prey for miles as the venom takes effect. 63. A spitting cobra's spit is actually venom that can cause pain and even blindness in humans. 64. A spitting cobra's range is about eight feet (2.4 m). 65. In 2015, scientists discovered the Greening's frog—the world's first known venomous frog. 66. Scientists discovered the first venomous crustacean, which is blind and only a few inches long, and lives in deep underwater caves in Mexico and Central America. 67. Grooves in Gila monsters' teeth release venom that seeps into their prey's wound with each bite. 68. Compounds found in tarantula venom are being studied for use as a pain killer for humans. 69. Molecules in Gila monsters' venom are being used to treat type 2 diabetes. 70. A bite from a brown recluse spider can take several months to heal. 71. Brown recluse spiders are also called violin spiders because of the dark violin-shaped design on their back. 72. Venomous Brazilian wandering spiders are also called banana spiders because they are often found on banana leaves. 73. In 2013, a family in London, England, had to fumigate their house after they unsuspectingly brought home a bunch of bananas containing an egg sac of Brazilian wandering spiders that opened. 74. Venomous brown widow spiders have an hourglass marking like the black widow, but it is orange, not red. 75. Brown widow venom is twice as powerful as the black widow's, but the spider only injects a small amount of venom when it bites, so it causes fewer fatalities. 76. The common iguana has venom glands, but its venom is weak and considered harmless to humans. 77. A boomslang, a venomous tree snake, is light green, helping it blend in with leaves. 78. Boomslangs, which live in sub-Saharan Africa, hunt for lizards, frogs, birds, and chameleons from the tree canopy. 79. The boomslang has fangs in the back of its mouth, which it wraps around its prey—then it bites down. 80. The puff adder snake gets its name from the way it inflates its body to appear bigger when threatened; it also hisses loudly. 81. Scientists discovered that caecilians may be the only amphibian to have a venomous bite. 82. Caecilians, which can grow to be five feet (1.5 m) long, look like large earthworms or smooth snakes. 83. Young caecilians use their teeth to tear off the outer layer of their mother's skin for food. 84. Ilha de Queimada Grande, an island off the coast of Brazil, is the only place golden lancehead vipers—one of the world's deadliest snakes—live. 85. Also known as Snake Island, it is

red lionfish

home to between 2,000 and 5,000 golden lancehead vipers. 86. The Brazilian government requires that a doctor be present when researchers visit the island in case a snake bite occurs. 87. There are more venomous fish in the ocean than there are venomous snakes on land. 88. The venomous decoy scorpionfish has a lure on its dorsal fin that looks like a tiny swimming fish, which tricks prey into coming close. 89. The venomous rhinoceros snake gets its name from a scaly "horn" at the tip of its head. 90. The golden head centipede can capture prey 15 times its body weight within 30 seconds using its paralyzing venom. 91. The buck moth caterpillar, which has venomous spines, causes burnlike blisters if you touch it. 92. Some venomous animals sport bright colors to warn potential predators that they won't taste good if eaten. 93. Because cone snails' venom works so quickly and effectively, scientists are studying it to see if they can replicate the reaction in human medicines. 94. A Portuguese man-of-war is made up of a colony of organisms called polyps that work together as one. 95. At least 1,250 species of catfish are venomous; they inject venom with sharp, bony spines found on the edges of their fins.

96. Portuguese man-of-war tentacles can stretch 165 feet (50 m). 97. Moon jellies' stinging tentacles shoot out tubes that harpoon prey floating by. 98. Crystal jellies light up like fireflies. 99. Lion's mane jellyfish are also called snotties because they are slimy. 100. Most jellyfish don't have stinging cells on their umbrella-like body, or bell.

black mamba

1 Hippos are the THIRD LARGEST LIVING LAND ANIMALS, after elephants and rhinos.

2 Hippos can be 16.5 feet (5 m) long and WEIGH NEARLY 10,000 POUNDS (4,540 kg).

3 Hippos live in slow-moving RIVERS and LAKES in Africa.

4 Hippos can eat 80 POUNDS (36 kg) of grass EVERY NIGHT.

5 Hippos can SLEEP UNDERWATER. A REFLEX allows them to BOB UP TO THE SURFACE to take a BREATH while still ASLEEP.

6 A GROUP of hippos is sometimes called a BLOAT.

7 In the wild, hippos LIVE AROUND 40 YEARS.

8 Hippos ROAR, GRUNT, and WHEEZE.

9 Hippos are ACTIVE DURING THE NIGHT, when they might TRAVEL SIX MILES (10 km) in search of food.

10 "Hippopotamus" means "RIVER HORSE" in Greek. But hippos AREN'T RELATED TO HORSES.

11 Hippos can BELLOW AT 115 DECIBELS— the same volume as a ROCK CONCERT.

12 The hippo is the WORLD'S DEADLIEST large LAND ANIMAL.

13 A hippo's YAWN is a WARNING TO BACK OFF.

14 Even though hippos spend most of their time in the water, THEY CAN'T SWIM.

15 Hippos OOZE AN OILY RED SUBSTANCE that acts like natural SUNSCREEN.

16 ANCIENT PEOPLE THOUGHT that hippos SWEAT BLOOD.

17 TURTLES sometimes SUNBATHE on a HIPPO'S BACK.

18 Hippos live in GROUPS of 10 TO 15 FEMALES and their young, led by a DOMINANT MALE.

19 Hippos can HOLD THEIR BREATH UNDERWATER for 30 MINUTES at a time.

20 Hippos' EYES, NOSES, and EARS are located on TOP OF THEIR HEADS so that they can SEE, BREATHE, and HEAR while IN THE WATER.

21 When FOOD IS SCARCE, hippos can STORE RESERVES IN THEIR STOMACHS and go up to THREE WEEKS WITHOUT EATING.

22 Experts once thought hippos were herbivores. But they actually EAT THE CARCASSES OF ANIMALS THEY FIND— INCLUDING OTHER HIPPOS'.

23 A hippo CALF is about 10 TIMES LARGER than a HUMAN BABY.

24 BABY HIPPOS NURSE from their mothers UNDERWATER.

25 A hippo can OUTRUN A HUMAN.

50 ROLY-POLY FACTS ABOUT HIPPOS

26
Hippos have a CLEAR MEMBRANE that COVERS THEIR EYES when they're underwater, like a pair of BUILT-IN SWIM GOGGLES.

27
Hippos can CHARGE at up to 30 MILES AN HOUR (48 km/h).

28
A hippo's STOMACH has FOUR COMPARTMENTS.

29
When it DIVES, a hippo's NOSE and EARS CLOSE so NO WATER GETS IN.

30
The hippo's CLOSEST LIVING RELATIVE may be the WHALE.

31
Hippos have the LARGEST MOUTH of ALL LAND ANIMALS at up to FOUR FEET (1.2 m) wide.

32
Hippos have STIFF WHISKERS on their UPPER LIP.

33
As many as 150 HIPPOS may use ONE WATERING HOLE at a time.

34
Hippo POOP FEEDS river- and lake-dwelling FISH in Africa.

35
In 2014, scientists sent ROBOT BOATS DISGUISED AS CROCODILES to STUDY the effects of hippos on WATER QUALITY in the Mara River.

36
The RARE PYGMY hippopotamus is about the SIZE OF A PIG.

37
The extinct *HIPPOPOTAMUS ANTIQUUS* weighed about FOUR TONS.

38
A hippo's body is so DENSE that the animal can WALK UNDERWATER.

39
Hippos have WEBBED TOES.

40
Hippos are considered AMPHIBIOUS ANIMALS because they spend up to 16 HOURS A DAY IN WATER.

41
Hippos have DEADLY SHARP CANINE TEETH that can be 28 INCHES (71 cm) LONG.

42
Hippos DON'T SWEAT, so they rely on BATHING in water to KEEP COOL.

43
FIONA the hippo became FAMOUS after she was BORN at the Cincinnati Zoo WEIGHING just 29 POUNDS (13 kg).

44
Because they spend a lot of time SITTING IN THE WATER, hippos EAT VERY LITTLE—just 1 to 1.5 percent of their body weight every day.

45
Hippos may use their POOP to SEND MESSAGES to other hippos.

46
George Washington wore DENTURES partly MADE OUT OF HIPPOPOTAMUS TEETH.

47
Hippos once LIVED in EUROPE, ASIA, and MADAGASCAR.

48
Hippos ONCE LIVED throughout SUB-SAHARAN AFRICA, but now can be found only in PROTECTED AREAS.

49
Hippos' LARGE CANINE TEETH are made from the SAME MATERIAL as ELEPHANTS' TUSKS.

50
Hippos begin a FIGHT by FLINGING THEIR POOP WITH THEIR TAILS.

1 Jewel wasps inject venom into cockroaches' brains, **paralyzing them,** and then lay eggs in the roaches' abdomens.

2 Mites have been found to live on every mammal except **Earth's two egg-laying mammals: platypuses and echidnas.**

3 When the eggs hatch, the larvae **feed on the cockroach.**

4 Fleas, bloodsucking parasites that live on birds and mammals, can **jump 100 times their body length.**

5 Leeches, a type of worm that lives in water and on land, **attach to frogs, fish,** and **even humans** to suck their blood for food.

25 FACTS ABOUT PARASITIC

6 Head lice, **which are the size of a sesame seed,** stick to human hair with their feet and **eat tiny amounts of blood** from their host as nourishment.

7 A parasite lives on or in the **body of another organism, harming it** and possibly causing death.

8 Mites, which are related to spiders and ticks, are **smaller than the period** at the end of this sentence.

9 Lice can lay **eight eggs a day** and live for **30 days** on a person's head.

10 An army of bedbugs can attack a person **500 times** in one night.

11 The Smithsonian National Museum of Natural History holds a collection of **120,000 jars of parasitic specimens.**

12

Brood parasites are animals that trick others to **raise their young**—like **cuckoo birds** that leave their eggs in warbler nests so the **warblers will tend to them as their own.**

13

Deer ticks eat only three times in their lifetime: when they molt from larva to nymph; when they turn from nymph to adult; and as adults when laying eggs.

14

Lice have been found in the hair of **Egyptian mummies.**

17

Deer ticks, which suck blood from dogs, deer, and people, can swell to twice their size while feasting.

18

Arctic skuas, a type of seabird, are also called **jaegers**—the German word for hunter—because **they steal food from other birds.**

15

The world's longest leeches grow to about **18 inches (0.45 m).**

16

In the Amazon, leeches crawl up swimmers' noses to feed on **mucus.**

ANIMALS

19

Thresher sharks sometimes jump completely out of the water, likely to help get rid of pea-size parasites called **copepods that cling to their gills.**

20

Bedbugs are **attracted to humans' body heat** and the carbon dioxide in our breath.

21

Goose barnacles got their name from medieval Europeans who first **thought the tiny crustaceans were fruit that turned into geese.**

22

Flea bites can cause skin to become itchy, but they can also transmit bacteria, **including—in rare instances—the plague.**

23

The U.S. Navy estimates that when a large number of barnacles are stuck to a ship, **they add substantial weight and drag, increasing fuel consumption by 40 percent.**

24

Bedbugs have lived among humans for some **250,000 years**—since before we had beds.

25

Humans can **ingest tapeworms** by eating **raw or undercooked pork;** the worms then attach to the intestines and grow.

»15 SUPERCOOL FACTS ABOUT SOCIAL MEDIA PETS

1

Reagan the Labradoodle is often photographed in **matching outfits with his best human friend.**

3

Celebrity chef Bobby Flay has a Maine coon cat named **Nacho Flay.**

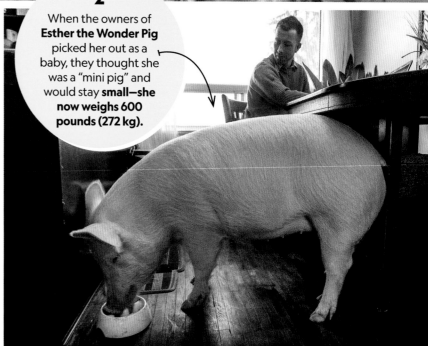

2

When the owners of **Esther the Wonder Pig** picked her out as a baby, they thought she was a "mini pig" and would stay **small—she now weighs 600 pounds (272 kg).**

4. **Maya Polar Bear, a Samoyed dog,** is famous for her recordings of **eating crunchy foods,** like **watermelon** and **popcorn.**

5

Doug the Pug often dresses up as musicians and movie characters—from **Taylor Swift to Harry Potter.**

7

The owners of **Nala the Cat,** who has **more followers on social media than any other cat,** adopted her from a **pet shelter** when she was a kitten.

6

Hamilton the Hipster Cat has gray fur, white paws, and white markings on his face that look like a **handlebar mustache.**

8. MacGyver, an **Argentine red tegu lizard,** is known for his videos of being **hand-fed snacks with chopsticks.**

9. Loki the Cat is famous for her **vampirelike teeth.**

10

Harlso, a dachshund, is known for his ability to **balance things on his head**—from pine cones to lattes.

11

Jim Pomm, a Pomeranian, holds two world records: for **fastest sprint on his front legs** and **fastest sprint on his hind legs.**

12. Smoothie the Cat has been named the **"world's most photogenic cat"** because of her emerald green eyes.

13. Henry and Baloo are cat and dog friends who are famous for their photos of **cuddling together during naptime.**

14. Rorschach, a Dalmatian, has spots around his nose that form **a heart.**

15. Miffy, a bunny model, has appeared on the **runway at New York Fashion Week.**

1. Elephants can **"hear" with their feet** by sensing sound waves that travel through the ground.

2. Ostriches are the **only birds with two toes.** (All others have three or four.)

3. A mole's **front feet** face sideways to help it **move dirt out of the way as it digs.**

4. Horses and their relatives are the **only animals with a single toe** (called a hoof).

5. Because **cat claws are retractable,** cat tracks usually don't show claw marks.

6. Ducks use their **webbed feet like paddles** to help them push through the water.

7. Mosquitoes can **walk on water.**

8. Mountain goats have **pads on their hooves** that provide grip, just like the soles of climbing shoes.

9. *Quetzalcoatlus northropi* **was a pterosaur**—a flying reptile related to dinosaurs—that was nearly as tall as a giraffe. When on land, it **walked with its wings** tucked like folded umbrellas.

10. The soles of the **flying lemur's feet** work like suction cups to help it grip.

11. For their size, rhinos have **surprisingly dainty feet.**

12. Some birds have a special, **serrated claw** that they likely use to clean their feathers.

13. **Jacanas** are birds that can **walk across floating lily pads** with their long, thin toes.

14. A fly's feet **produce a gluelike substance** that helps them cling to surfaces—even upside down.

15. Geckos get their gravity-defying grip from **hundreds of hairs** that cover their feet.

16. Just like house cats, lions have **retractable claws** they can push out when hunting or pull back in to keep them protected.

17. Butterflies "taste" with their feet.

18. Penguins can adjust **blood flow** to their feet to keep them from **freezing on the ice.**

19. The **giant armadillo's longest claw measures eight inches (20 cm)**—more than a quarter of the animal's body length!

20. Elephants can walk **nearly silently thanks to cushions of thick skin** on the soles of their feet.

21. A **dinosaur** named *Bambiraptor* had **opposable thumbs**—just as humans do.

22. Some dogs bred for swimming—**such as retrievers—have webbing between their toes** to help them move through the water.

23. Some whales have **nonfunctional feet bones** in their skeletons—the remains of hind legs their ancestors used to walk on land.

24. Dogs **sweat through their paws.**

25. Claws are **made of keratin,** the same substance that makes up your hair and nails.

26. **Tapirs** have **multiple hooves** on each foot.

27. You can **buy dog nail polish.**

28. The Norwegian Lundehund is a dog that **has six or more fully functioning toes** on each foot.

29. **Sloths** use their **long claws** to dig into the earth and pull their bodies along the ground.

30. The **cassowary** has a sharp, four-inch (10-cm)-long claw on each of its feet that it uses to **slice open predators** with a single kick.

31. Frogs' toes **ooze a sticky mucus** that helps them cling to surfaces.

32. Humans, bears, and great apes are among the few animals that **walk with their heel touching the ground first.**

33. **Hooves** are modified toenails.

34. The gray fox is the only member of the dog family that can **retract its claws.**

35. Many mammals, such as cats and dogs, are **"digitigrade"**—they walk on their toes.

36. A polar bear's wide, furry feet **act like snowshoes** to help the bears move across the Arctic.

37. An owl can **swivel its third toe to face either forward** or backward.

38. An osprey's feet **are covered with spiky "scales"** that help it hold on to slippery fish.

39. Some experts think peregrine falcons use their closed **talons like a fist to punch their prey out of the sky.**

40. A certain bacteria can cause dog paws to smell like corn chips.

41. The American coot bird has lobes of flesh on its feet that help **push through the water** but fold back when on land.

42. Birds called **blue-footed boobies** show off their teal-hued feet to potential mates. **The bluer the foot, the more attractive the booby.**

75 FABULOUS FACTS ABOUT FEET

43. The Virginia opossum has a toe, much like your thumb, **that it uses to hang upside down from branches.**

44. The eastern spadefoot toad is named for the structure on its hind feet that **resembles the garden tool.**

45. Female turtles use their **claws to dig a hole,** which they lay their eggs in.

46. The North American beaver has **a claw on each hind foot that's split in two.** It uses it like a comb to groom its fur.

47. The fiddler crab is so named because the male crab holds its one oversize claw—**a bit like a person holds a violin, or fiddle.**

48. Geckos can turn the **"stickiness"** of their feet on and off.

49. Mole crickets have **shovel-like front legs**—just like moles.

50. Frogfish use their **fins to "walk" on the ocean floor.**

51. Fossilized footprints are called **ichnites.**

52. Flamingos can **sleep while standing on one leg.**

53. Snails and slugs are gastropods, **a Greek word meaning "stomach-foot."** They're named this because they look like they're walking on their bellies.

54. Kangaroos use their big feet to propel themselves **30 feet (9 m) in a single leap.**

55. Bats clench their feet while sleeping, which allows them to **hang upside down.**

56. Mountain goats have **two toes,** which spread apart to help the goats balance.

57. Basilisk lizards can walk on water by unfurling flaps of skin on their feet. The **flaps trap air pockets underneath, which keeps the lizards from sinking.**

58. Horseshoes are attached by nails, but the nails don't hurt the horse because their hooves have **no nerve endings.**

59. Harpy eagles use their **huge talons** to crush their prey.

60. Armadillos use their enormous claws to **dig into termite mounds.**

61. The scaly-foot snail has a **squishy foot that's covered with iron plates.**

62. The longest claws in history may have belonged to the dinosaur *Therizinosaurus.* **Its three-foot (0.9-m)-long claws were the length of baseball bats!**

63. Collared lizards are one of the few lizards that can run upright on their hind legs.

64. A bird of prey's sharp, hooked claws are called talons.

65. Hooves **never stop growing.**

66. The **gluelike substance** that coats flies' feet is so sticky that **flies have special claws** to pry their feet free before taking a step.

67. The **red-handed tamarin** is named for the **bright red-golden fur** on its hands and feet.

68. The largest dinosaur footprint ever found was made by **a long-necked sauropod.** It measures 5 feet 9 inches (1.8 m) across.

69. Alpacas don't have **hooves.** Instead, they have **two pads similar to a dog's** that are protected by tough toenails.

70. The **aye-aye** has a **special claw** perfect for **hooking grubs** and scooping them into its mouth.

71. Birds' feet lock around their perch so they can **sleep standing up.**

72. The neck and front legs of the **male northern river terrapin,** a turtle found in Southeast Asia, turn bright pink when it's time to find a mate.

73. Squirrels and their relatives have **four toes** on their **front feet** and **five toes** on their **back feet.**

74. One species of extinct kangaroo was **heavier than a lion** and **walked on two feet instead of hopping.**

75. Water striders' feet repel water, allowing them to **walk across its surface.**

1 Gorillas have the **largest eardrums** of any animal.

2 **Gorilla babies** are born after **their moms are pregnant** for **about nine months**—just **like** human babies.

3 When **gorillas are having fun,** they can **make a purrlike** *huuuuh* **sound**.

4 Scientists **identify different gorillas** by the **unique shape of their noses.**

5 Gorillas **sleep** in the **treetops** in **nests made of bent branches.**

6 The **largest adult gorillas** can **eat 60 pounds** (27 kg) **of food in a day.**

7 Gorilla **poop,** which contains a lot of fiber, helps **fertilize the land in their forest homes.**

8 **In their forest homes** in East and Central Africa, **gorillas can live for 35 to 40 years.**

9 Gorillas make **low rumbling sounds** to **greet one another.**

35 FACTS ABOUT GLORIOUS GORILLAS

10
When a **gorilla grunts**—making a **sound** that's a little **like a cough**—it can **mean** "back off."

11
To **raise money for** gorilla **conservation**, people in Denver, Colorado, U.S.A., have run a **race** in either **banana** or **gorilla costumes**.

12
Gorillas are **usually shy and peaceful.**

13
The **Phoenix Suns gorilla mascot** got his **start in 1980,** when Henry Rojas, who **dressed up** as a gorilla **to deliver a singing telegram** to a fan in the arena, **danced under the basket** during **a time-out** in the **basketball game.**

14
To search **for food,** gorillas **can climb 50 feet** (15 m) up into trees.

15
A **large gorilla can weigh 400 pounds** (180 kg)—that's the **same as about 46 gallons** (174 L) **of milk.**

16
Gorillas are mainly **vegetarians**—they eat **fruits, wild celery, bark,** and also insects and worms.

17
Gorilla babies learn **how to walk and climb** when they are about **six months old.**

18
Baby gorillas develop twice as fast as human babies; they learn to **crawl** when they are around **three months old.**

19
When born, a **baby gorilla weighs** about **as much as two pineapples.**

20
Some adult **western lowland gorillas** have **a patch of red hair** on the **top** of their **heads.**

21
Kidogo, a silverback gorilla living at a zoo in Germany, **became famous when he walked across a tightrope** in his **enclosure.**

22
Gorillas are the **largest of all primates** (and that includes humans).

23
Since **gorillas** can **catch diseases** from **humans, baby** gorillas **in zoos** are **given vaccines.**

24
Scientists think **human ancestors and gorilla ancestors split** apart about **10 million years ago.**

25
A **silverback gorilla** is named for the **white-silver stripe of fur** on his back.

26
A **group of gorillas** is called a **troop.**

27
Both gorilla species **are critically endangered**—their **main threats** are **loss of habitat, poaching** by humans, and **diseases.**

28
The way **gorillas walk** is a **gait** that scientists think our **human ancestors** also used many **millions of years ago.**

29
In the wild, gorillas **like to eat the core** from **banana plant stems,** not the bananas themselves.

30
Mountain gorillas live in Africa's **first** designated **national park** in the **Democratic Republic of Congo.**

31
Zookeepers at a **London zoo** scatter chunks of **watermelon** on a **climbing structure** in the gorilla enclosure **for a tasty treat.**

32
Male gorillas **beat their chests** and **walk upright** to **intimidate other male gorillas.**

33
Koko, a western lowland gorilla, **learned how to use more than 1,000 signs** in American Sign Language **to talk with humans.**

34
Koko appeared twice on the **cover of** *National Geographic* **magazine,** once holding her pet kitten.

35
In the 1933 movie *King Kong,* six men inside the 50-foot (15-m)-tall model ran **85 different motors** to create the **gorilla's tantrums.**

100 HARD-CORE
FACTS ABOUT ANIMALS
WITH ARMOR

1. The purpose of shells, like the ones on snails, turtles, and crabs, is to protect the animal's soft body. 2. A turtle's shell continues to grow in relation to its body size until the turtle is full grown.

3. Scales—like the kind found on alligators and snakes—help make an animal's skin tough and also keep it from drying out. 4. During attacks, Roman soldiers got into a formation called a testudo—Latin for "tortoise"—in which they held shields in front of or above themselves to shelter as a group. 5. Some land snails have hairy shells, which might help them get a better grip in wet environments.

6. Armadillo is a Spanish word meaning "little armored one."

7. One type of hermit crab makes its home inside a coral, then walks around with it. 8. A mantis shrimp's claws are so strong that they can break aquarium glass. 9. Nine-banded armadillos nearly always have litters of identical quadruplets. 10. Thorny desert lizards can puff themselves up to appear larger than they actually are.

11. Armadillos' "armored" overlapping bands are tough but flexible and covered in scales. 12. The barbs on a porcupine's quills make the quills harder to pull out once they're embedded in an animal's skin. 13. Porcupines can't "throw" their quills at enemies, but they can quickly shed them, pricking their attacker. 14. Roman soldiers in the third century A.D. made helmets and body armor out of crocodile skin. 15. The ironclad beetle can't fly, but its rocklike exoskeleton makes it almost predator-proof. 16. To dissect an ironclad beetle after it has died, scientists have to use a hammer or drill to cut through its tough exterior. 17. Hedgehogs have about 5,000 spines—they roll into a sharp ball that is unappetizing to a predator. 18. Hedgehogs usually sleep curled in a ball to keep safe. 19. Unlike their snail cousins, which carry their shells on their backs, some slugs have internal shell plates that are hidden within their bodies. 20. The sea snail was considered a symbol of rebirth for Mesoamericans, people of pre-16th-century Indigenous cultures who lived in parts of Mexico and Central America. The whirled shape of its shell represented the cycle of life and death.

21. People have used conches, large sea snails with especially tough shells, as musical instruments for thousands of years. 22. In ancient Greek mythology, Triton calms the waves with a conch-shell trumpet.

23. Researchers are studying the structure of conch shells to make better body armor for the military. 24. Snails can repair minor injuries to their shells. The mantle just under the shell produces calcium and protein to mend damage. 25. Turtle shells have nerve endings—which means a turtle can feel when its shell is rubbed. 26. The world's smallest land snail, *Angustopila dominikae,* is so tiny it can fit inside the eye of a sewing needle. 27. Before it molts, or sheds its old shell, a lobster absorbs lots of water, which forces the shell open. 28. When a lobster walks out of its old shell, a new one is fully formed underneath.

29. After a lobster molts its shell, it goes into hiding to regain its strength and to let the new shell harden. 30. Sea urchins have pointy spines for protection, but their teeth are even tougher—they can chew through stone without getting dull. 31. A turtle's shell is part of its skeleton and is made up of more than 50 bones. 32. A giant clam can be four feet (1.2 m) long and weigh more than 500 pounds (227 kg). 33. Once a giant clam has found a good spot on a reef, it fastens itself there and stays for the rest of its life. 34. A pufferfish's spines lie flat, but to fend off predators, it gulps water to make the spines poke out. 35. Pangolins are the only mammal covered in true scales. 36. Even though the pangolin resembles an armadillo and eats insects with its sticky tongue like an anteater, it is more closely related to bears and cats.

37. Crocodiles and alligators have thick skin, but some parts of their bodies, like around their mouths, are more sensitive than human fingertips. 38. Almost all species of turtles can bring their heads and legs inside of their shells when they sense danger.

39. Porcupines rattle their quills when they sense a predator nearby. 40. *Glyptotherium,* a distant relative of the armadillo that lived 1.8 million to 12,000 years ago, was the size of a small car. 41. *Glyptotherium* had a hard shell and a spiked tail, which it swung like a club. 42. All sea turtles have hard shells except the leatherback turtle, which has a somewhat flexible and rubbery shell. 43. Thorny devil lizards' spikes help protect them against predators, but they also help absorb water in the lizards' dry desert habitat. 44. When startled or scared, nine-banded armadillos can jump as high as five feet (1.5 m). 45. Some hermit crabs attach stinging anemones to their shells as extra protection against predators. 46. When a hermit crab moves into a new shell, it removes the anemones from its old shell and sticks them on its new one. 47. X-rays of Komodo dragons showed that under their skin they are covered in tiny bones that look like medieval chain mail. 48. Adult Komodo dragons' strong skin helps protect them when they are fighting for mates and food.

49. The three-banded armadillo can bend its shell to curl into a hard ball, protecting it from predators. 50. The three-banded armadillo's teardrop-shaped head plate is just the right size and shape to seal off any openings when it curls into a ball.

51. When a mantis shrimp's claws wear out, the shrimp molts and grows a new exoskeleton, which includes new claws. 52. Researchers are studying the strong claws of

Coahuilan box turtle

mantis shrimps to improve sports helmets. 53. The scrawled cowfish is covered in six-sided scales that are fused together to form a hard shell. 54. Sharks are covered in millions of tiny toothlike scales that work like a suit of armor to protect their skin and body.

55. Crocodile scales, called scutes, don't overlap like fish and snake scales do, and crocodiles shed them one at a time as they wear out.

56. Pangolins are believed to be the most heavily trafficked wild animal in the world. They are poached for their scales, which are used in traditional Asian medicine, and meat. 57. Baby porcupines have soft quills at birth, but they harden in a few days. 58. Alligator gars, a type of megafish, get their name for their hard, interlocking, alligator-like scales. 59. Native Americans used to make arrowheads, sharpened tips added to arrows, out of alligator gar scales.

60. When pangolins roll into a ball, it's nearly impossible for a predator—even a lion—to bite into them. 61. Indian rhinos have thick hide plates that African rhinos don't have. Flexible skin between the plates allows them to shift as the animal moves. 62. Abalones make pearls by secreting a shell over a parasite that gets stuck in their flesh. 63. Spiny brittle sea stars deter predators with their spikes, but their main form of defense is to bury themselves in the sand, leaving just one or two arms free to catch food that passes by.

64. The jeweled top snail's colorful cone-shaped shell caught the eye of 18th-century explorer Captain James Cook, who collected the snails for study. 65. In 2010, a remote-operated underwater vehicle discovered a 2.5-foot (0.76-m)-long hard-shelled giant isopod 8,500 feet (2,590 m) below the ocean's surface. 66. Giant isopods, which are related to pill bugs, or roly-polies, can survive four years without eating. 67. The scaly-foot snail, which lives near hydrothermal vents on the ocean floor, has an armored shell made of iron. 68. Scaly-foot snails use their iron shells to protect themselves from hydrothermal vents, which heat the seawater to 750°F (399°C) or more. 69. One species of deep-sea snail, *Alviniconcha strummeri,* is named after Joe Strummer, the lead singer of the punk rock band The Clash, because researchers thought its spiky shell looked like the singer's hair. 70. Chitons, a type of mollusk, are covered by a hard shell of eight overlapping plates that are dotted with hundreds of eyes. 71. North American porcupines' 30,000 quills each contain 700 to 800 barbs. 72. Armadillos' shells protect them from thorny shrubs, where they hide from predators.

73. Arapaimas, freshwater fish, live with piranhas in the Amazon River but are protected by layers of hard, flexible scales that even the sharp-toothed piranhas can't penetrate. 74. The armadillo girdled lizard, which is covered in platelike scales, rolls on its back and bites its tail when in danger. 75. Thanks to their size, tough hide, and strong horns, adult rhinos have no natural predators.

76. *Hirondellea gigas,* a type of crustacean found in the deepest part of the ocean, creates a type of aluminum gel that covers its body to protect it from the harsh environment. 77. A worm fossil discovered in China had 30 legs, 18 of which were tipped with claws to help it attach to surfaces. 78. Researchers think the worm, which was covered in spikes, was one of the first armored animals. 79. The larvae of the caddisfly, a type of aquatic insect, produce a sticky silk from their mouths to make hard cases that they walk around in. 80. They attach stones and shells to their cases, which provides extra protection against predators. 81. Hermit crabs protect their soft tails by placing discarded shells from other animals on top of it. 82. When some hermit crabs molt, they eat their shells for extra vitamins and minerals. 83. Researchers are studying arapaimas' scales to make human-made armor, like bulletproof vests, even stronger and more lightweight. 84. The crown-of-thorns starfish is named for the long spines that cover its body. 85. Sea urchin spines are so sharp that they can easily puncture a thick wet suit. 86. Because of microscopic textured patterns on their skin, sharks are resistant to barnacles, algae, and human bacteria. 87. A biotech company created a material that mimics the shape and pattern of shark skin and used it to make germ-deflecting medical equipment and computer keyboards. 88. When hedgehogs fall to the ground from the trees where they sometimes live, they curl up into a ball, their spines providing a cushioned bounce when they hit the ground. 89. Sand dollars have hard, outer shells and are covered in fine hairs, which help them move along the seafloor. 90. The exoskeletons of sand dollars found on the beach are usually white, but live ones are gray or purple. 91. The sperm whale has the thickest skin of any animal—the skin on its back and neck is up to 14 inches (35 cm) thick. 92. Most turtle shells are covered in hard scutes—overlapping pieces of keratin, which is the same material as your fingernails. 93. Discarded oyster shells are sometimes used to make cement. 94. You can estimate a turtle's age by counting the rings on its scutes. 95. The matamata, a South American turtle, has a rough and knobby shell with growth rings that look like cones. 96. Nautiluses are cousins to squid, octopuses, and cuttlefish, but they live inside hard external shells. 97. A nautilus moves in a seesaw motion by pulling water into the mantle cavity within its shell and blowing it out a siphon beneath its tentacles.

98. Researchers discovered that the teeth of limpets, aquatic snails with a cone-shaped shell, consist of one of the strongest biological materials. 99. Scientists think the structure of limpet teeth, which are made of thin, tightly packed fibers, could be replicated to make high-performance cars, boats, and aircraft. 100. Sea urchins, which live on the seafloor, can withstand the same amount of pressure as being stood on by 20 stacked elephants—but they don't develop cracks in their shells.

Brazilian porcupine

1
There are more chickens than PEOPLE IN THE WORLD.

2
Chickens are DESCENDED from wild JUNGLE BIRDS.

3
Chickens were first domesticated about 8,000 YEARS AGO.

4
A young hen is called A PULLET.

5
A family of chicks is called A BROOD.

6
There are at least 10 TIMES more chickens than any OTHER BIRD ON EARTH.

7
Chickens are OMNIVORES: They eat plants as well as insects and small animals.

8
Roosters pick up and drop MORSELS OF FOOD on the ground during a mating dance called tidbitting.

9
The skin flap on top of a chicken's head is called A COMB.

10
THE FIRST CHICKEN IN HISTORY hatched from an egg born to REPTILE-LIKE PARENTS.

11
The record for the MOST CHICKEN EGGS LAID in the shortest amount of time is 371 in 364 days.

12
THE AYAM CEMANI is a rare chicken that's COMPLETELY BLACK, including its ORGANS, MUSCLES, and BONES.

13
Some breeds of hen can lay more than 300 EGGS A YEAR.

14
The HEAVIEST CHICKEN EGG ever laid weighed ONE POUND (454 G).

15
A fear of chickens is called ALEKTOROPHOBIA.

16
A mother hen TURNS HER EGGS about 50 TIMES A DAY.

17
It takes chicken eggs about 21 DAYS TO HATCH.

18
Most hens will STOP LAYING EGGS if they experience fewer than 12 HOURS OF DAYLIGHT.

19
A chicken eggshell is covered with up to 17,000 TINY PORES, or holes.

20
It takes about 26 HOURS for a hen to FORM AN EGG.

21
Chickens can only fLY A FEW YARDS—their WINGS ARE TOO SMALL and their flight muscles too heavy for takeoff.

22
Americans eat about 100 BILLION EGGS A YEAR—about 300 PER PERSON!

23
About 72,000 people participated in the WORLD'S LARGEST CHICKEN DANCE.

24
The highest an egg has been dropped WITHOUT BREAKING IS 700 FEET (213 m)—about the height of the Space Needle in Seattle, Washington, U.S.A.

25
Chickens can remember more than 100 HUMAN FACES.

26
Hens usually LAY THEIR EGGS in the MORNING.

27
Chickens, like other birds, can't TASTE SPICINESS.

28
It's ILLEGAL TO EAT FRIED CHICKEN with anything other than your hands in Gainesville, Georgia, U.S.A.

29
The joke "WHY DID THE CHICKEN CROSS THE ROAD?" was first printed in a New York City, U.S.A., magazine in 1847.

30
Chickens with white earlobes lay WHITE EGGS; chickens with dark earlobes lay BROWN EGGS.

31
A rooster announces to his flock that he's found food with A *TOOK, TOOK, TOOK* SOUND.

50
FEATHERED FACTS
ABOUT CHICKENS

32

The mushroom *LAETIPORUS SULPHUREUS* is called the "CHICKEN OF THE WOODS" because some people think it TASTES LIKE CHICKEN.

33

Chickens have THREE EYELIDS.

34

BUFFALO WINGS—chicken wings fried and coated in butter and hot sauce—were invented in 1964 in Buffalo, New York, U.S.A.

35

THE LONGEST RECORDED FLIGHT of a chicken lasted 13 seconds.

36

The skin that hangs under a rooster's neck is called A WATTLE.

37

Chickens clean themselves by TAKING DUST BATHS.

38

A 15-year-old farmer in Nova Scotia PLAYED CLASSICAL MUSIC to chickens as part of a science fair project. They laid BIGGER EGGS when they listened to it.

39

Chickens can run about NINE MILES an hour (14.5 km/h)—about as fast as the average human.

40

Mother hens "TALK" TO THEIR CHICKS while they're still in the eggs—and the CHICKS PEEP BACK!

41

There are more FRIED CHICKEN RESTAURANTS in SOUTH KOREA than there are McDonald's in the entire world.

42

Only one in every 1,000 eggs has TWO YOLKS.

43

In 2016, a man cracked open a dozen eggs to discover that they all had DOUBLE YOLKS—the odds of that happening are ONE IN A THOUSAND TRILLION.

44

The record for most yolks in ONE EGG IS NINE.

45

Roosters have A STRONG INSTINCT to protect hens from PREDATORS.

46

Chickens can see color BETTER THAN HUMANS CAN.

47

Chickens in a flock have a STRICT SOCIAL HIERARCHY called a PECKING ORDER.

48

Chickens make at least 24 DIFFERENT CALLS.

49

At the annual White House Easter Egg Roll, CHILDREN COMPETE IN A RACE to PUSH AN EGG through the grass with A LONG-HANDLED SPOON.

50

Some scientists think chickens could be as INTELLIGENT AS HUMAN TODDLERS.

Brahma rooster

1
Scientists think that some eagles have **two structures in their eyes** that act like a **telephoto lens,** helping them **spot prey** from more than **a mile (1.6 km) away.**

2
The **platypus's bill,** which looks like a duck's, has **special nerves** that can **sense** the **movements** of its prey.

3
Silkworm moths use **cells** on their **antennae** to **detect a mate** from more than a mile (1.6 km) away.

4
Some animals sense the world around them by **making a sound** and then **listening for its echo** as it **bounces off objects**—a skill known as **echolocation.**

5
Special hairs on the **legs** of **bumblebees** can pick up slight **electrical charges,** which they use to find flowers in bloom.

25 SENSATIONAL FACTS
ABOUT ANIMALS'
SPECIAL

6
Special **"pit" organs** on the faces of boas, pythons, and vipers allow these **snakes** to **sense** their **prey's body heat** so that they can **"see"** it at night.

7
To communicate, **toothed whales** send air through small structures in their heads called **"phonic lips,"** which act like **vocal cords.**

8
To **sense changes** in water pressure, **fish** have **sense organs** that sit in mucus-filled canals.

9
Electric eels use special **muscle cells** to send out **electric pulses** that stun their prey.

10
Some scientists think that **homing pigeons** use **ultra-low frequency sounds,** which humans can't hear, to **return to their home roost.**

11
Mantis shrimps are the only animal known to have **special filters in their eyes** that can detect a kind of **light** that other animals can't see.

12 When diving deep, **pilot whales** make **sounds** using **tiny bursts of air** that are the size of a drop of water.

13 **Wedge-tailed eagles** are smaller than humans, but their **eyes** are about the same size, giving them **excellent vision.**

14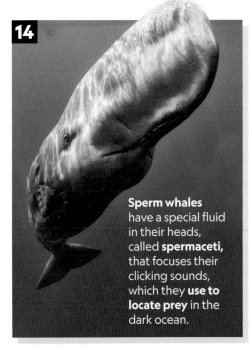

Sperm whales have a special fluid in their heads, called **spermaceti,** that focuses their clicking sounds, which they **use to locate prey** in the dark ocean.

15 Many fish have **special organs** underneath their skin that they **use to "see"** in a dark environment.

16 **Grasshoppers' "ears"** are on their **abdomen**—a pair of membranes that **vibrate** in response to sound waves.

17 **Toothed whales** have been using **echolocation** for millions of years.

18 **Bats** can send out **sound waves from** both their **mouths** and their **noses** to sense their environment.

SENSES

19 Some **flies** use their **antennae** to **sense vibrations** from male flies' beating wings, which they move to attract mates.

20 **A bluefin tuna** senses light and dark with its **pineal organ,** which acts like a **third eye.**

21 Used to locate prey, **muscles** in the **throats of Daubenton's bats move** about **20 times faster** than the muscles we use to blink.

22 **Salmon** can pick up **Earth's magnetic field,** which allows them to **find their way** from the ocean back to the **streams where they hatched.**

23 **Sea turtles** can pick up on **Earth's magnetic field,** too, using it to **navigate** back to the **beaches** where they hatched to **lay their own eggs.**

24

Bottlenose dolphins use **clicks**—each one lasting only about 50 to 128 microseconds— to **locate prey.**

25 **Mouse-size shrews** make high-pitched **"twittering" sounds** that scientists think help them **find their way** through the forests and meadows where they live.

1 Some species of **sea star** can have **40** arms.

2 Individual **gray whales** can be identified by the **scars** that **barnacles** leave on their skin.

3 **Sea anemones** are named after the **anemone flower,** which they resemble.

4 Some species of **pearlfish** make their **homes** inside sea cucumbers' **rear ends.**

5 **Clams, mussels,** and their **relatives** make the ocean cleaner by **filtering water** through their **gills.**

6 Instead of teeth, **sea snails** have a rough tonguelike organ called a **radula** that they use to scrape algae off rocks.

7 **Sea stars** have **suction cups** on their **feet.**

8 **Bat stars** are so named because their arms appear to have **webbing** in between, like a bat's wings.

35 FACTS ABOUT TIDE POOL ANIMALS

9

Experts think the **spiny shell** of the **scorpion spider conch** keeps the animal from rolling around in the waves.

10

New species of **nudibranchs,** colorful members of the sea slug family, are **discovered** nearly **every day.**

11

Sea anemones protect themselves by firing harpoonlike stinging cells called **nematocysts.**

12

Nudibranchs' bright colors come from the **pigment** they absorb from the corals, sponges, and other **food** they eat.

13

The **teeth** of some **sea otters** are **stained purple** from eating purple sea urchins.

14

The **sticky substance** barnacles use to attach to surfaces is considered the **strongest glue** found in nature.

15

A large **abalone,** a type of fish, can release more than **20 million eggs** at one time.

16

Turban snails can close the entrance to their shells for protection.

17

Some **sea stars** can **regrow** an entirely **new body** from just one piece of a severed arm.

18

A **pistol shrimp** snaps its **claw** so hard that it briefly **heats** the surrounding **water** to 8000°F (4427°C).

19

Octopuses occasionally **crawl on land** when they **visit tide pools** to hunt.

20

Sea stars have **no brain** and no blood.

21

Shore crabs glue their **eggs** to the **underside** of their **shells** to protect them.

22

The average **sea star** lives to be **35 years old** in the wild.

23

If the tide goes out and leaves them stranded, **tidepool sculpin fish** can **breathe air.**

24

Some **feather stars** can **ripple** their featherlike **arms** to **swim** through the water.

25

Sea cucumbers breathe through their **rear ends.**

26

The **giant green anemone** can grow to more than **three feet** (1 m) across.

27

Scallops swim by swiftly opening and closing their shells.

28

To keep from drying out at low tide, **mussels** close their shells to **hold in water.**

29

Sandcastle worms build **structures** out of **sand** that can be as big as a dining room table.

30

Moon jellies are see-through.

31

The **black sea hare,** the world's largest slug, can be 38 inches (97 cm) long and weigh **30 pounds** (13.6 kg).

32

The **two-spot octopus** can "see" with its **skin.**

33

If oxygen levels in a tide pool's water are low, **sculpin fish** can **survive** by **gulping air** at the surface.

34

The **ochre sea star** can **survive out of the water** for 50 hours.

35

Every **wave** that **splashes** into a **tide pool** carries **plankton** to feed the creatures that live there.

»15 DISPLAY-ABLE FACTS ABOUT ANIMAL ARTISTS

1
Nudibranchs, a type of sea slug, have **brilliant and bright gills** on their backs to warn predators they are dangerous.

2
Elephants have painted artworks holding **paintbrushes in their trunks.** Zoos sold the works to raise money for conservation.

3
Beluga whales blow bubbles of different shapes that scientists think **may reflect their mood.**

4. Elephants in captivity **paint in a number of colors,** but they can only see in shades of **blue** and **yellow.**

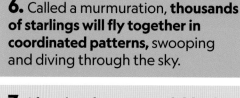

5

Female cochineal insects, small bugs about the size of a grain of rice, produce a special acid that has been used to dye clothes and lipstick red.

6. Called a murmuration, **thousands of starlings will fly together in coordinated patterns,** swooping and diving through the sky.

7. After their **hooves are dabbed in paint,** goats at some zoos run across poster board to **create works of art to raise money for conservation.**

8. Ancient Egyptians used the dried bodies of insects called kermes, which live on oak trees in the Mediterranean, **to dye clothes red.**

9. In the Great Salt Lick contest, **cows, horses, and deer lick 50-pound (23-kg) blocks of salt into beautiful sculptures,** which also adds minerals to their diets that can be lacking from the foods they usually eat.

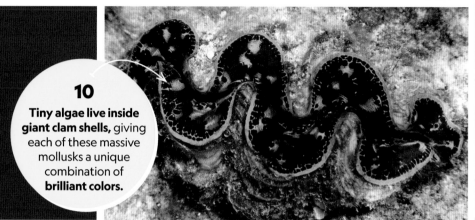

10

Tiny algae live inside giant clam shells, giving each of these massive mollusks a unique combination of **brilliant colors.**

11. When a **small irritant like a grain of sand gets inside their shells,** some mollusks protect themselves by repeatedly secreting a fluid that builds up, **creating a pearl** in the process.

12. A **marine shell** living in the **Mediterranean Sea** produces a **clear (and toxic) fluid** that turns a **vivid purple** when **exposed to air.** It has been used to **dye fabrics** for centuries.

13

Rare gemstones known as ammolites are made from ammonites, **fossilized shells of creatures** that lived in the seas millions of years ago.

14

Pearls have been worn as jewelry for more than 6,000 years.

15

Glowworms lure insects to caves by emitting blue bioluminescent light, then trap them in sticky weblike lines they've made and hung from the cave ceiling.

1
Animals that eat animals they haven't killed themselves or that died of natural causes are known as scavengers.

2
Scavengers eat carrion, which is a term for dead animals.

3
Dead animals are also broken down by insects such as flies and beetles.

4
Insects are the first animals to arrive to scavenge, usually flies that are then followed by beetles.

5
A 2018 study found 154 ant species that tear into and eat dead animals.

6
Vultures can clean a dead animal down to its bones in less than an hour.

7
While known as scavengers, hyenas get most of their food by killing it themselves.

8
Flies are able to locate a dead animal within just a few minutes after the animal has died.

9
Some species of eyeless carrion beetles live in dark caves and eat bat droppings.

10
Black bears and grizzly bears are able to kill animals themselves but will also eat dead animals they find.

11
Bearded vultures—the only animal whose diet consists mostly of bones—eat the soft marrow inside.

12
Some jackals live in family groups called packs.

35 FACTS

TO SCROUNGE UP ABOUT SCAVENGERS

13
When **turkey vultures** locate a **dead skunk**, they have been known to **avoid eating** their smelly **scent glands.**

14
Some carrion beetles, or **burying beetles**, **dig out** the **dirt** around a small **dead animal** like a mouse and **bury it.**

15
Vultures' bald heads help **keep** their **faces clean** when they put their heads inside dead animals.

16
A **vulture** can **eat more** than **two pounds** (1 kg) of **meat** in **60 seconds.**

17
A study of **spotted hyenas** in Kenya found that they **successfully caught** an animal about **one-third** of the time they **hunted.**

18
Blowflies eat the **decaying flesh** around wounds on cattle and other livestock, which can **help** the **animal heal.**

19
Crayfish hide under rocks during the day and come out at **night** to look for dead animals that have sunk to the bottom of the water.

20
Sometimes **jackals bury meat** to hide it from other scavengers.

21
Tenacious predators, **wolverines** rely on **carrion** during the **winter** when food is scarce in their cold forest habitats.

22
Carrion flies lay thousands of **eggs** in a **carcass** so that when they hatch, the larvae have a ready meal.

23
Carrion beetles can **climb underneath dead animals** and **feed** without getting injured.

24
Jackals "sing" a **haunting cry** as the sun sets, **calling out** to their **family members.**

25
Turkey vultures use their great sense of **smell**—an unusual trait for birds—to **find dead animals.**

26
Some **carrion beetles** live in **beehives** so they can **eat dead bees.**

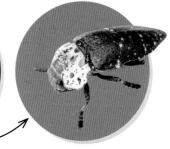

27
The **California condor** almost went extinct from eating animals that had been shot with lead bullets and from toxins in the environment.

28
Superstrong **stomach acids** help **vultures digest** decaying meat without getting sick.

29
Vultures can **throw up** everything in their stomachs to **fly away** from a predator more **quickly.**

30
Jackals will try to **steal** animals that other carnivores, such as cheetahs, have killed.

31
Turkey vultures lack a voice box, so the only **sounds** they can make are **hisses** and **grunts.**

32
Spotted hyenas are also known as **laughing hyenas** because their **calls** can sound like **cackles.**

33
Zebra moray eels use **sharp, backward-curving teeth** to feed on dead animals in coral reefs.

34
Active hunters like **coyotes** and **foxes** will **eat carrion** if they have **trouble** finding **live prey.**

35
American eels scavenge, but they also can **rip apart prey**, spinning some 14 times a second to tear it apart.

1

There are more than 100,000 DIFFERENT SPECIES of WASPS.

2

Bees are COVERED in an OIL that keeps them WATERPROOF.

3

ONLY FEMALE WASPS CAN STING—and they can sting more than once.

4

WASPS range in color from YELLOW to BROWN to BLUE to RED.

5

Hornets eat LEAVES and TREE SAP but also FLIES and BEES.

6

A wasp's NEST is the TEXTURE OF PAPER.

7

WASPS are CARNIVORES—they use their stinger to kill and eat insects and caterpillars.

8

WORKER HONEYBEES make wax called HONEYCOMB that they use to build their hives.

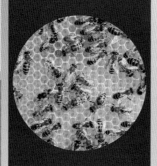

9

There are more than 20,000 SPECIES OF BEES.

10

BUMBLEBEES are also called HUMBLE-BEES.

11

To PROTECT THEIR CROPS, some farmers bring in WASPS to EAT PEST INSECTS.

12

To WARD OFF ATTACKS by giant hornets, some HONEYBEES DECORATE THE ENTRANCE TO THEIR NEST with other ANIMALS' POOP.

13

ONE BEE makes ONE-TWELFTH A TEASPOON of honey in its lifetime.

14

WASPS make their NESTS out of pieces of WOOD that they chew into a pulp and spit out.

15

When BEES STING PEOPLE, their STINGER GETS STUCK in the skin, KILLING the BEE.

16

Bees are POLLINATORS of FRUIT, VEGETABLES, AND PLANTS, transferring pollen between male and female plant parts, which allows the plants to grow seeds and fruit.

17

BUMBLEBEES flap their wings BACK AND FORTH rather than up and down.

18

HORNETS are a type of wasp but are generally ROUNDER and BIGGER than a common wasp.

19

A HONEYBEE COLONY can have as many as 60,000 HONEYBEES.

20

Queen bees SHIVER to WARM UP.

21

NOT ALL WASP SPECIES STING, but generally the BRIGHTER COLORED ONES DO.

22

VESPA-BRAND SCOOTERS are NAMED AFTER WASPS—*vespa* means "wasp" in Italian.

23

QUEEN BEES LIVE up to FIVE YEARS.

24

If a queen honeybee dies, WORKERS CREATE A NEW QUEEN by feeding a female worker a special food called "ROYAL JELLY."

25

Bumblebees usually BUILD NESTS CLOSE TO THE GROUND under wood or dead leaves.

26

AFRICANIZED KILLER BEES are more AGGRESSIVE than regular honeybees and are PROTECTIVE OF THEIR HIVE.

27

A QUEEN HONEYBEE's job is to LAY THE EGGS that will become the NEXT GENERATION OF BEES.

28

The TINY HAIRS all over a BEE'S BODY make them FUZZY.

29

Some WASPS that are IN DISTRESS RELEASE A CHEMICAL that WARNS NEARBY COLONY MEMBERS to be on alert.

30

An AVERAGE WORKER BEE lives just FIVE WEEKS.

31

HONEYBEES live on every continent EXCEPT ANTARCTICA.

32

AFRICANIZED KILLER BEES are smaller than regular honeybees, and their VENOM IS LESS POWERFUL.

33

The ASIAN GIANT HORNET'S STINGER is long enough to PIERCE a BEEKEEPER'S SUIT.

34

BUMBLEBEES are larger than honeybees but DON'T PRODUCE AS MUCH HONEY.

35
An 8,000-YEAR-OLD CAVE PAINTING in Spain depicts a HUMAN REMOVING HONEY FROM A HIVE.

36
WASPS also use their STINGERS to LAY EGGS inside their prey.

37
Bees perform a "WAGGLE DANCE" to indicate the direction of a NECTAR SOURCE.

38
Since WORKER HONEYBEES ARE THE ONLY BEES THAT LEAVE THE HIVE, they are the ones we see flying around us.

39
The ASIAN GIANT HORNET's main prey is honeybees—ONE HORNET can KILL 300 HONEYBEES in an HOUR.

40
A BEE'S HONEY NEVER SPOILS—edible honey has been found in EGYPTIAN TOMBS.

41
WORKER HONEYBEES RETURN to the hive at DUSK.

42
GEORGIA TECH university's MASCOT is a YELLOW JACKET NAMED BUZZ.

43
YELLOW JACKETS sometimes BUILD THEIR NESTS UNDERGROUND, and the nests can be the SIZE OF A SOCCER BALL.

44
HONEYBEES beat their wings 200 TIMES PER SECOND.

45
When a HORNET finds a bee colony, it LEAVES A CHEMICAL SCENT to ATTRACT other hornets.

46
In Japan, FRIED HORNETS are EATEN AS A DELICACY.

47
DRONE HONEYBEES are always MALE and DON'T HAVE STINGERS.

48
BEEKEEPERS IN FRANCE found their HONEY TURNED SHADES OF BLUE AND GREEN after their BEES FED ON COLORFUL CANDY that had been discarded by a nearby factory.

49
The ASIAN GIANT HORNET can grow to TWO INCHES (5 cm) long.

50
To produce ONE POUND (.45 kg) of HONEY, a colony of bees must COLLECT NECTAR from approximately TWO MILLION FLOWERS.

honeybee

50 BUZZWORTHY FACTS ABOUT *BEES, WASPS,* AND *HORNETS*

5,000 AWESOME FACTS ABOUT ANIMALS **113**

100 FURRY FACTS ABOUT DOMESTIC CATS

Abyssinian cat

1. Cats spend up to half their day cleaning themselves. 2. Cats purr when they're content, but also when they're hungry, injured, or frightened. 3. The world's wealthiest cat was a cat named Blackie in the United Kingdom. When Blackie's owner died, he left his pet $12.5 million (£7 million). 4. Cleaning themselves helps cats stay cool: It spreads saliva that evaporates, carrying heat with it. 5. To see if cats respond to music, scientists tested which beats and tempos made felines in their study purr, walk toward the speaker, and rub against it. 6. When asked if her husband, U.S. president Abraham Lincoln, had a hobby, Mary Todd Lincoln responded "Cats." 7. A group of kittens is called a kindle. 8. Ancient Egyptians worshipped a cat goddess named Bastet. 9. According to English superstition from the Middle Ages, brides who receive a black cat as a wedding gift will have a lucky marriage. 10. Cat saliva may contain chemicals that help wounds heal. 11. Author Ernest Hemingway had a white, six-toed cat named Snow White whose descendants still live at his home in Key West, Florida, U.S.A. 12. Some scientists think that cats might purr at a frequency that helps their bones heal from injury. 13. A cat's tongue is covered in tiny hooks that act like a comb. 14. Cats groom each other to bond. 15. Catnip is a member of the same plant family as mint. 16. The technical term for "cat lover" is ailurophile. 17. Catnip affects most big cats like lions and leopards as it does domestic cats. 18. The first and only cat to travel to space was a French feline named Félicette, who blasted off in 1963. 19. Cats can drink salty seawater if they have to. 20. Cats like to sit in cardboard boxes because they have an instinct to hide. 21. The oldest cat ever, Creme Puff, lived 38 years. 22. Cats have an excellent sense of balance and extremely flexible backbones that allow them to twist right side up when falling so that they almost always land on their feet. 23. The longest cat on record is a Maine coon that measures 3 feet 11.2 inches (120 cm) long. 24. About 70 percent of domestic cats are affected by catnip. 25. A group of cats is called a clowder. 26. The Ragdoll is one of the most popular cat breeds in the world. 27. Cats can't chew their food. 28. Indigenous Americans once used catnip to treat headaches and stomachaches in babies. 29. When a cat died in ancient Egypt, its owners would shave off their own eyebrows in mourning. 30. Iceland has a TV show called *Keeping Up With the Kattarshians* that follows kittens with hidden cameras. 31. The smallest cat on record was a Himalayan-Persian named Tinker Toy that was only 2.75 inches (7 cm) tall and 7.5 inches (19 cm) long. 32. Cats can be allergic to humans. 33. A Scottish cat named Towser caught nearly 30,000 mice in her lifetime. 34. A cat named Dusty holds the record for having the most kittens of any cat on record: 420. 35. Cats probably recognize their names. (They just sometimes choose not to listen.) 36. Taiwan has a Hello Kitty–themed hospital. 37. Most people who are allergic to cats aren't allergic to their fur but to a substance in their saliva. 38. The effects of catnip—rolling, flipping, rubbing, and meowing—last for around 10 minutes. 39. In ancient Egypt, killing a cat was a crime punishable by death. 40. Cats may bring their owners dead animals to try to teach them hunting skills, just as they would for their kittens. 41. Florence

tabby cat

Egyptian Mau cat

Nightingale, the founder of modern nursing, owned about 60 cats in her lifetime. 42. Cats were domesticated about 10,000 years ago. 43. Felix the Cat was the first animated movie star. 44. Experts aren't sure why adult cats knead with their paws. 45. A house cat can run as fast as Olympic sprinter Usain Bolt. 46. While humans typically have 33 vertebrae, cats have up to 53. 47. A painting of one woman's 42 cats sold for more than $820,000 in 2015. 48. In 1966, the first sphynx—a type of hairless cat—was born to a furry domestic cat in Toronto, Canada. 49. Ancient Egyptians mummified their cats when they died. 50. Cats have tiny collarbones, which allow them to squeeze through tight spaces. 51. Most female cats are right-pawed, while most male cats are left-pawed. 52. In Japan, black cats are considered good luck. 53. A cat's nose has bumps and ridges that are as unique as a human fingerprint. 54. Cats can't taste sweetness. 55. The first cat show—in which cat owners entered their cats to compete for best of breed—was held in London, England, in 1871. 56. Cats have 244 bones. (Adult humans have 206.) 57. Some cats have extra toes, a condition called polydactyly. 58. The record for the most toes on a cat is 28. 59. Sailors often kept cats with extra toes on their ships, believing they were good luck. 60. The ancient Aztec may have kept hairless cats. 61. The Turkish Van is a breed of cat that likes to swim. 62. Adult cats meow only at humans, not at each other. 63. Siamese cats' color is determined by temperature. Their body temperatures are coolest at their paws, nose, and tail. That makes the fur there dark brown. 64. The world's most expensive cat breed is the Ashera, which has characteristics of the African serval, the Asian leopard cat, and the domestic house cat. 65. Rome, Italy, has more feral cats per square mile than any other city in the world. 66. Cats sweat through their paws. 67. Cats sleep an average of 15 hours a day. 68. Feral cats roam Disneyland, where they keep the rodent population under control. 69. In the 1870s, cats were trained to deliver the mail in Liège, Belgium. 70. Cats can jump five times their own height. 71. The first cat to be cloned, named Little Nicky, was born in 2004. 72. The tufts of hair that grow out of a cat's ears help direct sound. 73. In 2012, a cat named Holly found her way home after being lost during a family vacation 200 miles (322 km) away. 74. As long as they have access to water, cats can tolerate temperatures of up to 133°F (56°C). 75. Cats have about 60,000 hairs per square inch (9,300 per sq cm) on their backs, and 120,000 hairs per square inch (18,600 per sq cm) on their bellies. 76. Cats can rotate their ears 180 degrees to pick up sounds—just like a satellite dish. 77. The technical term for a hair ball is a bezoar.

78. Owning a cat can help make people healthier. 79. Some people have trained their cats to use the toilet. 80. Cats' vertical pupils may help them gauge distance to pounce on prey—or a toy. 81. Cats use their tails for balance. 82. Kittens begin to purr when they are a few days old. 83. When cats rub against objects, they leave a scent from glands in their cheeks, foreheads, and tails. 84. Cats can't climb down a tree headfirst—they have to go backward. 85. A female cat is called a queen. 86. Experts think cats may be able to make 100 different sounds. 87. The world's oldest known pet cat is a 9,500-year-old cat found buried with a human on the Mediterranean island of Cyprus. 88. About 38 percent of Americans own a pet cat. 89. The house cat shares 95.6 percent of its DNA with the tiger. 90. Scientists aren't exactly sure how cats purr. 91. In 1888, an Egyptian farmer uncovered a grave containing thousands of cats. They had been carefully mummified and some even had faces gilded with gold. 92. The largest known cat litter had 19 kittens. 93. The ancestor of all cats lived about 30 million years ago and looked like a mongoose. 94. The Singapura is the smallest cat breed, weighing as little as four pounds (1.8 kg). 95. Cats can spread out their bodies like a parachute to help them survive falls from great heights. 96. The Egyptian Mau is one of the world's oldest cat breeds. 97. Cats usually have 12 whiskers on each side of their face. 98. Most cats like milk, but many are lactose intolerant. 99. Cats can see in color, but not as well as humans can. 100. Walt Disney's first animated animal was not Mickey Mouse but Julius the Cat.

kitten

1

BOTH JAGUARS AND LEOPARDS HAVE SPOTTED COATS, but jaguars live in Central and South America, and leopards live in Africa and Asia.

2

JAGUARS CAN WEIGH some 75 POUNDS (34 KG) more than their smaller leopard cousins.

3

Because LEOPARDS ARE NOT the LARGEST PREDATOR in their habitat, they tend to be MORE ATHLETIC than jaguars, which can rely on their powerful muscles and jaws.

4

MOTHS have antennae that are FEATHERY on the end; BUTTERFLY antennae are TOPPED with a BULB.

5

BUTTERFLIES tend to be MORE COLORFUL than moths.

6

BUTTERFLIES FOLD THEIR WINGS so they STICK UP above their bodies in a straight line; MOTHS often fold their wings to FORM A TENTLIKE SHAPE.

7

Both moths and butterflies can grow to be QUITE LARGE: The GOLIATH BIRDWING BUTTERFLY has a wingspan of 11 INCHES (28 cm), while the ATLAS MOTH'S wingspan can reach 12 INCHES (30.5 cm).

8

BUTTERFLIES FLY from flower to flower DURING THE DAY, while many MOTHS VISIT PLANTS and flowers that bloom AT NIGHT.

9

BROWN BEARS have a DISTINCTIVE HUMP on their shoulders; BLACK BEARS DON'T.

10

BLACK BEARS are SMALLER than BROWN BEARS, which can stand FIVE FEET (1.5 m) tall at the shoulder compared to about TWO AND A HALF FEET (0.8 m) for BLACK BEARS.

11

AS THEY GROW from a caterpillar into an adult, both moths and butterflies form a PROTECTIVE COVERING called a PUPA: A butterfly pupa is HARD, while a moth pupa is a SOFT COCOON made of silk.

12

BROWN BEARS have SHORTER and ROUNDER EARS than BLACK BEARS' more POINTED ones.

13

BROWN BEARS have much LONGER CLAWS, about TWO TO FOUR INCHES (5–10 cm) in length; BLACK BEARS have SHORTER and more curved claws.

14

The RUMP of a BLACK BEAR SLOPES UP from its front shoulders; the rump of a BROWN BEAR IS LOWER than its shoulders.

15

DOLPHINS have CONE-SHAPED TEETH while PORPOISES' teeth are TRIANGLE-SHAPED.

16

There are more than 30 SPECIES of DOLPHINS but ONLY SIX SPECIES of PORPOISES.

17

A DOLPHIN HAS a BEAK, or LONG NOSE; a PORPOISE has a ROUNDER FACE without a beak.

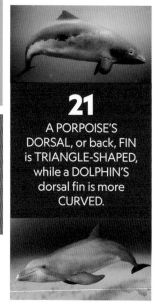

18

DOLPHINS are "CHATTIER," communicating more often USING SOUND than porpoises do.

19

DOLPHINS are MORE STREAMLINED and LONGER than porpoises, about SIX to 12 FEET (1.8–3.6 m) in length.

20

DONKEYS have a REPUTATION for being STUBBORN, but they are less likely to show they are uncomfortable than horses are.

21

A PORPOISE'S DORSAL, or back, FIN is TRIANGLE-SHAPED, while a DOLPHIN'S dorsal fin is more CURVED.

50 FACTS TO GET STRAIGHT ABOUT ANIMAL LOOK-ALIKES

22
SHEEP hang their TAILS DOWN, while GOATS hold their TAILS UP.

23
A wool sweater comes FROM SHEEP'S wool; GOATS HAVE HAIR.

24
SHEEP EAT vegetation that grows CLOSE to the GROUND, but GOATS can CLIMB TREES to pick off leaves.

25
An ANGRY MALE SHEEP lowers his head and tries to bump his opponent, while an ANGRY MALE GOAT rears up on his legs and then hits with his head.

26
GOATS are more INDEPENDENT than SHEEP, which like to flock together.

27
LIZARDS HAVE EAR OPENINGS on their bodies, but SALAMANDERS DON'T.

28
LIZARDS have SCALY SKIN and have LUNGS FOR BREATHING, while SALAMANDERS lack scales because they BREATHE THROUGH THEIR SKIN.

29
SALAMANDERS DON'T HAVE CLAWS on their feet, while MOST LIZARDS DO.

30
LIZARDS HAVE FIVE FINGERS on their front legs; SALAMANDERS HAVE FOUR.

31
Lizards and salamanders LOOK ALIKE, but LIZARDS ARE REPTILES and SALAMANDERS ARE AMPHIBIANS.

32
Most SALAMANDER MOMS LAY their JELLYLIKE EGGS in water; LIZARD moms LAY LEATHERY EGGS that they often bury in loose soil or sand.

33
Both hedgehogs and porcupines are COVERED IN hard hairs called QUILLS, but PORCUPINES ARE RODENTS; HEDGEHOGS ARE NOT.

34
HEDGEHOG QUILLS are about ONE INCH (2.5 cm) LONG and don't easily detach, whereas most PORCUPINES have quills about TWO TO THREE INCHES (5–7.5 cm) LONG that they can easily lose.

35
PORCUPINES HAVE much LONGER TAILS than hedgehogs, which they USE TO CLIMB TREES; hedgehogs stay on the ground.

36
When threatened, a HEDGEHOG ROLLS INTO A BALL; when a PORCUPINE is threatened, its QUILLS STICK UP, making its body look larger.

37
HEDGEHOGS HAVE about 3,000 TO 5,000 QUILLS, while SOME PORCUPINES CAN HAVE as many as 30,000!

38
HEDGEHOGS EAT insects, worms, snails, and frogs; PORCUPINES ARE HERBIVORES that eat fruit and plants.

39
PENGUINS have SOLID BONES and CAN'T FLY, while PUFFINS, which have HOLLOW BONES, can TAKE TO THE AIR.

40
All PENGUINS LIVE in the SOUTHERN HEMISPHERE—PUFFINS make their homes in the NORTHERN HEMISPHERE.

41
PUFFINS CAN FOLD THEIR WINGS, while PENGUINS CANNOT.

42
The LARGEST penguin species, the EMPEROR PENGUIN, is as tall as a six-year-old kid; PUFFINS ARE ONLY about as tall as a gallon of milk.

43
The FASTEST PENGUIN species underwater, the GENTOO, can zip along at 22 MILES an hour (35 km/h), while PUFFINS cruise underwater at about THREE MILES an hour (5 km/h).

44
There are FOUR SPECIES of PUFFIN but at least 17 DIFFERENT SPECIES of PENGUIN.

45
DONKEYS HAVE LARGER ears than horses, and they also HAVE STIFFER HAIR on their manes and tails.

46
ALLIGATORS tend to be DARKER IN COLOR than crocodiles, which can be tan.

47
CROCODILES can SWIM in the OCEAN— they have a special gland that helps them get rid of excess salt— but ALLIGATORS CAN'T do this as well and swim in freshwater.

48
A CROCODILE has a V-SHAPED SNOUT; an ALLIGATOR'S jaw is more U-SHAPED.

49
SMALL CROCODILES have been seen GALLOPING in the wild, which small ALLIGATORS CAN'T DO.

50
If you see teeth when the mouth is closed, it's a CROCODILE— its TEETH STICK UP from its lower jaw.

1 At up to **18 feet** (5.5 m), **giraffes** are the **world's tallest animals**—they could **peer** into a second-story window!

2  **Giraffes** can go **days without drinking water.**

3 Giraffes **give birth standing up.** The newborn giraffe **falls more than five feet** (1.5 m) to the **ground!**

4  Giraffes **pick their noses** with their **tongues.**

5 A **giraffe's heart** is **two feet** (0.6 m) **long** and weighs about **25 pounds** (11 kg)—big enough to pump blood all the way up to the giraffe's head!

6 A **single giraffe kick** can **kill** a **lion.**

7 Scientists discovered that there are **four species of giraffe,** not just one.

25 TALL FACTS
ABOUT GIRAFFES

12 No two giraffes have the same pattern of spots.

9 The **veins** in a giraffe's **neck** have a series of **one-way valves** that **prevent too much blood** from **flowing** to the **brain** when the animal **lowers its head.**

13 Giraffes' **tongues** are **purplish-black** to protect them from **sunburn.**

8 Giraffes **hum** to each other at **night.**

10 A giraffe's **neck** has **seven vertebrae,** just like a human's.

11  A giraffe's feet are the **size of dinner plates.**

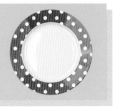

14 Giraffes use their **21-inch** (53-cm)-**long tongues** to **strip** the **leaves** off acacia trees and **maneuver** around the **large thorns.**

15

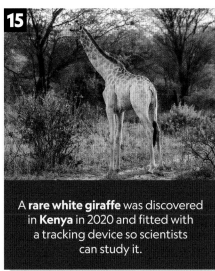

A **rare white giraffe** was discovered in **Kenya** in 2020 and fitted with a tracking device so scientists can study it.

16

To **drink,** a giraffe has to **spread its front legs wide** to **reach** the **water.**

17

When **ancient Romans** first saw a giraffe, they called it a **"cameleopard"** because they thought it looked like a combination of a camel and a leopard.

18

Newborn giraffes can **run** with their mothers just **10 hours after birth.**

19

NASA has **studied giraffe blood vessels** to create a **device** that helps keep **astronauts** from blacking out due to blood flow changes in **zero gravity.**

20

Fossil evidence shows that long ago, the **giraffe's ancestors** had **short necks.**

21

Guests at the **Giraffe Manor** in Nairobi, Kenya, get to **feed the hotel's resident giraffes,** which poke their heads through the windows for treats.

23

In 2020, the **Memphis Zoo** named a baby giraffe **Ja Raffe** in honor of Memphis Grizzlies basketball player **Ja Morant.**

22

Like cows, **giraffes regurgitate,** or cough up, their **food** and **chew it.**

24

Male giraffes fight by **slamming** their **necks together.**

25

Giraffes sleep no more than **30 minutes a day.**

»15 MATURE FACTS ABOUT HOW LONG ANIMALS LIVE

1
Greenland sharks can live to be **400 years old.**

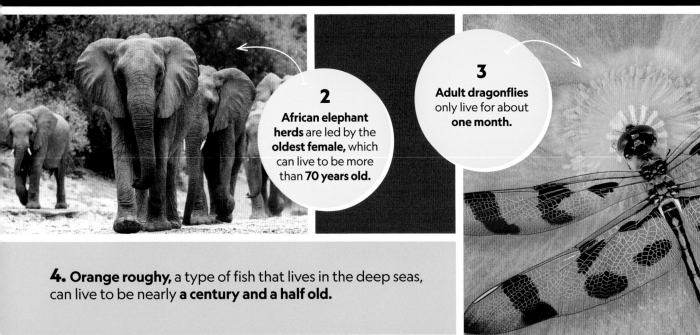

2
African elephant herds are led by the **oldest female,** which can live to be more than **70 years old.**

3
Adult dragonflies only live for about **one month.**

4. Orange roughy, a type of fish that lives in the deep seas, can live to be nearly **a century and a half old.**

5
Kakapos, flightless parrots that live in New Zealand, **live longer than most humans.**

6. A **41-year-old male Brandt's bat** that lives in caves in Siberia is the **world's oldest known bat.**

7. Scientists studied an **11,000-year-old glass sponge,** a type of deep-sea animal, to look at how water temperatures have changed over the centuries.

8. Jonathan, an **Aldabra giant tortoise** that lives in the Seychelles in the Pacific Ocean, turned **189** in 2021.

9. Fruit flies can hatch from eggs and grow into adults in just **eight days.**

10
The **pygmy goby,** a fish that lives among coral reefs, **dies after just two months.**

11. Bowhead whales are the longest lived mammals—they can live to be **more than 200 years old.**

12. Researchers think that **Greenland sharks' longevity** is due to a **slow metabolism and the cold waters** of the North Atlantic and Arctic Oceans where they swim.

13
A type of clam called an **ocean quahog** can live to be **500 years old.**

14
After a female mayfly lays her eggs, she lives for **less than five minutes.**

15
The owner of the **world's oldest domestic cat** fed her a daily breakfast of **eggs, broccoli, and turkey bacon.**

5. Bigfoot **has an official file with the** United States Federal Bureau of Investigation (FBI).

WARNING BIGFOOT IN THIS AREA

20. Ancient Roman scholar Pliny the Elder thought the rhinoceros was a mash-up of a deer, elephant, and boar.

1. Some people think the **Loch Ness Monster** is a plesiosaur, an **ancient marine reptile** that went **extinct** about **66 million years ago.**

2. When **Christopher Columbus** spotted **manatees** in the ocean near what is now the Dominican Republic, he thought they were **mermaids.**

3. In Greek mythology, the **chimera** is a **fire-breathing creature** with **three heads:** a lion's, a goat's, and a snake's.

4. A monastery in Nepal claims to have a **piece of scalp** from an **abominable snowman.** Experts say it's really an animal hide.

6. Zombie ants are **infected** with a **fungus** that takes over their brains.

7. In Greek mythology, the **Minotaur** has the **head** and **tail** of a **bull** and the **body** of a **man.**

8. The myth of the **werewolf** might have originated with **rabies**—a disease spread when the infected bit a victim.

9. The basilisk **is a mythical reptile able to kill with a single** glance.

10. Thor's hero shrew, named after the mighty Norse god, has a **nearly unbreakable spine.**

11. The mythical monster called the **chupacabra** may have come from sightings of **coyotes** with **mange,** a disease that causes them to lose their hair.

12. The Japanese myth of the **river monster** called the **Kappa** may have begun with sightings of the **giant salamander,** which can grow to be five feet (1.5 m) long.

13. The **one-horned Indian rhinoceros** may have **inspired** the myth of the **unicorn.**

14. The myth of the **three-eyed cyclops** may have come from discoveries of **ancient elephant skulls**—they have a **hole** in the **middle** right where a **third eye** could have been.

15. The superhero **Wolverine** is **immune to poison.** In real life, the **opossum** is **immune** to **snake venom.**

16. The **sphinx,** a mythical ancient Egyptian creature, has the **head** of a **human** and the **body** of a **lion.**

17. The **Greek god Orion** was said to be able to **walk** on **water**—just **like** the real-life **basilisk lizard.**

18. In the **Middle Ages,** people purchased **narwhal tusks** for huge sums, believing they were **unicorn horns.**

19. Some dragon myths **may have begun when ancient people** discovered dinosaur fossils.

21. Sasquatch isn't real. But until 300,000 years ago, an **ape** the **size** of a **polar bear,** *Gigantopithecus,* did **roam** South Asia.

22. The mythical **Mongolian death worm** kills its **victims** with **electric shocks**—just as the **electric eel** does.

23. In Native American myth, the **coyote** is a **"trickster,"** just like real-life coyotes, which are clever, savvy animals.

24. Legends of the Lenape and Iroquois people say that the **world** was **created** on the **back** of an **enormous turtle.**

25. Wood frogs have an ability that seems mythical—they can **survive being frozen.**

26. The **oarfish,** which can be more than 50 feet (15 m) long, may have **inspired myths** of **enormous sea serpents.**

27. The **real-life blue dragon** isn't a dragon at all—it's a **tiny,** one-inch (2.5-cm)-long **sea slug.**

28. The **bunyip,** a lake monster in Aboriginal myth, may have been **inspired** by the now-extinct *Diprotodon,* a three-ton (2,700-kg) relative of the wombat.

75 UNREAL FACTS ABOUT MYTHICAL ANIMALS

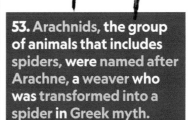

29. **Centaurs** are mythical creatures from Greek legend with the **body of a horse** and the **head** and **chest of a human.**

30. In Arabic myth, the **roc** is a **gigantic bird** that **ate people.** Fossils show that thousands of years ago, huge birds really did eat people.

31. **Half fish** and **half woman, sirens** are Greek mythological figures whose **songs** could **lure sailors** to their **deaths.**

32. **Some experts believe that the** myth **of the half-eagle, half-lion griffin came from fossils of** *Protoceratops,* **a dinosaur with a giant beak.**

33. In Scandinavia, Scotland, and Ireland, **selkies** are **seals** that can **transform** into **humans.**

34. **Nile crocodiles,** which can be up to 18 feet (5.5 m) long, may have **inspired** some **dragon legends.**

35. For about **1,500 years,** many **people believed** that **salamanders** could **not be hurt** by **fire.**

36. **Sightings of the** giant squid **may have inspired the** myth **of the enormous** sea monster **called the** kraken.

37. The striped-legged, horselike **okapi** is so elusive it's **nicknamed** the **"African unicorn."**

38. In the folklore of England, **spotting** the **giant monster dog** called the barghest **means death is coming.**

39. In Peruvian mythology, **Amazon river dolphins** are shape-shifters that can **transform** into **humans.**

40. Some real-life animals can also change their shape to copy other animals, like the **mimic octopus,** which can **impersonate** sea snakes, lionfish, and more.

41. **Invisibility** is a **fictional superpower,** but the **reticulated glass frog** does have a **see-through underside.**

42. Aztec legend told of a **"clawed butterfly"** creature named Itzpapalotl (ITZ-papa-lot-l). Real-life butterflies really do have tiny claws.

43. The mythical, many-headed **Hydra** could **regrow a head** if it lost one. The **real-life hydra** can **regrow body parts**—including its head—if they are lost.

44. **Fairies aren't real—but the pink fairy armadillo, a five-inch (12.7-cm) desert dweller, is.**

45. A bit like the mythical serpent the Ouroboros, the **armadillo lizard** *Ouroboros cataphractus* **bites its own tail** and **curls into a ball** when **threatened.**

46. **Chameleons** can't change form like the rakshasas of Hindu mythology, but **many can change color** to trick and avoid predators.

47. An **extinct prehistoric rhinoceros** the **size of an SUV** is nicknamed the "Siberian unicorn."

48. **Satyrs** are **half-human, half-goat** or **half-horse** creatures in Greek mythology.

49. The **phoenix** is a **legendary bird** with the ability to be **reborn again and again.**

50. The **manticore** is a **mythical beast** with the ability to **shoot lethal stingers** from its **tail.**

51. When faced with a threat, the **"immortal" jellyfish** can **return** to its **juvenile** state over and over again.

52. In Greek mythology, **Cerberus** is a **many-headed dog** that **guards** the **entrance** to the **underworld.**

53. **Arachnids, the group of animals that includes spiders, were named after Arachne, a weaver who was transformed into a spider in Greek myth.**

54. Ancient Babylonian myths tell of the **Aqrabuamelu,** creatures that were **half human** and **half scorpion.**

55. **Komodo dragons** are the **largest living lizards.** They can weigh more than **300 pounds** (136 kg).

56. Like the basilisk, an enormous mythical snake, *Titanoboa* was a **now-extinct snake** that could be as long as a city bus.

57. **Harpy eagles** are named after the **half-woman, half-bird monsters** from Greek mythology.

58. The **Ouroboros,** a snake that eats its own tail, is a **mythical symbol** of the **cycle of life.**

59. In Welsh myth, the Cwn Annwn are **phantom dogs** that come from the **world of the dead.**

60. **Lord Ganesha,** a god with an elephant's head, is the **Hindu god of beginnings.**

61. Several species of **goblin spiders** have **horns.**

62. Legend says the qilin, or **Chinese unicorn, appears** when an **important ruler** is about to be **born** or **die.**

63. **Anansi,** a character from West African folklore, most often appears as a **giant spider.**

64. **Cyclops** is a group of **small crustaceans** that, like the mythical cyclops, have a **single eye.**

65. **Medusa** is a mythological Greek character who had **hair made of snakes.**

66. The **sea mouse** *Aphrodita aculeata* is **named after Aphrodite,** the Greek goddess of love.

67. A group of **wormlike nematodes,** the *Cloacina,* **live** only in the **stomachs** of **kangaroos.** They're named after the Roman goddess of the sewers.

68. The dinosaur species *Sacisaurus* is named after a **one-legged creature** from Brazilian folktales because only the right leg bones of the animals have ever been found.

69. **In Japanese folklore, foxes have the ability to shape-shift into humans.**

70. The **world's heaviest stick insect,** the **jungle nymph,** is named after the nymphs, goddesses of nature in Greek mythology.

71. The many **two-headed creatures** of myth occur in real life too: in fish, snakes, cats, and more. This **rare phenomenon** is called **bicephaly.**

72. **Australian kelpie dogs** are named after mythological water creatures from Scottish folklore.

73. In Greek mythology, **Echidna** is a **half-woman, half-snake monster.** In real life, echidnas are spiny mammals that resemble porcupines.

74. During the **19th century, people paid to see** the **remains** of **"mermaids"** that were really just the upper bodies of apes sewn to the tails of fish.

75. The **jackalope** of North American folklore is a **rabbit with antlers.**

1 In Latin, *centi* means "a hundred" and *pede* means "foot," but **centipedes** don't have 100 feet—they have **70**, on average.

2 In Latin, *mille* means "a thousand," but **millipedes** have at the most **750** legs.

3 **Millipedes** are mostly **vegetarian**, eating decaying leaves and other plants.

4 **Centipedes** are **predators**, feeding on insects and spiders—and even other centipedes.

5 The largest **centipedes eat small animals** like mice and birds, first **paralyzing them** with **venom**.

6 The **leggiest millipede**, *Illacme plenipes*, is just 1.2 inches (3 cm) long but has **750 legs**.

7 It can **spin silk** from **hairs** that cover its **back**.

8 **Millipedes** sometimes **curl up** into a tight **spiral** with their heads in the center to protect their soft undersides.

9 A **millipede's legs are tucked** under its body and are **hard to see**.

10 **Centipede mothers coil around** their **eggs** and groom them, possibly protecting them from mold and bacteria.

11 **Millipedes** are normally solitary, but young millipedes sometimes **swarm together** to **hunt** for **food**.

12 In California, U.S.A.'s **Sierra Nevada Mountains**, there are **blind millipedes** that **glow in the dark**.

13 **Scientists** think the **millipedes glow** to **warn predators** to keep away.

14 A **Southeast Asian millipede** that looks like **pink bubble gum** uses its bright color to warn predators that it's toxic to eat.

centipede

35 LEGGY FACTS ABOUT CENTIPEDES AND MILLIPEDES

15

A **newly discovered centipede** from Southeast Asia is about eight inches (20 cm) long. It **lives on land** and in **water.**

16

Each **pair** of a **centipede's legs** are **longer** than the **pair** in **front** of them.

17

A **centipede's legs** are **attached** to the **side** of its **body segments,** rather than underneath, which lets it move quickly.

18

Millipedes and **centipedes** both **molt,** shedding their hard outer layer and adding more segments and more legs.

19

When a **yellow-spotted millipede** feels **threatened,** it releases a chemical that **smells** like **toasted almonds.**

20

Both **centipedes** and **millipedes breathe** through **tiny holes** on the **sides** of their **bodies.**

21

A **centipede's front two legs** work like venomous **claws** to **capture prey.**

22

Centipedes have **long antennae** that they use to **locate prey.**

23

Centipedes can move **forward, backward,** and **sideways.**

24

If a **centipede's legs** are **attacked,** it can **drop them** and **escape** using the **remaining legs.**

25

Centipedes have **one set** of legs per segment; **millipedes** have **two.**

26

One type of **millipede sheds** its bristly **hairs** to irritate attacking ants.

27

Millipedes are second only to earthworms at being able to **quickly break down** and **eat dead plant matter.**

28

Millipedes typically have only **three pairs of legs** when they **hatch.**

29

Centipede was a popular **video game** in which the player fought off centipedes, spiders, and scorpions.

30

Giant centipedes in **Venezuela** sometimes **hang** from cave ceilings and **catch bats to eat.**

31

You can buy **centipede-shaped gummy candy.**

32

In Madagascar, **lemurs squeeze millipedes** to release their **toxin,** and then smear it on their **fur** to **repel** mosquitoes.

33

After the **Peruvian giant yellowleg centipede** sheds its **exoskeleton,** it eats it.

34

Arthropleura, a six-foot (1.8-m)-long invertebrate that resembled a millipede, **lived** almost **300 million years ago.**

35

The **Amazonian giant centipede** has **46 clawed feet** that it uses to grab on to prey.

1. More than 360 different species of birds have been seen in Everglades National Park, part of a vast wetland in southern Florida nicknamed the "river of grass."   2. Water rats can close their noses to keep water out when searching for fish and insects to eat in rivers, lakes, and ponds.   3. Mangroves, trees that grow stiltlike roots in salt water, serve as nurseries for thousands of fish species, from small gobies to 10-foot (3-m)-long sharks.   4. The platypus has a soft, leathery bill—it's the only mammal with one.   5. When a giant marine toad swallows something, its eyes sink into the roof of its mouth, which helps the food move into its stomach.   6. Red-eyed tree frogs spend most of their time high in the trees, but during breeding season, the males gather around streams and loudly call to females.   7. Marsh rabbits flee from predators by diving underwater.   8. Male Florida panthers use their hind legs to kick up grass and dirt into mounds called "scrapes" that mark their territory.   9. Mangrove skinks, a kind of lizard, seek out sunny spots in mangrove forests, but if startled, they scurry into narrow openings in rocks.   10. Squirrel treefrogs get their name from their call, which sounds like a squirrel chattering.   11. They are also nicknamed rain frogs because they often call out during and after rainstorms.   12. At about four inches (10 cm) long, full-grown bog turtles are the smallest turtles in North America.   13. The maned wolf likes to eat the small red berries of the lobeira plant, whose name means "fruit of the wolf."   14. Barnacle larvae swim through mangroves until attaching headfirst to a solid object, such as a tree trunk or an animal's shell.   15. Home to migrating birds, caribou, and fish, tundra environments are cold wetlands, where the little precipitation that falls saturates the ground above the layer of permafrost or bedrock.   16. To ward off wolves on the Arctic tundra, musk oxen arrange themselves in a circle with their young inside and the adults facing outward.   17. Capybaras have partially webbed feet to help them swim in the South American wetlands where they live.   18. Hundreds of years ago, Times Square in New York City, U.S.A.—a bustling area full of people and shops—was a pond filled with beavers.   19. The gulf toadfish gets its name for the toadlike grunts it uses to attract a mate.   20. Gulf toadfish hide in seaweed or sand to stay safe, but they can live for an extended period of time out of the water.

21. The muskrat and its bigger cousin, the beaver, are the only mammals that build their homes in water.   22. To find prey in muddy water, wood storks use their bill, quickly snapping it closed when they feel fish or insects, and then swallowing their catch whole.   23. Water rats, one of Australia's largest rodents, build their burrows along lake and riverbanks, the entrances hidden by plants and trees.   24. Caribou can be so bothered by biting insects on the Arctic tundra that they will run for miles (km) to escape them.   25. Dragonflies have been on Earth for 325 million years—since before the time of the dinosaurs.   26. White ibises use their bills like tweezers to pinch and pull up worms, crayfish, and crabs, cleaning off really muddy prey before eating it.   27. They remove the claws from crabs and crayfish before eating them.   28. The southern bell frog, found in Australia, lives under grass, rocks, or fallen logs, but during breeding season, it floats on top of the water in rice fields, lagoons, and marshes.   29. Sunda woodpeckers, which live in parts of Southeast Asia, peck at trees with powerful beaks, but the noise from these five-inch (12-cm)-long birds is quiet compared to larger woodpeckers'.   30. Today, dragonfly wingspans average about three inches (7.6 cm), but a dragonfly ancestor that lived before the time of the dinosaurs had a wingspan of nearly 2.5 feet (0.8 m).   31. Proboscis monkeys that live on the Southeast Asian island of Borneo have specialized digestive systems that make their bellies look large and bloated.   32. The crab-eating frog is the only amphibian that can live its entire life in salt water.   33. Great blue herons guard their territories, and if another heron approaches, they throw up their heads and stretch out their wings as a warning to back off.   34. Water moccasins, venomous snakes that live in the southeastern United States, are also called cottonmouths: When threatened, they open their mouths wide to reveal the white coloration inside.   35. Carmine bee-eaters, small birds that live in Africa, catch bees, rub them against tree branches until their stingers fall out or are crushed, and then swallow them whole.   36. The great egret, a wading bird with long legs, has an S-shaped neck.   37. During breeding season, a patch of skin near the great egret's eyes turns bright green and long plumes grow from its back.   38. Great egrets were hunted to near extinction for these plumes, leading to some of the first laws to protect birds.   39. Crocodiles have been around for some 80 million years—since the time of the dinosaurs.   40. Vernal pools, wetlands that occur for only part of the year, provide the perfect place for amphibians to lay their eggs—fish aren't around to eat them.   41. A man in Suriname, a country in South America, trained a capybara to be his guide animal.   42. Radjah shelducks, which live in Australia and parts of Southeast Asia, squabble and call to each other before feeding.   43. American alligators can grow

red-eyed tree frog

100 SPLASHY FACTS ABOUT WETLAND ANIMALS

to be about 15 feet (5 m) long, and their strong tails are about half that length.   44. Anhinga, which are water birds, are also called "water turkeys" and "water snakes" for their turkeylike tails and snakelike necks.   45. A single dragonfly can eat 100 mosquitoes a day.   46. Marsh-dwelling nutria, rodents about the size of a small dog, are messy eaters and can ruin about 10 times more plants than they eat, damaging wetlands and even causing riverbanks to collapse.   47. The Murray cod, Australia's largest freshwater fish, can grow to be six feet (1.8 m) long and weigh as much as 200 pounds (100 kg).   48. Green anacondas can stretch their jaws to swallow jaguars, capybaras, and wild pigs whole.   49. Beavers can stay underwater for 15 minutes without coming to the surface to breathe.   50. Mangrove periwinkles, small snails about one inch (2.5 cm) long, use their teethlike radula to feed on algae that grows on tree trunks and branches.   51. Caribou travel to the tundra wetlands in northern North America to have their calves and fatten up on the summer grasses and plants.   52. Muskrats make raised areas out of mud and plants, and carry small fish and turtles there to eat.   53. The platypus lacks teeth, so it crushes up insects, worms, and shellfish in its mouth with pebbles it slurps up from the bottom of rivers and wetlands.   54. The "trilling" call of the eastern gray treefrog is similar to that of the red-bellied woodpecker.   55. Great egrets wade through wetlands looking for fish to jab with their bright yellow beaks.   56. Garter snakes have glands on their tails that release a bad-smelling liquid when the snake is surprised.   57. Depending on where they live, crab-eating frogs don't just eat crabs—they eat insects and even other small frogs.   58. South Florida, U.S.A., is the only place in the world where American alligators and American crocodiles live in the same habitat.   59. Unlike most snakes, moccasins don't lay eggs; they give birth to live little snakes.   60. The endangered Florida panther, the only puma (or mountain lion) found east of the Mississippi River, preys on white-tailed deer in marshes and wetlands of southern Florida.   61. Anhinga swim slowly underwater and use their bills to stab fish through their sides.   62. Storks don't have voice boxes, so they clack their bills together when excited.   63. In the Arctic, lemmings, small micelike rodents, stockpile plants in underground burrows so they have food during the winter.   64. Beavers' teeth and jaws are strong enough to cut down trees.   65. They use the wood to build dams that block streams and create ponds.   66. The black howler monkey's large hyoid bone, which helps produce its loud call, restricts its arm movement, so it relies on its strong tail to navigate through the trees.   67. Nutria gather in groups to keep warm during the winter.   68. White ibis couples bond by crossing their necks together.   69. Male white ibises collect most of the sticks needed for the nest and give them to the female to build it.   70. The hyacinth macaw, a bright blue parrot that lives in South America, can be about as tall as a four-year-old kid.   71. Excellent climbers, Cuban treefrogs have been known to hop up utility poles, short-circuiting switches and causing power outages in cities.   72. River otters live in burrows along the edge of marshes, rivers, and lakes, and can hold their breath underwater for about eight minutes.   73. The bright orange color of nutria and beavers' front teeth comes from iron in their tooth enamel, which makes their teeth stronger.   74. Caribou are the only member of the deer family in which both males and females have antlers.   75. Common musk

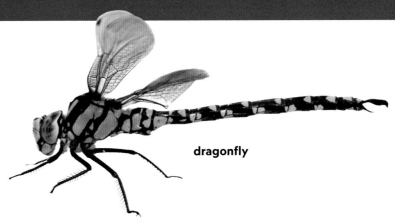

dragonfly

turtles walk along the bottom of ponds, looking for plants, insects, and small fish to eat.   76. Sheepshead fish, which live in mangroves along coasts in the western Atlantic Ocean, have teeth that look like human teeth.   77. To track the migration patterns of green darners, a kind of dragonfly, scientists fitted them with tiny transmitters, and then followed them from the ground and from airplanes.   78. American snake neck turtles, found in the southeast United States, have long, striped necks that are almost as long as their shells.   79. Crocodiles can go for months without eating.   80. River otters' stiff whiskers are so sensitive they can sense fish moving underwater.   81. Male green darners guard a small area of a pond, aggressively ramming into any intruders.   82. A swimming platypus is on Australia's 20-cent coin.   83. Dragonflies have two sets of rigid wings and can hover, fly backward, and even fly upside down.   84. During hot weather, capybaras keep cool by staying in shallow water or muddy spots—they'll even sleep there.   85. They have earned the nickname "water pigs."   86. The largest Nile crocodiles can reach lengths of 20 feet (6 m)—that's about the height of a two-story building.   87. Carmine bee-eaters fly alongside moving cars to catch the insects that are startled into the air.   88. Giant marine toads can be nine inches (23 cm) long—that's longer than a 10-year-old's foot.   89. When threatened, giant marine toads release a milky poison from the bumpy warts that cover their bodies.   90. The mangrove salt marsh snake curls up in the limbs of mangrove trees, flicking its tongue to lure fish.   91. Capybaras act as moving "chairs" to the animals that like to perch on their backs, such as birds and small monkeys.   92. Beavers build underground entrances to their lodges, which are made with mud and branches.   93. Only about one inch (2.5 cm) in size, mangrove tree crabs scurry up to the top of mangrove trees during high tide and down to the exposed ground during low tide.   94. A female mangrove tree crab carries as many as 35,000 eggs on her belly; when they're ready to hatch, she shakes her body over the water to release the larvae.   95. Predators like fish and barnacles easily prey on the larvae—only about .04 percent of the larvae will become juvenile crabs.   96. Anhinga have dense bones, and feathers that are not waterproof, both of which help them stay submerged when hunting for fish.   97. Howler monkeys can eat acidic plants that would bother other animals because their saliva breaks down the acids before they reach their stomachs.   98. Green anacondas lie in wait for their prey, which they coil around and squeeze to death.   99. With the largest bill in the world, hyacinth macaws can eat nuts and seeds that other animals can't crack into.   100. Mana Pools National Park, a wetland along the Zambezi River in Africa, is home to Zimbabwe's largest population of crocodiles and hippos.

1

SHARKS' NOSTRILS are used only for SMELLING, NOT BREATHING.

2

A LEMON SHARK can DETECT TUNA OIL at one part per 25 million—the same as 10 drops in a backyard swimming pool.

3

A GREAT WHITE SHARK can DETECT BLOOD at one part per 10 billion—the same as one drop in an Olympic-size pool.

4

Some BLOODHOUNDS have STAYED ON A SCENT TRAIL for more than 130 MILES (209 km).

5

A bloodhound's DROOPY EARS AND LOOSE FACIAL SKIN help COLLECT ODORS for better scent detection.

6

A BLOODHOUND'S SENSE OF SMELL is so accurate that its TRACKING RESULTS are CONSIDERED ADMISSIBLE EVIDENCE in a court of law.

7

A Kentucky BLOODHOUND named Nick Carter helped lead to the CAPTURE of 600 CRIMINALS.

8

An elephant shrew has a LONG, BENDABLE NOSE that helps it find insects.

9

An elephant's TRUNK is an EXTENSION of its UPPER LIP and NOSE.

10

The PIGMENTATION around a KOALA'S NOSE is as UNIQUE as a human fingerprint.

11

An ELEPHANT'S TRUNK isn't used only to breathe and to smell—it CAN LIFT HEAVY OBJECTS like logs, spray water, and pluck small objects like leaves.

12

Elephants RAISE and WAVE THEIR TRUNKS in the air to GATHER and DETECT SCENT PARTICLES.

13

ELEPHANTS can SMELL WATER 12 miles (19 km) away.

14

TURKEY VULTURES' sense of smell is better than any other bird. They also have a BONY STRUCTURE OVER THEIR NOSTRILS that keeps food from going in when they eat.

15

INSECTS SMELL with their ANTENNAE and LEGS.

16

A SNAKE has a strong sense of smell, but it DOESN'T USE ITS NOSE—it catches scent particles on its TONGUE.

17

A SNAKE has an organ in its mouth called a JACOBSON'S ORGAN that DETECTS FOOD and PREDATORS' SCENTS.

18

MALE SILK MOTHS can SMELL FEMALES six miles (10 km) away.

19

Scientists are STUDYING SILK MOTHS to invent SCENT-DETECTING ROBOTS.

20

A BEAR'S BRAIN is a THIRD THE SIZE of a human's, but the area that CONTROLS ITS SENSE of smell is FIVE TIMES LARGER.

21

A BEAR can DETECT A CARCASS 20 miles (32 km) away.

SNIFF OUT THESE 50 FACTS ABOUT ANIMAL NOSES

22

MANDRILLS, a type of primate, are one of the MOST COLORFUL MAMMALS, with bright red noses and blue and purple ridges along their noses.

23

A MALE POLAR BEAR can follow a FEMALE, which LEAVES A SCENT THROUGH HER PAWS, for 60 miles (100 km).

24

ELEPHANTNOSE FISH, African freshwater fish, use their LONG NOSES to POKE THE BOTTOM OF LAKES TO FIND FOOD.

25

PIGS have been used for centuries to sniff out UNDERGROUND TRUFFLES, a type of rare mushroom.

26

PIGS can DETECT ODORS in the air SEVEN MILES (11 km) AWAY and FOOD buried 25 FEET (7.6 m) UNDERGROUND.

27

WANDERING ALBATROSSES FOLLOW SCENTS like a blood-hound, TRACKING PREY from 12 miles (20 km) away.

28

BUMBLEBEES can tell the DIFFERENCE BETWEEN SMELLS left behind by FAMILY members and STRANGERS.

29

WALLABIES are born with a good sense of SMELL, which helps them FIND THEIR WAY to their MOTHER'S POUCH.

30

CHINESE SOFTSHELL TURTLES have the BEST SENSE OF SMELL OF ALL REPTILES. They use it to search for food in water at night.

31

TRAINED DOGS are used to SNIFF OUT THE POOP OF THREATENED or ENDANGERED SPECIES, like wolves or tigers, to help scientists keep track of their health and populations.

32

A KOALA uses its sensitive nose to SNIFF OUT the amount of TOXINS in EUCALYPTUS LEAVES before choosing which ones to eat.

33

The PINOCCHIO LIZARD, which lives in forest canopies in Ecuador and has a long nose, is NAMED AFTER THE FICTIONAL PUPPET whose nose grows when he lies.

34

The SWORD-NOSED BAT has a distinct nose leaf, a SWORD-SHAPED protrusion, which is believed to help improve its ECHOLOCATION.

35

A sword-nosed bat's NOSE LEAF can be ALMOST AS LONG AS ITS EARS.

36

Researchers don't know why GOBLIN SHARKS have such long noses, but they think it could help detect ELECTRICAL SIGNALS from prey in the water.

37

In 2019, scientists discovered a tree frog in New Guinea with a SINGLE SPIKE on its nose, which they named the northern PINOCCHIO FROG.

38

With more than 450 species of frogs in New Guinea, scientists think the SPIKE might help the frogs DISTINGUISH one species from another.

39

The STAR-NOSED MOLE'S NOSTRILS are ringed with 22 TENTACLES that help it SEARCH FOR FOOD.

40

STAR-NOSED MOLES are the world's fastest eaters—they can SNIFF OUT and EAT an insect or worm in a QUARTER OF A SECOND.

41

The STAR-NOSED MOLE has five times more TOUCH SENSORS ON ITS NOSE than the human hand has.

42

Star-nosed moles and water shrews can SMELL UNDERWATER.

43

They BLOW BUBBLES, then SUCK THEM BACK into their noses to smell for food.

44

EASTERN MOLES smell in stereo—EACH NOSTRIL OPERATES INDEPENDENTLY—which helps them determine the location of their prey.

45

The GOLDEN SNUB-NOSED MONKEY, which lives in snowy regions of China, has FLAPS OVER ITS NOSTRILS that may protect it from FROSTBITE.

46

At up to 6.8 inches (17.5 cm) long, the NOSE of a PROBOSCIS MONKEY is the LONGEST of any primate.

47

The MALE, which has a longer nose than the female, makes a loud HONKING SOUND.

48

The UNICORNFISH has a BONY HORN on its forehead that LOOKS LIKE A NOSE.

49

BONOBO MOTHERS SUCK SNOT out of their babies' noses so they can breathe better.

50

A HAMMERHEAD SHARK has NOSTRILS on EITHER END OF ITS HAMMER-SHAPED HEAD, which allows it to take in smells from a WIDER RANGE.

»15 FACTS TO GROUP TOGETHER

A GROUP OF ...

1
... fish is a
SCHOOL.

2
... owls is a
PARLIAMENT.

4. ... wombats is a **WISDOM.**

3
... elephants is a
HERD.

5
... flamingos is a **FLAMBOYANCE.**

6. ... hippos is a **BLOAT.**

7. ... ravens is an **UNKINDNESS.**

8. ... lizards is a **LOUNGE.**

9. ... ladybugs is a **BLOOM.**

10
... lemurs is a **CONSPIRACY.**

11. ... geese is a **GAGGLE.**

12. ... bats is a **CAULDRON.**

13
... penguins is a **COLONY.**

14
... jellyfish is a **SMACK.**

15
... baboons is a **TROOP.**

1 Axolotls, a type of salamander, can **regenerate their limbs, lungs, heart, spines**, and even parts of their **brain**.

2 Scientists are studying **axolotls** to one day use that **superpower** to **help humans**.

3 A **wild boar's lower tusks** are called **cutters** because the teeth are sharp and are used to cut rival boars or predators.

4 **Wolves** sometimes **begin eating prey** before it is dead.

5 Aggressive **cape buffalo,** which live in sub-Saharan Africa, **charge** at speeds up to **35 miles an hour** (56 km/h).

6 A **shoebill bird** has a one-foot (30-cm)-long **bill** that has **sharp edges** and a **hook** on the end.

7 **Shoebills** use their **fierce bills** to snag fish, eels, snakes, and even baby crocodiles.

24 BURLY FACTS
ABOUT ANIMAL
TOUGH GUYS

8 On rare occasion, **meerkats** kill and **eat venomous scorpions,** but they don't get hurt thanks to a **venom immunity**.

9 **Meerkats** can **survive without drinking water;** they get all the moisture they need from roots and fruit, like melons.

10 During the dry season, **overcrowding** from too many animals **competing for water and territory** causes **hippos' tempers to flare**.

11 Bearded vultures drop the bones of dead animals from as high as 260 feet (80 m) onto rocks, **cracking them open** and then eating the marrow inside.

12

The **northern goshawk** has **red eyes** and **sharp talons** that it will use to attack humans who get too close to its nest.

13

Tiger sharks have been known to **eat everything** from other **sharks** to **license plates** to **tires.**

14

A **naked mole rat's front teeth** can operate separately, like **chopsticks.**

15

A **bite** from the **gooty sapphire tarantula** can cause **pain** that lasts a **week.**

16

Thanks to **strong jaws,** Tasmanian devils are able to **eat all of their prey,** including their **bones.**

18

Sun bears have **four-inch** (10-cm)-long **sickle-shaped claws** that they use to tear open tree bark to look for insects.

17

The **mountain stone weta,** one of the **world's largest insects,** can **survive** being **frozen** in **snow and ice** for **weeks** at a time.

19

The **talons** of a **great horned owl** have a clutch force as **strong as a guard dog's bite.**

20

Slow-moving **opossums aren't afraid of rattlesnakes**—they have a compound in their blood that makes them resistant to their venom.

21

Aggressive **male betta fish flare their gills** and **nip** at the **fins** of other males.

22

During dry season, when streams disappear, **betta fish** survive by **puddle-hopping.**

23

Pound-for-pound, **bull sharks** have a **stronger bite** than any other shark.

24

A **hammerhead shark** sometimes **uses** the sides of its head to pin down stingrays—and then it eats their wings.

1. **Barn owls store** dozens of captured **prey** to **feed** their **young** when they **hatch.**

2. When a female horse and a male donkey have a baby, that animal is called a mule, but when a female donkey and a male horse have a baby, it's called a hinny.

3. If given a **clean pool of water, ducks** will **bathe** themselves, but **chickens won't.**

4. A **horse's eyes** are about **eight times larger** than **human eyes.**

5. Since a **horse's eyes** are on the **side** of their **heads,** they can **see** in almost every **direction.**

6. To attract a mate, **male barn owls hover in the air** for a few seconds in front of a female barn owl.

7. **Llamas** will **"adopt" a herd** of sheep or goats as their own and **protect** them from predators such as coyotes.

8. **Goat milk** is **easier** for **humans to digest** than **cow milk.**

9. The **wild horses** that live on **Assateague Island,** a sandy barrier island near Virginia and Maryland, are **descendants** of **horses** brought to the island by settlers in the **late 1600s.**

10. **Businesses and home-owners rent goats**—some companies bring 100 goats or more—as an **environmentally** friendly way to **trim their lawns.**

11. One **female rabbit** can have a **litter** of babies **every month,** and a litter can number as many as **14 babies.**

12. **Mules** can **kick** their **legs** sideways.

13. According to **Norse mythology, Thor,** the **god of thunder and agriculture,** rode in a **chariot pulled** by **two goats.**

14. **Ducks** produce **more eggs** on average than **chickens,** and their eggs are also **slightly larger** and **more nutritious.**

15. Many domestic pigs have curly tails, **but** potbellied pigs **have** straight tails.

16. The extremely **soft and curly hair** of the **Angora goat,** called **mohair,** grows about 12 inches (30 cm) a year.

17. When a **horse gallops,** all **four of its legs** briefly **lift off the ground.**

18. **Goats** can **understand facial expressions** and **prefer** to hang around **happy people,** a study found.

75 FACTS ABOUT FARM ANIMALS

19. A **horse's teeth** take up **more space** in their heads **than** their **brains** do.

20. The **Inca**, who lived in the Andes mountain range of South America hundreds of years ago, burned **dried llama poop** for **fuel**.

21. **Cows** don't have **teeth** in their upper jaw, but rather a **thick dental pad** that helps them crush the tough plants they eat.

22. **Llama** have special **"fighting" teeth** that can grow into one-inch (2.5-cm)-long fangs.

23. **Female barn owls** eat their **nestlings' poop** for about 10 days after they hatch to **keep** the **nest clean**.

24. **Barn owls** like to nest in building towers and water silos, and have even been **spotted** in **Yankee Stadium** in **New York City, U.S.A.**

25. **Alpacas** and **llamas hum**.

26. **Historians think that English colonists brought goats on the** *Mayflower* **during their 1620 voyage to North America.**

27. About as tall as a four-story building, a **giant Holstein cow sculpture** named **Salem Sue** towers over the countryside in **New Salem, North Dakota, U.S.A.**

28. Some **mules** make a **whimpering sound** if **excited** or **anxious**.

29. The **"lionhead" rabbit** gets its name from the **ruff of fur around its head,** but it only weighs about as much as three cans of soup.

30. **Baby goats** are called **kids,** and a **female goat** giving **birth** is known as **kidding**.

31. The word **"donkey"** comes from their usual grayish color (known as "dun") and "ky," which means "small."

32. **Rabbit teeth** never stop growing.

33. Some **pigs salivate** when they anticipate **getting treats,** such as carrots, grapefruit, or snow peas.

34. **Chickens** can **fly** for **short bursts** to escape from danger.

35. **Horses and donkeys have excellent memories.**

36. In some parts of **Africa, cows** are **sometimes used** instead of **cash**.

37. **Rabbits sleep** with their **eyes open**.

38. **One pound** (0.5 kg) of **sheep wool** can create a piece of **yarn** that stretches for **10 miles** (16 km).

39. Some **farms** use **robots** to **milk dairy cows**.

40. **Ducks** are known as **waterfowl** because they are birds that **need to live near water**.

41. Some **"mini" mules** weigh only about **200 pounds** (90 kg).

42. **Rabbits** sometimes **eat** their **poop** to get more **nutrients** from their food.

43. **Goats** can be **taught** to **surf, skateboard,** and **paddleboard**.

44. The oldest known horse, **Old Billy,** was born in England in 1760 and died **62 years** later.

45. **Chariot racing,** in which four horses pulled a rider in a wooden-wheeled carriage around a stadium, was an **Olympic sport** beginning in **680 B.C.**

46. **Companies** make **raincoats** for **horses** and **goats**.

47. **To warn of danger, rabbits thump their feet.**

48. In 1931, a **farmer** on Long Island, New York, U.S.A., **sold ducks** from the belly of a giant duck-shaped structure.

49. **George Washington** rode Nelson, one of his **favorite horses,** during the American Revolution because the loud noises of battle didn't scare the horse.

50. **Barnyard ducks** can lay **greenish** or **bluish colored eggs.**

51. **Cows** make **friends** with other cows and are **less stressed** when they can **stay** with their **friends** if separated from the herd, a study found.

52. A **very productive dairy cow** can produce enough milk in one day to make **10.5 pounds** (4.8 kg) of **cheese**.

53. **Chickens make at least 24 different sounds to communicate with other chickens.**

54. When **chickens coo softly,** that means they're ready for **bed,** and a **short shriek** means they've spotted **danger**.

55. **A goat** has a **four-part stomach,** which helps it **digest** the **tough vines** and **bushes** goats eat.

56. **Alpacas** are **smaller** than **llamas,** only about three feet (1 m) tall at their shoulder.

57. A **horse's hooves** are always **growing;** they grow a **new set** of hooves **every year**.

58. **Donald Duck's** middle name is **Fauntleroy**.

59. An **adult horse drinks** about **12 gallons** (45 L) of **water** every **day**.

60. **Pigs "rut"** around in **soil** searching for **tasty things to eat,** a behavior that also helps them get the iron they need to be healthy.

61. There are more than **200 different breeds** of **goats**.

62. **Cows can spend up to eight hours a day chewing food such as grasses and hay.**

63. A group of **miniature therapy horses** in Los Angeles, California, U.S.A., has helped **cheer up** more than **50,000 people** by **visiting hospitals** and other locations.

64. Shaped like a corkscrew, an **18th-century barn** in Leixlip, Ireland, may have been **designed** as a place for **birds to nest**.

65. A **horse's tail** acts as a **flyswatter,** but to keep **flies out** of their **ears,** some owners put cloth covers over them.

66. Both **male** and **female goats** can have **"beards."**

67. **Llamas** and **alpacas** are related to **camels**.

68. **Horses** and **ponies** blow a **gentle puff of air** as a friendly **"hello."**

69. **Potbellied pigs** can learn how to **open** a **refrigerator** to eat the food inside.

70. **Horses** like to **munch** on special treats of **carrots, apples, sugar cubes,** and even **ginger-snap cookies**.

71. **Donald Duck** has an **asteroid** named after him.

72. In one study, **cows** would **jump, kick,** and **buck** excitedly after figuring out that **pressing a panel** with their **noses** gave them access to **food**.

73. **Llamas** are **pack animals,** but if asked to carry too much weight, they will lie down and refuse to budge.

74. Every day, a **horse** produces about **10 gallons** (38 L) of **saliva**.

75. **Rabbits** can learn how to use a **litter box**.

1 Orcas stun stingrays with a **slap** of their **tails.**

2 When **scorpions** fight over a territory, they use their **tails** as **swords;** the winner stings, then eats its opponent.

3 The **blue whale** is the **largest predator** that has ever lived on Earth.

4 **Net-casting spiders** make a **stamp-size net,** hold it in their two front legs, and quickly **wrap** unsuspecting **prey** in it.

5 When **male kangaroos** fight over females, **one powerful kick** can kill an opponent.

6 **African wild dogs** can travel more than **30 miles** (48 km) in **one day** to find a **meal.**

7 In the **spring,** it takes a **polar bear** an average of **three days** of **hunting** before it catches a seal; in the **summer** it takes **five.**

8 **Kiwi birds** kick logs with their **powerful legs** to dislodge bugs that are inside.

9 **Velvet worms** squirt a **sticky slime** at their **prey,** then suck it up.

10 **Archerfish** are able to **recognize individual human faces,** a skill that likely helps them hunt specific prey in the wild.

11 Amazonian **giant centipedes** use their **claws** to **stab bats** in caves, **paralyzing** and then **eating** them.

12 **Trapdoor spiders** cover their underground home with twigs and leaves to capture insects moving above.

13 **Tentacled snakes** use their **tails as bait** to distract fish, then eat them.

14 **Green herons** have been observed **dropping bread crusts** and **insects** in water as **bait** to attract fish.

15 When chasing prey, **bobcats** place their **back feet** in the **same place** their **front feet landed** to reduce noise.

16 **Bobcats** can **jump** high enough to **catch low-flying birds.**

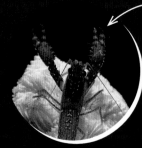

17 A **pistol shrimp** stuns its **prey** by quickly closing its extra-large powerful **claw,** which makes a **shock wave.**

18 A **blue whale** can hold up to **110 tons** (100 t) of **krill** and **water** in its **mouth.**

35 AWESOME FACTS
ABOUT ANIMALS ON THE
OFFENSE

19
Wolf spiders are named for the wolflike way they chase and pounce on their insect prey.

20
Crocodiles have been seen covering their snouts in sticks and lying still in the water to lure birds to rest on them.

21
Cichlid fish play dead in lake water and then eat the fish that come to investigate.

22
A crocodile's powerful bite isn't because of its large teeth, but rather because of its strong jaw muscles.

23
Red foxes dive into the snow headfirst and can catch prey buried three feet (1 m) deep.

24
Humpback whales hunt in groups, using air bubbles to herd small fish and then lunging upward through the circular "net" to engulf them.

25
If a harpy eagle's prey is too heavy to carry to its nest, it cuts it up into pieces.

26
Trumpetfish change colors to sneak up on prey and then vacuum them up with their long snouts.

27
Colossal squid have rotating hooks on the end of their tentacles to hold on to prey.

28
Bottlenose dolphins catch fish in shallow water by stirring up mud, causing the fish to jump into their mouths.

29
Pelican spiders have jaws that look like a pelican's bill and are used to bite into prey and then hold on to it until it dies.

30
A pelican spider grabs and pulls other spiders' webs close to itself, and then eats them.

31
Margays mimic the sound of a baby monkey, then attack the adult monkeys that come to investigate.

32
Megalodon, an extinct shark that lived 2.6 million years ago, had a bite that could crush a small car.

33
The larvae of *Epomis* beetles lure frogs and salamanders; when they're in range, the larvae bite and kill them.

34
Golden eagles sometimes attack fully grown deer.

35
Komodo dragons have been known to swallow a goat whole.

giant
anteater

100
FACTS
ABOUT
RAINFOREST
ANIMALS

1. More than half the world's animals live in rainforests. 2. Jaguars, the third largest cat after lions and tigers, typically live in tropical rainforests, but are also found in savannas and grasslands. 3. The short-eared wild dog *Atelocynus microtis,* the only canine that lives in the Amazon rainforest, is known as a "ghost dog" because it is rarely seen by people. 4. Sloths move so little that algae and fungi grow on their fur. 5. Sloths' diet, which mostly consists of leaves, contains so few calories and has such little nutritional value that the animals have to move slowly to conserve energy. 6. The toco toucan's colorful bill makes up almost half of its body length. 7. Toco toucans can regulate blood flow to their bills, helping them move heat away from their bodies. 8. Toucans flick food down their throats with their featherlike tongues. 9. Mountain gorillas live in rainforests of Central Africa at elevations between 8,000 and 13,000 feet (2,440–3,965 m). To adapt to the cold, they grew thicker hair than their lowland relatives. 10. A group of mountain gorillas is called a troop. 11. Just as humans have unique fingerprints, gorillas have unique nose prints. 12. The Malay word for orangutan means "person of the forest." 13. When orangutans stand, their arms can nearly touch the ground. 14. Orangutans spend 90 percent of their day in trees and use leaves as umbrellas when it rains. 15. As male orangutans move through the forest, they make a howling call to make sure they stay out of each other's way.

16. Tapirs, which look like pigs but are more closely related to horses and rhinos, sometimes wallow in the mud, which can help remove ticks. 17. Tapirs have flexible snouts that they use to grab branches and pick fruit from trees. 18. Tapirs help plant new fruit trees: After eating fruit, they poop out the seeds in different locations. 19. Anteaters lick up as many as 35,000 ants and termites every day. 20. An anteater's sense of smell is 40 times better than a human's. 21. Giant anteaters have four-inch (10-cm)-long claws that they use to fight off predators—including jaguars. 22. Of all the big cat species, the leopard is the only one that lives in both deserts and rainforests. 23. Leopards drag their kills up into trees to keep hyenas and other animals from stealing them. 24. Leopards can jump 10 feet (3 m) straight up in the air. 25. Harpy eagles, the world's largest eagle, have talons longer than a grizzly bear's claws. 26. Harpy eagles bring fresh twigs to their nest after chicks have hatched, which scientists think helps provide a cooler environment. 27. Harpy eagles use their powerful talons to snatch monkeys and sloths out of rainforest trees. 28. Chimpanzees have the widest range of all the great apes, living in rainforests, grasslands, and savannas from central to western Africa. 29. Chimpanzees bond by picking ticks and dirt off of each other. 30. Scientists think chimps might eat certain plants to help cure an upset stomach or headache. 31. Okapi, known as the "forest giraffe," is the giraffe's only living relative. 32. Okapi stripes are sometimes called "follow me" stripes, as their pattern helps calves follow their mothers through the shady rainforest. 33. Okapi have thick oily fur that helps them stay dry in the rain. 34. Okapi can lick their own eyes and ears. 35. Macaws have colorful feathers that blend in with flowers and fruit. 36. Some macaws mimic human speech. 37. Macaws sometimes eat dirt, which can help ease stomachaches brought on by the fruits they eat. 38. The southern cassowary, a flightless bird that lives in the rainforests of Queensland, Australia, can eat hundreds of fruits and berries in a single day. 39. Male cassowaries, not the females, sit on eggs and raise the chicks for nine months or more. 40. Cassowaries, which stand five feet (1.5 m) tall, can jump nearly seven feet (2 m) in the air and swim across rivers. 41. African pygmy hippos look like a miniature version of hippos and weigh about one-tenth as much. 42. Found in rainforests in West Africa, pygmy hippos spend more time out of water than their larger relatives, foraging for food on the forest

jaguar

floor.   43. Ring-tailed lemurs, which live in the rainforests of Madagascar, are known for their long, striped tails, but they can't grip with them like other primates can.   44. Some green tree pythons have more than 100 teeth.   45. When scared, the hawk-headed parrot raises its neck feathers, which look like a fan around its head.   46. The red-ruffed lemur has a special, long grooming claw that it uses to keep its fur clean.   47. The blue morpho butterfly, one of the largest butterflies in the world, has a wingspan of up to eight inches (20 cm).   48. Blue morpho butterflies aren't actually blue. Microscopic scales on the back of their wings reflect blue light, making them appear blue to human eyes.   49. Pilots flying over the Amazon have spotted large groups of blue morpho butterflies on the top of the rainforest canopy, warming themselves in the sun.   50. Capybaras are closely related to guinea pigs, but at twice the size of a beaver, they are the largest rodent on Earth.   51. An Amazon language calls the capybara *kapiyva,* or "masters of the grasses."   52. Capybaras eat their own poop. The grasses they eat are hard to digest, so by eating their poop, they can digest the grass twice.   53. The green anaconda, a member of the boa family, is the heaviest snake in the world, weighing more than 550 pounds (250 kg).   54. Green anacondas, which are semiaquatic and live in the Amazon and Orinoco rainforests, can grow longer than a school bus.   55. Newborn green anacondas are about the length of a skate-board.   56. Two-inch (5-cm)-long golden poison frogs pack enough poison to kill 10 people.   57. Golden poison frogs move their tad-poles onto land by carrying them piggyback.   58. Poison frogs' Latin family name, Dendrobatidae, means "one who walks in the trees."   59. Black howler monkeys, the largest monkeys in Latin American rainforests, make one of the loudest calls of any land animal.   60. Only male black howler monkeys are black—females have a blond coat.   61. Black howler monkeys, which rarely come down to the forest floor, use their tail to grip on to and hang from branches.   62. Jaguars eat 85 different types of animals—from turtles to deer to monkeys to fish.   63. Bats that live in Central and South American rainforests sometimes cut banana leaves into tentlike shelters.   64. Nectar bats drink from flowers with their long snouts and tongues, making them important pollinators in rainforests.   65. Vampire bats drink blood from cows, pigs, and other animals; they make a cut with their teeth and lap the blood with their tongues.   66. Up to 30 percent of the Amazon's animal biomass is made up of ants.   67. Leaf-cutter ants live in massive colonies of up to three million.   68. Leaf-cutter ants remove about 15 percent of the Amazon's vege-tation and take it back to their nests to grow fungus, the ants' food.   69. One-quarter of all butterfly species live in South American rain-forests.   70. Brown-headed spider monkeys, which live in South American rainforests, gather in groups of up to 100.   71. During its caterpillar stage, the Queen Alexandra's birdwing butterfly eats its toxic host plant, making itself toxic to predators.   72. The gibbon, a type of ape, has such long arms that it holds them over its head for balance when it walks.   73. Tree frogs blink their eyes to help force their food down when swallowing.   74. The white dots on the solid black back of the white-blotched river stingray resemble the sun hitting the bottom of a river, helping camouflage it in the water.   75. When threatened, the Brazilian wandering spider assumes an attacking stance, putting its front legs in the air and swaying from side to side.   76. The pygmy marmoset, the world's smallest mon-key, survives mostly on tree sap.   77. Amazon milk frogs got their name for the poisonous, sticky, white substance they secrete.   78. Kinkajous are sometimes called honey bears because they raid bees' nests for honey.   79. The kinkajou, which has a tail that can grip branches like a monkey's, is actually related to raccoons 80. Golden lion tamarins are primates, but they get their name from the thick, manelike hair around their faces.   81. Red-legged pademel-ons, a type of wallaby that lives in the Australian rainforest, thump their feet when they sense danger.   82. The Brazilian rainbow boa gets its name from its iridescent skin, which refracts light, producing a rainbow effect.   83. Sugar gliders, palm-size possums that live in tropical forests in Australia, Indonesia, and Papua New Guinea, can glide through the air using thin skin that stretches from their hands to their ankles.   84. Sugar gliders use their bushy tails as rudders to steer while gliding through the air.   85. The hoatzin, a bird found in the Amazon River Basin, is born with claws at the end of its wings, which disappear as they grow.   86. When hoatzin chicks feel threat-ened, they hop out of their nest, which is built on a branch over water, and use their wings to paddle to shore.   87. The Madagascan flying fox, a type of bat that lives only on Madagascar, chews on fruit to release and swallow the juice, then spits out the seeds, skin, and pulp.   88. Draco lizards, which live in tropical forests of Southeast Asia, can leap 100 feet (30 m) between trees—the skin between their ribs opens up like an umbrella.   89. Male Draco lizards chase each other while gliding in the air from tree to tree.   90. To impress females, male caimans, relatives of the American crocodile, do a special dance by spinning in the water.   91. Spectacled caiman get their name from a bony ridge between their eyes that makes them look as if they are wearing glasses.   92. Scientists think that the pink color of some male Amazon river dolphins could be scar tissue from fighting for females.   93. Male Amazon river dol-phins beat the water's surface with a branch to impress females.   94. Tomato frogs, which are named for their reddish color, are poi-sonous, but they can also inflate themselves to look bigger to deter predators.   95. Nile crocodiles mostly eat fish but will also eat zebras, wildebeests, small hippos, and porcupines.   96. The Amazon rainforest is the world's largest tropical rainforest, home to nearly 1,300 bird spe-cies, 3,000 types of fish, 427 species of mam-mals, and 2.5 million different insects.   97. Red-bellied piranhas nip fins from the tails of larger fish, which accounts for a good portion of their diet.   98. Aggressive red-bellied piranhas make a barking sound to tell other fish to back off.   99. Electric eels that live in the Amazon River generate an electric charge that stuns prey.   100. Electric eels aren't eels. They are more closely related to catfish and carp.

channel-billed toucan

1 Female lions do **most** of the **hunting.**

2 Male lions **guard** the **cubs** while the lionesses hunt.

3 Lions are the **only cats** that **live** in **groups.**

4 A **male lion** can **eat** about **140 pounds** (64 kg)—a quarter of his body weight—in a **single sitting.**

5 The **Swahili word** for lion, *simba,* means **"king."**

6 A **lion's tongue** is so **rough** it can **peel the skin** off its **prey.**

7 **Lions** are the **only predators** powerful enough to **kill** an elephant.

8 The **darker** a male lion's mane, the **more attractive** females find him.

9 **Lions** in the **Kalahari Desert** have been spotted **eating melons** to get **water** in dry conditions.

10 A **lion's roar** can be **heard five miles** (8 km) **away.**

35 ROARING FACTS ABOUT LIONS

11
Lionesses often kill by **clamping** their **jaws** down over their **prey's mouth** and **nose.**

12
Some **ancient Egyptian pharaohs** kept **lions** as **pets.**

13
Lion yawns are **contagious.**

16
The **lion** is called the **"king of the jungle"** but it actually **lives** in **grasslands.**

14
Both **male** and **female lions roar.**

15
Lion cubs are **born** with **blue eyes.**

17
To be **"lionhearted"** means to be **courageous** or **brave.**

18
The pair of **lion statues** outside the New York Public Library are named **Patience** and **Fortitude.**

19
Lions can **roar** at **114 decibels,** about 25 times **louder** than a gas-powered **lawn mower.**

20
The extinct **Barbary lion** was even **bigger** than modern lions, weighing up to **600 pounds** (272 kg).

21
By working together, **lions** can **take down** animals as large as **giraffes.**

22
Hyenas and **lions compete** for the same prey.

23
Lionesses in a **pride** often have their **cubs** at the same time.

24
Lions can **run 50 miles an hour** (80 km/h) for **short distances.**

25
Only a **few hundred Asiatic lions** are left in the wild, all living in **India's Gir Forest.**

26
A **pride,** or group, of lions is made up of **mother, sister,** and **cousin lionesses** and their cubs, along with a **few adult males.**

27
Experts can **identify individual lions** by the **pattern** of **spots** at the **base** of their **whiskers.**

28
Lions in **cool climates** have **longer, thicker manes.**

29
Lions sleep up to **21 hours a day.**

30
Lions in captivity are able to **solve puzzles** that leopards and tigers can't.

31
Lions once lived across Africa, Asia, and Europe but now **exist** mainly in **Africa** (and a few hundred live in **Asia**).

32
A **male lion** can **weigh** up to **500 pounds** (230 kg), as much as an empty Dumpster.

33
Like house cats, **lions** often **sleep in strange positions**—sometimes on their backs with all four paws in the air.

34
Domestic cats' pupils are **vertical slits,** but **lions** have **round pupils** like humans.

35
Zookeepers sometimes **feed** captive lions frozen **"bloodsicles"** in hot weather.

1

Large animals known as MEGAFAUNA have been DECLINING since the end of the PLEISTOCENE, a period of time that ended 11,700 years ago.

2

Generally, scientists describe MEGAFAUNA as animals WEIGHING MORE THAN 100 POUNDS (45 kg), such as elephants, hippos, and polar bears.

3

By the END of the PLEISTOCENE, nearly three-quarters of the MEGAFAUNA in North America became EXTINCT as the climate changed.

4

WOOLLY RHINOS lived throughout Europe and Asia until about 14,000 years ago and had THICK COATS to keep them warm in cold climates.

5

Woolly rhinos weighed as much as THREE TONS (2.7 t) and were SIX FEET (1.8 m) TALL at their shoulders.

6

A GIANT TORTOISE that lived some FIVE MILLION YEARS ago had the LARGEST SHELL of any known turtle: It was 9.8 feet (3 m) long.

7

GIANT SLOTH LEMURS the size of today's gorillas once lived on MADAGASCAR.

8

Scientists think that SABER-TOOTHED ANIMALS used their giant canine TEETH to TEAR into their prey instead of using the teeth to pin it down.

9

An EGG from the extinct elephant bird, found on MADAGASCAR, could weigh 22 pounds (10 kg).

10

An ANCIENT BUFFALO found in TANZANIA had LONGER limb bones than the cape buffalo living today, which stand almost 60 inches (150 cm) tall at their shoulders.

11

Fossils of MAMMOTHS, an EXTINCT group of elephants, have been FOUND on every CONTINENT except Australia and South America.

12

Smilodon, the SABER-TOOTHED BIG CAT that was nearly twice as heavy as today's lion, is the STATE FOSSIL of California, U.S.A.

13

SMILODON is NOT RELATED to TIGERS that live today.

14

The SUMATRAN RHINO is the LAST RELATIVE of the woolly rhino still alive.

15

CAVE DRAWINGS suggest that MALE CAVE LIONS, which were larger than lions today, did not have MANES.

16

Known as the IRISH ELK, the largest deer species that ever lived was TALLER at its SHOULDER than the AVERAGE NBA PLAYER.

17

The LARGEST HYENA that ever lived, *Pachycrocuta brevirostris*, WEIGHED about 220 POUNDS (100 kg) and lived in Europe, Asia, and Africa until about half a million years ago.

18

CAVE BEARS in Europe and SHORT-FACED BEARS in North America were about the SAME SIZE as BROWN BEARS today.

19

The GIANT CROCODILE *QUINKANA*, which could grow to be 23 feet (7 m) long, lived on land in Australia and used its SHARP TEETH to tear into prey.

woolly mammoth

50 TOWERING FACTS ABOUT *GIANT* PREHISTORIC ANIMALS

20
The IRISH ELK had ANTLERS that stretched 12 FEET (3.65 m) across.

21
They lived throughout Europe, northern Asia, and northern Africa, but the name "IRISH ELK" stuck because well-preserved FOSSILS of the GIANT DEER are commonly found in peat bogs in IRELAND.

22
In 2018, FISHERMEN at a Northern Ireland lake reeled in a six-foot (1.8-m)-wide Irish ELK SKULL and ANTLERS that were more than 10,500 years old.

23
Ice Age animals that became TRAPPED in the LA BREA TAR PITS in California attracted hungry animals, which could then become trapped, too.

24
More than ONE MILLION BONES have been found at the LA BREA TAR PITS.

25
Hancock Park in Los Angeles, California, near the La Brea Tar Pits, has life-size SCULPTURES of giant ICE AGE mammals.

26
The FLAT-HEADED PECCARY, a piglike mammal that lived in North America, likely lived in HERDS, just like peccaries today. These mammals all CHATTER THEIR TEETH when alarmed.

27
LARGE DUCKS related to mallards lived in the HAWAIIAN ISLANDS until they died off about 1,000 years ago, some 200 years after people arrived on the islands and caused the birds to go EXTINCT.

28
Called MOA-NALO, these ducks could stand three feet (1 m) high and COULDN'T FLY.

29
The GIANT SHORT-FACED BEAR, which lived in South America about half a million years ago, WEIGHED as much as 3,500 POUNDS (1,590 kg)—1,000 pounds more than the heaviest polar bear today.

30
A GIANT CHEETAH that lived in Europe more than two million years ago was about TWICE as BIG as cheetahs today.

31
BONES of a GIANT HYENA found in a Spanish cave showed that the scavenger—which could crack open bones, including human skulls, with their teeth—preferred bones with a lot of MARROW in them.

32
Scientists looking at a MAMMOTH TOOTH in 2015 found that a small population LIVED on an ISOLATED ISLAND in the Arctic Ocean before going extinct some 4,300 years ago.

33
The HAAST'S EAGLE, which lived on the island of New Zealand and chased giant birds, had a WINGSPAN of nearly 10 feet (3 m).

34
The TALONS of the Haast's eagle were THREE INCHES (7.5 cm) LONG—the same size as a modern-day tiger's.

35
CAVE PAINTINGS in France some 30,000 years old depict WOOLLY RHINOS, which means they LIVED ALONGSIDE HUMANS.

36
Workers digging an extension to the Los Angeles metro system found a JUVENILE MAMMOTH FOSSIL—which they nicknamed "Hayden"—that still had his BABY TEETH.

37
Standing about two feet (0.7 m) at the shoulder, the GIANT WOMBAT *RAMSAYIA* weighed about 550 POUNDS (250 kg), more than six times that of today's wombats.

38
AMERICAN MASTODONS had DENSE HAIR to keep them WARM during the last ice age.

39
MALE AMERICAN MASTODONS, which were bigger than females, could WEIGH FIVE TONS (4.5 t).

40
Scientists think that CAVE LIONS ate reindeer and young cave bears.

41
The enormous AMERICAN GROUND SLOTH, which lived from what is today Texas, U.S.A., throughout South America, was about as LONG as a MEDIUM-SIZE LIVING ROOM.

42
GIANT SLOTHS may have sat on their enormous hind legs and pulled down leaves from trees.

43
The VOAY, a crocodile-like reptile that lived during the time of the dinosaurs, had TEETH the SIZE of a *TYRANNOSAURUS REX* and ate the same prey as the dinosaur.

44
Unlike ostriches today, scientists think that a GIANT OSTRICH-TYPE BIRD, which stood 11 feet (3 m) tall and lived in Europe until the end of the last ice age, probably WASN'T A VERY FAST RUNNER.

45
One ancient type of MUSTELID (the group that includes weasels and otters) was the size of a leopard.

46
Giant armadillo-like animals known as *GLYPTODONS* went extinct around 11,000 years ago, and just like armadillos today, they could TUCK THEIR HEADS into their SHELLS to keep safe.

47
In 2015, scientists discovered a BABY WOOLLY RHINO, which they nicknamed Sasha, preserved in a RIVER-BANK in Siberia.

48
GIANT BEAVERS the size of black bears lived in North America during the last ice age.

49
The GIANT BEAVER isn't closely related to beavers today.

50
The GIANT BEAVER had SIX-INCH (15-cm)-LONG TEETH it used to mash up plants.

»15 GROSS-OUT ANIMAL FACTS THAT WILL MAKE YOU SAY *EWW!*

1
Short-horned lizards defend themselves against predators by **shooting blood out of the corner of their eyes.**

3
When parts of ribbon worms are chopped off, the pieces can grow into **new worms.**

2
Apes and monkeys pick each other's lice and eat them.

4. The **Amazon leech can grow to be 18 inches (46 cm) long**—that's as long as two pencils.

5

To scare away predators, **wood snakes can turn their eyes red** and release drops of blood from their mouths.

6. **Ambergris,** a waxy substance **found in the digestive system of sperm whales,** is used in some **perfumes.**

7. **Crocodiles** sometimes **foam around the eyes** when they eat.

8. Slugs use their own slime trail to find their way back home.

9. **Capuchin monkeys** use sticks to **pick their noses.**

10

A **blue whale's poop** is the consistency of **bread crumbs.**

11. **Sea pigs,** a type of sea cucumber, **feast on dead animals** deep on the ocean floor.

12. **When a camel spits,** it's actually **flinging partly digested food** that it burped up.

13

Bedbugs have been found preserved in some **ancient Egyptian tombs.**

14

A **hagfish uses teethlike structures to burrow a tunnel into its prey's flesh** and then starts eating.

15

After a **West Indian manatee passes gas,** the animal sinks in the water.

1 In 2012, a **cheetah** at the **Cincinnati Zoo** was **clocked running 328 feet** (100 m) in **5.95 seconds.**

2 **Pronghorns,** antelope-like creatures that live in western North America, **can run nearly as fast as cheetahs can,** and they can **sustain that speed** for much **longer.**

3 **Birds "catch" tailwinds** while flying, which **boosts their speed.**

4 Female Brazilian free-tailed bats can **fly** at nearly **100 miles an hour** (161 km/h).

25 FACTS THAT WILL GET YOU UP TO SPEED

5 While chasing tuna, **shortfin mako sharks,** the **fastest** sharks in the ocean, can **swim** at speeds **eight times faster** than swimmer **Michael Phelps.**

6 **Dragonflies grab prey** with their **feet** as they **dart** through the **skies** at up to **35 miles an hour** (56 km/h).

7 **Pigeons "see" the world several times faster** than humans can, which **helps them chase speedy prey** and **avoid quick predators.**

8 **Leatherback turtles swim** at the **highest speeds** at the **start** and **end** of their **dives.**

9 When flying to impress a mate, the **common swift** can reach **speeds** of **69 miles an hour** (111 km/h).

10 Moose can weigh more than two tigers but can still **run** at **speeds** of **35 miles an hour** (56 km/h).

15 African ostriches can sprint at **43 miles an hour** (69 km/h)—their leg tendons let them store and release energy much more efficiently than humans can.

16 To catch fish, bald eagles can **dive** into lakes and rivers **at 100 miles an hour** (161 km/h).

20 The long-legged **Australian tiger beetle** is the **fastest running beetle in the world**—they can run at **5.6 miles an hour** (9 km/h).

23 The **black mamba,** considered to be the **world's deadliest snake,** will **quickly strike at humans in defense** and can **slither at speeds of 12 miles an hour** (19 km/h).

11

A **cheetah's flexible spine** allows it to **step 22 feet** (6.7 m) in **one stride.**

19 The **lower jaws** of **green darner dragonflies** have special **hooks** that can **shoot out** in **a hundredth of a second to seize prey.**

21

Gentoo penguins can **swim underwater** as much as **three times faster** than other kinds of penguins.

24 Roadrunners can **sprint** at speeds of almost **20 miles an hour** (32 km/h).

12 When **"stooping,"** or attacking **prey** from the sky, **peregrine falcons** have been clocked at **speeds of 186 miles an hour** (299 km/h).

13 **Red kangaroos** can **hop** at **speeds** of around **35 miles an hour** (56 km/h) for about a mile.

14 To **escape predators** such as coyotes, foxes, and hawks, **hares** can **dart at speeds of 40 miles an hour** (64 km/h).

17 With **two wingbeats per second, great egrets** can **cruise** through the **air** at around **25 miles an hour** (40 km/h).

18 **Alpine swifts** aren't fast as their name implies, but they do **fly long distances**—a single nonstop flight can last 200 days.

22 To attract a mate, male **Anna's hummingbirds** swoop toward the ground, making a **loud popping sound with their feathers** at the bottom of the dive.

25 Roadrunners easily **avoid rattlesnake bites** by spreading their wings wide and **leaping into the air.**

1. Situated 600 miles (966 km) from the mainland of South America, the **Galápagos Islands** are home to **animals** that have had to **adapt** to the **conditions** there in order to **survive**.

2. Found only on the Galápagos, marine iguanas evolved to be able to swim underwater, using special claws to grip rocks.

3. When food is scarce, **marine iguanas** adapt by **absorbing bone** and **reducing** their **size** by **20 percent;** they regrow once food is plentiful.

4. Naturalist **Charles Darwin** called **marine iguanas** the **"most disgusting, clumsy lizards."**

5. Magnificent **frigatebirds** have **webbed feet,** but they don't have waterproof feathers, so they **spend little time** in the **water.**

6. **Galápagos penguins** live farther north than any other penguin.

7. **Galápagos penguins** build **nests** in **holes** found in **lava rocks.**

8. Galápagos tortoises have been living on the Galápagos Islands for three million years.

9. **Painted locusts** can **leap 9.8 feet** (3 m).

10. **Waved albatross** court one another by **nodding their heads, clacking bills,** and letting out a cowlike moo.

11. **Galápagos tortoises** are as **heavy** as at least **three St. Bernards.**

12. The **Galápagos hawk's nest,** which is **used year after year,** can be up to **9.8 feet** (3 m) **deep.**

13. The **oldest** Galápagos tortoise **lived to be 152.**

14. **Flightless cormorants** used to fly but have **evolved** to no longer need their wings for flight—they **dive underwater for food.**

15. They still have a use for their wings: to **steer their way through water.**

16. **Giant tortoises** sometimes **soak** in **pools of water** in **volcano craters** on the islands.

17. The **waters off** the **Galápagos** are **home** to the **densest shark population in the world**—31 tons (28 t) of sharks per acre (0.4 ha).

18. **Galápagos penguins pant** like dogs.

19. Every time a **Sally Lightfoot crab** molts, it becomes a little more **colorful.**

20. **Blue-footed boobies touch bills** when they've **found** their **mate.**

21. The **Galápagos** are **home** to **half** of all **breeding pairs** of **blue-footed boobies.**

22. The **Spanish word** for **"tortoise"** is *galápago.*

23. Galápagos **land iguanas' color varies** based on **where they live** on the islands: ones that live near **lava rock** are **darker** and ones that live near **sandy beaches** are **lighter.**

24. **Researchers** think **iguanas came to the Galápagos** from the South American continent millions of years ago on rafts of vegetation.

25. Green sea turtles can sleep underwater for a few hours at a time.

26. **Hoary bats** typically **hang from one foot** and **look like** a **dead leaf** in a tree.

27. **Galápagos tortoises sleep** up to **16 hours a day.**

28. The **Galápagos green sea turtle** is the **only sea turtle** that **nests** on the **islands.**

29. **Galápagos sea lions** can **"gallop"** across the **rocky shore faster** than a **human** can **run** on rocky terrain.

30. Galápagos fur seals have large eyes that help them hunt for fish at night.

31. **Galápagos tortoises** can **grow** to be **five feet** (1.5 m) long and **weigh 550 pounds** (250 kg).

32. **Studies** have found that **Galápagos fur seals** hunt less frequently **during full moons,** probably because they are more visible to sharks.

75 FACTS ABOUT ANIMALS OF THE GALÁPAGOS

33. Sally Lightfoot crabs sometimes **eat ticks** that they **pick off** of **marine iguanas.**

34. To **rid** their **bodies of salt** from the ocean, **green sea turtles cry** from **special glands** under their **eyes.**

35. Magnificent frigatebirds can glide on air currents for days at a time.

36. Magnificent frigatebirds chase **booby birds,** grabbing their feathers and shaking them until they regurgitate their recently eaten food.

37. Magnificent frigatebirds have been **nicknamed "pirate birds"** for their habit of **stealing** other birds' **food.**

38. Vampire finches hop on the backs of Nazca boobies, peck on their wings, and then drink their blood.

39. Studies show **vampire finches don't do any lasting harm to the birds** and only feed on blood when other food is hard to find.

40. Because **Galápagos hawks** don't have any natural predators, they have **little fear** of **people** on the **islands.**

41. Galápagos flamingos get their **bright pink color** from the **crustaceans** they **eat.**

42. Sixty percent of the **150 spider species** on the Galápagos **occur nowhere else** in the **world.**

43. Darwin's goliath centipede, one of the largest centipedes in the world, can **grow** to be **as long as two pencils lined up end to end.**

44. Giant manta rays, which swim off the Galápagos Islands, sometimes **leap out of the water** and **land** on their **backs.**

45. The Galápagos batfish has red lips that make it look as if it is wearing lipstick.

46. The **Galápagos batfish** uses its **fins** as **legs,** propping itself up on the ocean floor to check out its surroundings.

47. Painted locusts likely **colonized** the Galápagos by **flying** from another **continent.**

48. Marine iguanas sneeze to **force out sea salt** from glands by their **noses.**

49. The **13 species of Darwin's finches** that live on the Galápagos **evolved** to have **different beaks from one another,** each suited to eating different foods—from seeds to insects.

50. Naturalist **Charles Darwin** called Galápagos tortoises **"inhabitants of some other planet."**

51. The **woodpecker** and **mangrove finches** use cactus spines as **tools** to **poke around for grubs.**

52. Baby sea lions hang out together in shallow water **nurseries** and are looked after by **one female.**

53. The **Pacific seahorse** has a fused jaw—it **sucks prey** up through its **strawlike snout.**

54. At more than a foot (30 cm) long, **Pacific seahorses** are **one** of the **largest seahorses** in the **world.**

55. To prevent overheating, **Galápagos penguins** have **less body fat** and **feathers** than other penguin species that live in colder climates.

56. The **Galápagos Islands' coat of arms** features a volcano, a sailboat, a cornucopia, the colors of its flag, and in the middle, a **tortoise.**

57. Galápagos tortoises have **two** different types of **shells:** either one with a **notch** in the **front** so they can lift their heads to reach food overhead, or a **dome-shaped** one that allows them to search for vegetation on the ground.

58. Scientists think **tortoises** arrived to the **Galápagos** by **floating** on the ocean's currents.

59. Scientists believed the **Pinta tortoise** had **gone extinct** until a **lone survivor** named Lonesome George was **discovered** in 1971.

60. When attacked, **Sally Lightfoot crabs spray water** as a defense.

61. The Darwin's goliath centipede feasts on lava lizards and young rats.

62. Blue-footed boobies are believed to take their name from the **Spanish word bobo,** which means **"fool."**

63. Blue-footed boobies use their **webbed feet** to **cover** their **chicks** and keep them **warm.**

64. The **pink iguana** is native to only one area around a volcano on the **Galápagos' Isabela Island.**

65. After **Galápagos sharks** are **born,** they flee **to shallow water** to avoid being eaten by other sharks.

66. Magnificent frigatebirds have the **world's largest wingspan relative** to their **body weight.**

67. A slow metabolism allows Galápagos tortoises to survive a year without eating or drinking.

68. If **threatened** by a predator, **Galápagos sharks** try to appear intimidating by **arcing** their **backs** and **swimming** in **figure-eight formations.**

69. The **Galápagos shark** is found **worldwide,** but the scientists who found it **named** it **after the Galápagos Islands,** where they first saw it swimming offshore.

70. The **waved albatross** gets its name from the **waved pattern** of its **feathers.**

71. Isabela Island, when seen from above, **resembles** a **seahorse.**

72. How to tell the **difference** between **Galápagos fur seals** and **sea lions: Fur seals** have **thicker, lighter fur** and more **pronounced ears.**

73. Magnificent frigatebird parents take care of their **chicks** longer than any other bird species—**males** care for **hatchlings** for the first **three months** and then **females** take over for another **nine months.**

74. Sailors in the **19th century captured** Galápagos **tortoises** and kept them on ships to provide **fresh meat** on their **voyage.**

75. Four of the original **seven rice rat species** that live on the islands **went extinct** after humans colonized and brought in black rats on their boats.

1
In the 1990s, a captive **beluga whale** mimicked **human speech.**

2
Without any training, **dogs** are capable of **following human gestures,** like **pointing** and **eye movements.**

3
Crows remember human faces, and they remember if a particular person was a threat.

4
Male palm cockatoos use twigs and seed-pods to **make drumsticks** to **attract a mate.**

5
A captive **African gray parrot** named Alex learned more than **100 words** and how to identify **shapes** and **colors.**

6
A **scrub jay** can **remember 200 spots** where it **hid** its **food.**

7
Some **crows carve hooks** at the end of **sticks** to **reach prey inside holes.**

8
Studies show that even though a **raven's brain** is the **size of a walnut,** the bird is about as **smart** as a **chimpanzee.**

9
African cichlid fish can tell the difference between **familiar fish** and **strangers** based on their **facial patterns.**

10
In a study, **African gray parrots** showed **selflessness**—one parrot **helped another get treats,** even if it meant it would get less.

11
A **border collie** named Chester knew **1,022 nouns,** the largest known **vocabulary** of any dog.

12
Captive African **elephants** have been observed **mimicking** the **sound** of **traffic.**

13
Giant Pacific octopuses in captivity are capable of **opening jars.**

35
WITTY FACTS ABOUT ANIMAL
INTELLIGENCE

14
Bottlenose dolphins, magpies, and manta rays are able to recognize themselves in mirrors.

15
Dolphins have been seen putting sponges on their noses to protect their beaks from getting cut on rocks and coral.

16
Bonobos, a type of primate, are willing to help bonobos they don't know even if there isn't anything in it for them.

17
Chimpanzees use grass as a tool to dig termites and ants from mounds.

18
They also fold leaves as a cup to drink water.

19
A study found that gray squirrels are better at problem-solving than red squirrels are.

20
A gorilla was once observed using sticks to measure how deep muddy water was before crossing it.

21
As a group, bees can detect and respond to situations that wouldn't be possible for a single bee.

22
"Potty-trained" cows use a special stall to go to the bathroom, which could help reduce pollution.

23
Elephants move rocks and logs onto electric fences to break the current to reach crops.

24
Dairy cows follow sounds in a maze to find food, showing they have heightened decision-making skills.

25
Pocket gophers use rocks as a spade to dig holes.

26
Researchers studied ants' behavior to improve data transfer on the internet.

27
Dolphins take care of each other: If one member of the pod is sick and heads to shallow water, the rest will sometimes follow.

28
A chimpanzee was better than a group of college students at a game of memory.

29
In one study, raccoons were taught how to pick complex locks.

30
Dogs often know a storm is coming before people do.

31
Chickens can tell the differences among shapes and colors.

32
Octopuses have one central brain, which controls their nervous system, plus eight others, which control movement.

33
Red-footed tortoises have been taught how to use a touch screen.

34
Sulphur-crested cockatoos can sync their body movements to the beat of music.

35
In one study, donkeys proved to be better at opening gates than horses were.

100 WILD FACTS ABOUT THE WEASEL FAMILY

1. The Mustelidae, or weasel family, is made up of about 55 carnivorous mammals, including weasels, badgers, otters, ferrets, martens, minks, polecats, and wolverines. 2. The weasel family lives on every continent except Australia, Antarctica, and most oceanic islands. 3. A badger once reportedly attacked a tractor after it ran over the entrance to its den. 4. Least weasels are the smallest in the weasel family, weighing just two ounces (55 g). 5. Because least weasels can't store much fat on their bodies, they have to eat often, consuming half their body weight in food every day. 6. At birth, a least weasel is as small and light as a paper clip. 7. Least weasels' hearts beat up to 400 times per minute. (That's four times faster than yours.) 8. Fishers, long-tailed members of the weasel

European Pine Marten

family, don't eat fish. They likely got their name from their resemblance to a European polecat, also known as a "fitchet." 9. In parts of Central America, weasels are called "furry snakes." 10. Sea otters' teeth aren't pointy—they're big and round—but they have a thick coat of enamel that allows these animals to crush and open clams and crabs. 11. Weasels are one of the few animals that play as adults. 12. Minks have 44,000 hairs—and humans just 350—in an area the size of a postage stamp. 13. Weasels often kill more than they can eat, so they stash the leftovers in an underground cache near their den. 14. Weasels and ferrets perform a dance when they corner their prey—they hop, twist, and dart. 15. Scientists aren't sure why weasels and ferrets dance, but they think it might confuse or distract their prey. 16. Young weasels and ferrets sometimes dance with their siblings. 17. A female ferret is called a jill and a male ferret is called a hob. 18. "Ferreting" is a hunting technique practiced since Roman times, in which ferrets are used to drive rabbits, rats, and other animals from their underground burrows. 19. Black-footed ferrets make their home in prairie dog burrows and almost exclusively eat prairie dogs. 20. Black-footed ferrets nearly went extinct in the 1980s, but in 1987, the last 18 were caught to begin a captive breeding program. Today several hundred live in the wild. 21. Black-footed ferret mothers make a whimpering sound to get their babies to follow them. 22. Weasels can jump four times their body length from a standing position. 23. Weasels have whiskers on their legs to help them feel their way in dark underground burrows. 24. To confuse predators, long-tailed weasels use their black-tipped tails to mimic their heads. 25. All members of the weasel family stink! They have glands at the base of their tails that make musk—a smelly substance. 26. Musk is used to attract mates and to mark territories—including stashes of dead prey to eat later. 27. Honey badgers get their name from their diet of honey and honeybee larvae, but they also eat amphibians, reptiles, birds, mammals, berries, and roots. 28. Honey badgers are good swimmers. They sometimes jump in rivers to chase turtles. 29. Wolverines sometimes dig into burrows and eat hibernating animals. 30. Badgers eat several hundred earthworms every night. 31. Honey badgers' thick skin helps protect them from their venomous prey species, like bees and cobras. 32. Michigan's traditional state nickname is the Wolverine State. Even though wolverines never had an established population in Michigan, U.S.A., their pelts were traded in the Michigan city of Sault Sainte Marie in the 18th century. 33. Mink have webbed feet and can swim up to 100 feet (30 m) underwater. 34. Weighing up to 99 pounds (45 kg), sea otters are the largest member of the weasel family, but they are the smallest marine mammal in North America. 35. A sea otter's lung capacity is two and a half times greater than similar-size land mammals'. 36. Sea otters can hold their breath for more than five minutes, while river otters can hold theirs for eight. 37. Wolverine teeth are so sharp they can eat bones and hooves. 38. Pine martens, which are the size of a domestic cat, live in holes in trees or take over old squirrel and bird nests. 39. Baby pine martens call to their moms by making a birdlike chirping sound. 40. A wolverine can travel 15 miles (24 km) a day to search for food. 41. Honey badgers release a sticky liquid from the base of their tails that's as smelly as a skunk's musk spray. 42. Wolverines often follow wolves to scavenge the remains of their kill. 43. A wolverine can bring down prey as large as an adult caribou all by itself. 44. When a mink is happy, it purrs like a cat. 45. The sea otter is the only marine mammal that can lift and flip over boulders on the ocean floor. 46. Wolverines are also known as "skunk bears" because of the smelly musk they use to mark their territory. 47. Wolverines have wide, webbed feet that work like snowshoes, helping them walk on snow. 48. In 2009, scientists tracked a wolverine that had trekked more than 500 miles (805 km)—crossing numerous highways in the U.S.—from its home in Wyoming to Colorado. 49. Wolverines' scientific name, *Gulo gulo,* comes from the Latin word *gulo,* which means "glutton," or "greedy eater." 50. River otters sometimes playfully slide down snowy or muddy hills and then splash into water. 51. When river otters are about two months old, their mother pushes them into the water to teach them to swim. 52. An otter's tail is called a rudder. 53. Otters use their whiskers in the water to detect the movement of fish. 54. Minks build their den with grass and fur left over from their prey. 55. Wolverines have two upper molars that sit sideways at 90 degrees—a helpful angle for ripping into ice-covered carcasses. 56. Mink store leftovers of their kills in their dens to eat later. 57. Mink have long been hunted for their luxurious fur, which has depleted their populations. 58. The Welsh name for badger translates as "earth pig." 59. According to ancient British folklore, badgers bring bad luck. 60. Badger hair was traditionally used to make shaving brushes. 61. Badgers are social and often groom one another. 62. A group of otters out of the water is called a romp. 63. Badger families live in about six complex burrows that have several rooms. 64. These burrows, called setts, can be hundreds of years old. 65. The largest badger burrow ever found had 2,883 feet (879 m) of tunnels, 50 rooms, and 178 entrances. 66. Badgers dig shallow holes outside of their den that they use as communal toilets. 67. Amazon weasels, which live in tropical rainforests in South America, sometimes raid bird nests and eat their eggs. 68. A group of ferrets is called a business. 69. Ferrets were domesticated about 2,500 years ago but are illegal to keep as pets in some U.S. states. 70. "Ferret" comes from the Latin word *furittus,* which means "little thief." 71. Ferrets are known to have a habit of stealing small items. 72. Weasel tail hairs are used to make paintbrushes. 73. Baby ferrets are born white

honey badger

and change color after a few weeks. 74. A honey badger's skin is loose, allowing it to twist and bite an animal that has grabbed it by the neck. 75. Domesticated ferrets have been trained to help workers pull wires through underground tunnels or pipes. 76. In England, spectators gather to watch domestic ferrets race through tubes. 77. Domestic ferrets don't sweat and can easily overheat. 78. Domestic ferrets sleep up to 20 hours a day. 79. Domestic ferrets can understand and respond to gestures like pointing just as dogs do. 80. Scientists ranked skunk odor as one of the worst smells found in nature. 81. Ferrets have extra-long vertebrae, allowing them to bend their bodies 180 degrees. 82. Most carnivores' legs and bodies are about the same length, but burrowing members of the weasel family, like ferrets, have legs that are half the length of their bodies. 83. Having short legs helps ferrets run in tunnels without tripping. 84. Ferrets can compress their rib cages to fit through small spaces. 85. Honey badgers have been observed moving and climbing on objects, like boxes, in order to reach food. 86. Pine martens have semi-retractable claws, making them good tree climbers. 87. If pine martens fall out of a tree, they twist in the air to land on all four feet. 88. When threatened, river otters make a screaming sound that can be heard up to 1.5 miles (2.4 km) away. 89. Sea otters have sensitive whiskers, which they use to locate prey hiding in underwater crevices. 90. Skunks may be smelly, but a lesser anteater releases an odor to ward off predators that is considered up to seven times smellier. 91. Ferrets can fit through a one-inch (2.5-cm) hole. 92. Most of a wolverine's diet is dead animals, sometimes buried in snow after an avalanche. 93. Wolverines hide their kill in the snow, spray it with their musk, and come back to eat it later. 94. Aggressive wolverines sometimes steal grizzly bears' kills. 95. Wolverines like to climb, and they sometimes rest in trees. 96. Venomous snakes make up as much as 25 percent of a honey badger's diet. 97. A bite from a cobra can slow down a honey badger, but because of their developed resistance to venom, they rarely die. 98. Fishers are one of the few animals that prey on porcupines. They run circles around the porcupine, then bite at its face until it grows tired and rolls over. 99. Fishers don't make noise very often, but when they do, it sounds like a chuckle. 100. Fishers can rotate their hind paws 180 degrees, allowing them to climb down from a tree headfirst.

European mink

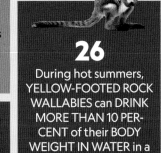

1

An ARABIAN CAMEL'S HUMP can store 80 POUNDS (36 kg) of FAT, which the animal uses as ENERGY.

2

FENNEC FOXES have BIG, BATLIKE EARS that help RELEASE BODY HEAT.

3

BENGAL TIGERS in India SWIM in WATERING HOLES to COOL OFF.

4

DESERT SNAILS that live in the Sahara can remain inactive FOR YEARS until rainfall revives them.

5

POMPEII WORMS live near deep-sea hydrothermal vents in TEMPERATURES that are almost hot enough to BOIL WATER.

6

SAHARAN SILVER ANTS travel their body length in LESS THAN A HUNDREDTH OF A SECOND—that's the equivalent of a human running 400 miles an hour (644 km/h)!

7

MALE DESERT TORTOISES sometimes battle by trying to FLIP ONE ANOTHER.

8

Scientists think POMPEII WORMS can survive high temperatures because they are covered in a HAIRLIKE BACTERIA that INSULATES them.

9

The SAHARA DESERT ANT'S body temperature can reach 122°F (50°C), making it one of the MOST HEAT-TOLERANT ANIMALS on Earth.

10

The ADDAX, a type of antelope, has WIDE, FLAT HOOVES that keep it from SINKING in the Sahara SAND.

11

The desert RÜPPELL'S FOX has concentrated PEE, which helps it SAVE WATER.

12

To cool themselves down, OSTRICHES flutter their wings to CREATE A BREEZE.

13

CAMELS can DRINK 30 GALLONS (114 L) of water in 13 MINUTES.

14

SAHARAN SILVER ANTS have TINY HAIRS on their BACKS that REPEL the SUN'S RAYS.

15

DUNG BEETLES, which live in African and Australian deserts, get MOISTURE from the POOP that they eat.

16

PUPFISH, a small fish that lives in Death Valley National Park, CAN SURVIVE in hot springs that are WARMER than HOT TUBS.

17

After a meal, SNAKES SUNBATHE to raise their body temperature, which helps DIGEST their FOOD.

18

DIBOKALI, which are closely related to zebras, can SURVIVE SEVERAL DAYS in the deserts of Ethiopia WITHOUT WATER.

19

On cool mornings, THORNY DEVIL LIZARDS are olive brown but GET LIGHTER IN COLOR as the day's TEMPERATURE RISES.

20

To survive sweltering hot conditions, AFRICAN BULLFROGS dig a burrow and shed layers of skin to create a HARD COCOON that keeps them from drying out.

21

COYOTES that live in North American deserts get some of their WATER from wild-growing MELONS.

22

The microscopic TARDIGRADE lives in the deep sea at temperatures as high as 302°F (150°C)—almost 100°F (55°C) higher than the BOILING POINT of WATER.

23

TARDIGRADES can SURVIVE up to 30 years without food or water.

24

When WESTERN BOX-ELDER BUGS sunbathe, they PRODUCE CHEMICALS that KILL GERMS that live on them.

25

The SAHARA DESERT ANT'S long legs keep its body off the hot sand.

26

During hot summers, YELLOW-FOOTED ROCK WALLABIES can DRINK MORE THAN 10 PERCENT of their BODY WEIGHT IN WATER in a few minutes.

27

SIDEWINDER SNAKES move SIDEWAYS so that only two points of their body are in contact with the hot desert sand at a time.

28

CAPE GROUND SQUIRRELS use their BUSHY TAIL as a PARASOL.

29

To avoid the heat, DESERT TORTOISES spend 98 percent of their time in BURROWS.

30

Even in 120°F (49°C) heat, CAMELS RARELY SWEAT.

31

FENNEC FOXES have FURRY FEET that PROTECT them from hot desert sand.

32

The GREATER BILBY, a marsupial that lives in Australian deserts, DIGS BURROWS almost seven feet (2 m) deep to avoid daytime HEAT.

33

CHICKENS PANT like dogs and LIFT THEIR WINGS away from their body to RELEASE HEAT.

34

MARINE IGUANAS lounge on lava rocks to WARM UP after they swim in the sea.

35

SIDEWINDER SNAKES have HORNS ABOVE THEIR EYES, possibly to keep out sand when they're buried.

36

PIGS ROLL in MUD to COOL OFF.

37

MEERKATS use the DARK SKIN on their STOMACHS to control their TEMPERATURE— they lie on their backs to warm up or facedown to cool off.

38

BABY GUANACOS, which are related to camels, can WALK within FIVE MINUTES of being BORN.

39

GUANACOS eat CACTUS and other PLANTS to get WATER.

40

During the summer, more BLOOD CIRCULATES through the blood vessels in ELEPHANTS' big ears, which helps RELEASE HEAT.

41

To stay hydrated, THORNY DEVIL LIZARDS absorb MOISTURE from WET SAND through their SKIN.

42

KANGAROOS lick their forearms to keep COOL.

43

SEA LIONS regulate their body TEMPERATURE by lifting a flipper out of the water; BLOOD VESSELS under their skin either absorb or release heat.

44

VULTURES use warm air currents to TAKE A REST when the rising air gives them a lift.

45

Because THERMAL POWER PLANTS, which use steam to produce power, create stronger and hotter air currents, VULTURES seek them out so that they can fly even faster.

46

The TEMPERATURE of the SAND where a SEA TURTLE nest is buried determines whether a turtle is born MALE or FEMALE.

47

Eggs that incubate below 81.86°F (27.7°C) will hatch MALE sea turtles; eggs that incubate above 87.8°F (31°C) will hatch FEMALE.

48

As DUNG BEETLES push a moist BALL OF DUNG, it COOLS the sand, creating a more COMFORTABLE walking surface for the beetles.

49

CAMELS can SHUT THEIR NOSTRILS during sandstorms to keep out sand.

50

ARABIAN CAMELS can TRAVEL up to 100 miles (161 km) in the desert WITHOUT WATER.

50

FACTS ABOUT ANIMALS THAT CAN *TAKE THE HEAT*

1 Bright-yellow **banana slugs move** along the moist forests in the Pacific Northwest at about **6.5 inches** (16.5 cm) **a minute.**

2 Banana slugs have only **one foot** and **one lung.**

3 An adult **sea star** can have **15,000 tubelike feet,** but it **crawls slowly** over sand, rocks, and shells.

4

Blue-tongued skinks, a kind of lizard, have **short legs** and **waddle** when they walk. They **rarely leave** the hollow logs or debris **where they live.**

5 **Slow lorises** are called the **"sloths of the primate world,"** but they **can move fast** through the trees **when necessary.**

25

NOT-SO-FAST FACTS

ABOUT SLOW-MOVING ANIMALS

6 Turtles don't move fast in part because of their **protective shells,** which are **made up of bones** that are **fused together.**

7 **Greenland sharks** are also known as **"sleeper" sharks** because they **swim slowly** through **chilly waters.**

8 A pond snail can use the **bottom of its foot to crawl** on the **underside** of the **water's surface.**

9 Because **turtles eat plants** and **don't have to chase down a meal,** they **don't need to be fast.**

10 **Desert tortoises** are able to **move only 20 feet** (6 m) **per minute,** so it **would take** them **more than four hours** to walk a **mile** (1.6 km).

11 A **scientist** found that it took a **three-fingered sloth** living in the **Costa Rican rainforest** about **half a month** to **digest its food.**

12 **Slow-swimming manatees** can only **reach speeds** of **five miles an hour** (8 km/h), but they are so large and their skin is so tough that other animals don't try to eat them.

14 **Scientists** think that sloths may have developed such **slow movements** to **avoid catching** the **eye** of **hawks** and **wild cats.**

13 **Sloths** can **slow down** their **metabolism** (how much energy their bodies use) **if it is too cold or too hot.**

15 Generally, **sloths move** about **123 feet** (38 m) a **day,** which is about half a city block.

16 **Scientists** aren't sure how **Greenland sharks** capture seals, but one theory suggests they **sneak up** on the **seals** when they are **sleeping.**

18

Sea anemones, known as flowers of the sea, are slow-moving saltwater animals that **attach themselves to rocks** and **other hard underwater surfaces.**

19 **Gila monsters walk slowly** on short legs, **swinging their tails** from side to side **for balance.**

20 Because these lizards are not very fast, **they have to sneak up on prey and bite them,** injecting powerful venom with their teeth.

17 **Koalas sleep** or **rest** in eucalyptus trees for about **18 hours a day.**

21 **Koalas** live in **small areas** made up of just a **few eucalyptus trees,** and they **slowly move between them.**

22 **Seahorses** move up and down by **adjusting** the **amount of air** in their **swim bladders,** tiny pockets inside their bodies.

23 It would take a **seahorse** about an **hour** to **swim five feet** (1.5 m)—and that's when swimming "fast"!

24

Water snails tend to **move faster** than **land snails.**

25 **Snails** move the **bottom** of their **single foot** in a **wavelike motion** to travel slowly along the ground.

15 PERFECT FACTS ABOUT PETS IN HISTORY

1

Socks, President Bill Clinton's cat, was the first presidential pet to have a website, and he signed fan mail with a paw print.

2

Wolfgang Amadeus Mozart had a pet starling, a type of small bird, that would sometimes mimic his piano playing.

3

The dog that played Toto, Dorothy's pup in *The Wizard of Oz*, was paid $125 a week—more than some of the human actors.

4. Charles Schulz, the creator of the "Peanuts" comic strip, had two dogs as a boy, named Snooky and Spike. In the comic, Snoopy's brother is named Spike.

5

Artist Frida Kahlo used her pet deer as a model for her famous painting "The Wounded Deer," in which her head appears on the body of a deer, injured by arrows.

6. **President Andrew Jackson had a pet parrot** that was known to speak curse words.

7. **Mary Queen of Scots, had up to 22 lapdogs at one time,** most of which were pugs, spaniels, and Maltese terriers.

8. **Freddie Mercury,** singer of the band Queen, **wrote a song about his cat Delilah.**

10

President George H. W. Bush's dog Millie had a best-selling book that made almost $1 million in royalties.

9. **British Prime Minister Winston Churchill watched films with his pet poodle, Rufus,** and covered the dog's eyes during scary parts.

11. **President Franklin D. Roosevelt's Scottie, Fala, attended secret meetings** and even gave up his toys to promote a rubber collection drive during World War II.

12. **President George W. Bush's Scottish terrier Barney once filmed the White House Christmas decorations** from the vantage point of his collar, which had a camera attached to it.

13

The **first dog to orbit Earth was Laika,** who was aboard the Soviet Sputnik 2 mission in 1957.

14

The **Beatles song "Martha My Dear"** was about **Paul McCartney's sheepdog.**

15

Bo, President Barack Obama's Portuguese water dog, had his own trading card.

lynx

1. Scientists think that **wild cats started living around farmers** in what is today part of the **Middle East** and, **over thousands of years,** became **domesticated.**

2. There are more domestic cats in the world than any wild cat species.

3. More than **30 species of wild cats** are alive today, and they live on **all continents except Antarctica.**

4. Domestic cats have been called **"the lion of mice"** for their **exceptional hunting** techniques.

5. Big cats—lions, tigers, jaguars, leopards, and snow leopards— **diverged from other smaller wild cat species** like cheetahs and pumas some **11.5 million years ago.**

6. Clouded leopards make their **homes** in the **cloud forests** of **Southeast Asia,** where they use special pads on their feet to grip tree branches.

7. Small wild cats are **solitary unless** they are **mating** or **raising kittens.**

8. The **sand cat** sleeps during the day in **underground burrows** to stay out of the intense Sahara heat.

9. Clouded leopards cannot purr or **roar,** but they **can growl** and **hiss.**

10. About the size of a domestic cat, the **endangered bay cat** is only found in the **forests** on the Southeast Asian island of **Borneo.**

11. Fishing cats have **tails** that act like **rudders** when they are swimming, **double-coated fur** to **repel water,** and **partially webbed front toes.**

12. The **fishing cat** and the **flat-headed cat dunk their heads** in **rivers** and **streams** to search for prey.

13. Flat-headed cats have **backward-facing teeth** to keep fish they've caught from escaping their mouths.

14. People started to **breed domestic cats** into **different cat breeds** in the 1800s.

15. In **ancient Egypt,** pet cats were thought to bring **good luck** to a household.

16. Wealthy ancient Egyptians **dressed** their pet **cats in jewels** and **fed** them **fancy treats.**

17. Small wild cats are almost fully grown by the time they are one year old.

18. Caracals can **swat a bird** from the sky with a single paw.

19. At less than two feet (0.6 m) tall, a **caracal can jump up to 10 feet** (3 m) **in the air.**

20. The **smallest wild cat,** the **rusty-spotted cat, weighs less** than many **laptop computers.**

21. Long fur on their **cheeks** makes **Canada lynx** look as if they have **beards.**

22. The **Chinese mountain cat**— the only wild cat from China— uses a **keen sense of hearing** to **dig rodents** out of their **underground** burrows.

23. A group of clouded leopards is called a leap.

24. Two **Iberian lynx,** an endangered species of lynx that lives on the Iberian Peninsula in Europe, **walked** some **1,500 miles** (2,400 km) **to find new territories**—that's about the distance from Chicago, Illinois, to Miami, Florida, U.S.A.

25. Servals, which live in Africa, use their **ultrasonic hearing** to find mice and shrews underground, **reaching** their **long legs** into the **burrows** to snatch them.

26. Servals are often **born** about **a month before** the local rodent population is at its highest.

27. Videos of the Pallas's cat's **grumpy-looking facial expression** made the **wild cat** an **internet star.**

75 PURR-FECT FACTS ABOUT (MOSTLY) WILD SMALL AND MEDIUM CATS

28. The **supersensitive whiskers** of wild cats are **located** on their **chins,** as well as beside their noses, on their **cheeks,** and **above** their **eyes.**

29. The small Japanese island of **Iriomote** is the only place where you will find **Iriomote cats,** a subspecies of leopard with a dark, spotted coat.

30. Iriomote cats have lived on the island for **90,000 years.**

31. Pallas's cats live in **snowy grasslands** at high elevations and have the **densest fur** of any cat species.

32. Africa's black-footed cat, which lives in abandoned termite mounds, is also called the **"anthill tiger"** because of how **ferociously** it **fights** if threatened.

33. About half the size of a domestic cat, the **güiña,** which lives in South America, **climbs** trees to **catch** and **eat birds.**

34. Unlike in humans, the **shoulder blades** of small wild cats are **not connected to their skeletons,** which gives them **excellent flexibility.**

35. Bobcats have **stubby** or **"bobbed" tails** that are black on the top and white on the underside.

36. The **black-footed cat** can **walk** about **20 miles** (32 km) **every night**—almost the length of a marathon—searching for food.

37. While much smaller than tigers, **clouded leopards** have **two-inch (5-cm)-long canine teeth**—about the same size as tiger teeth.

38. Small wild cats **can see** blues **and greens but** not reds.

39. A **blind cat** can use its whiskers to **sense** the **air currents flowing** around **objects** to avoid walking into them.

40. Wild cats have **claws** and **flexible wrists** they use to grab and tear apart prey.

41. In zoos, **flat-headed cats** will **play** for hours in **pools.**

42. Servals are nicknamed the **"giraffe cat"** for their **extra-long necks** and **legs.**

43. Only about **700 Eurasian lynx** were **alive** in the **mid-20th century,** but **today** the population is around **50,000.**

44. The **rough feel** of a cat's **tongue** comes from **tiny "hooks"** made from the same material as your fingernails.

45. Fluffy cottontail rabbits are bobcats' favorite **prey.**

46. Some people in the **United Kingdom** call domestic cats **"moggies."**

47. Living in the Andes mountain range of South America, the **Andean cat** wraps its **tail** around its **face** to keep its **nose warm** while it sleeps.

48. Some ancient Egyptians kept servals as pets.

49. Pallas's cats' scientific genus name, *Otocolobus,* means **"ugly-eared."**

50. Sand cats are able to live in areas where the **temperatures** range from about **120°F** (49°C) to **freezing.**

51. In bright **sunlight,** most cat **pupils close up** into vertical slits, but the **Pallas's cat's pupils contract** into small, round dots.

52. Domestic cats can **leap up to nine times their body length** straight up in the air to **grab a toy.**

53. When living around people, güiñas are **active at night,** but if people aren't around they are **active during the day.**

54. Based on 30-million-year-old fossil fragments found in southern France, **scientists** think that the **first "true" cats evolved** in **Europe.**

55. With short limbs and long bodies, **jaguarundis,** which live in Central and South America, are sometimes called **"weasel cats."**

56. All **small wild cats** have about **24 whiskers.**

57. Jaguarundis communicate with at least 13 different calls, from whistles to birdlike chirps.

58. In 2015, a **bobcat** was **photographed dragging a shark out of the ocean** and onto a Florida beach—the first time a bobcat was seen fishing in salt water.

59. Rusty-spotted cats, which usually live in the forests of India and Sri Lanka, have been found **living** in the **rafters** of **abandoned houses.**

60. The **marbled cat,** which lives in the forests of Southeast Asia, is so **elusive** that so far only one has been studied in the wild.

61. Five different wild cats share the same region in **Suriname,** a small country in South America: **puma, ocelot, margay, jaguar,** and **jaguarundi.**

62. But only **three** different kinds of wild cats are found in the **United States: Canada lynx, bobcats,** and **ocelots.**

63. Margay cats **grab prey with their paws** while **hanging** from a tree branch.

64. The domestic cat breed Selkirk Rex—or **poodle cat**—has **extra-fluffy, three-layered fur.**

65. In the **United States,** the **bobcat** is the **most numerous wild cat** species.

66. Canada lynx are strong enough to **chase down caribou.**

67. Chinese mountain cat moms hide their **kittens** in burrows to keep them **safe** from predators such as bears and wolves.

68. In 2018, **Waffle the Warrior,** a 10-year-old pet cat in California, U.S.A., **jumped seven feet** (2.1 m), the longest jump by a house cat.

69. Margay cats can **climb down trees headfirst.**

70. Africa's sand cat has **sand-colored fur** that even grows on its **paws,** probably to keep its feet from burning on the hot desert ground.

71. A **museum** dedicated to cats in **Krakow, Poland,** showcases about **1,000 cat-themed trinkets.**

72. Since the **Iberian lynx** relies on European hares as its main food, the wild cat became **critically endangered** when a virus wiped out most of the hares where the lynx lives.

73. Pallas's cats hide behind rocks, waiting to pounce on the rodentlike pikas, hares, and squirrels they eat.

74. A successful hunter, **Africa's black-footed cat catches its prey** about **60 percent** of the time, whereas a **lion** only catches its prey about **25 percent** of the time.

75. Female bobcats pile moss and leaves to make their dens comfortable, moving their kittens between a few different dens to keep them safe.

1
Up to **4,000 coyotes** live in the Chicago, Illinois, U.S.A., area.

2
A **coyote** in downtown **Chicago** spent its life **living in a cemetery,** eating food that people left on graves.

3
A pair of **coyotes** raised a **litter of pups** in the parking lot of the **Chicago Bears** football team's **Soldier Field Stadium.**

4
In **Tokyo, Japan,** *tanuki,* also called **raccoon dogs,** scavenge at night. They are portrayed as pranksters in folktales.

5
In one area of **New York City,** ants ate **2,100 pounds** (950 kg) of **food** left on the **sidewalk** in a year.

6
That's the equivalent of **60,000 hot dogs.**

7
There are about **18 foxes per 0.4 square mile** (1 sq km) living in **London, England.**

8
In 2016, a **seal pup** wandered into a **restaurant** in San Diego, California, U.S.A.

9
The world's **pigeon** population is more than **400 million,** most of which live in cities.

10
Rat sightings reported to **New York City's** non-emergency hotline **increased 37 percent** between 2014 and 2019.

11
There are **leeches** in **freshwater ponds** in New York City.

12
About **30 pairs** of **peregrine falcons** fly in the skies above **London, England.**

13
As long as **5,000 years ago,** people put out **birdhouses** to encourage **pigeons** to live close to them.

35 FACTS ABOUT CITY-SLICKER ANIMALS

14
In a problem-solving experiment with **finches**, urban birds were better at getting food.

15
Trained falcons are used in cities to keep other birds from pooping on buildings or bothering outdoor diners.

16
In one study, 80 percent of **city raccoons** could **get into a secured trash can**, but none of the country ones could.

17
About **35 leopards** live on the edge of **Mumbai, India**—a city with a population of more than 20 million people.

18
So many **pigeons pooped** into the **ocean** in Venice, California, that officials issued a **no-swim policy** in the area.

19
Mountain lions that live in **rural areas** have **14 times** the amount of territory that **urban mountain lions** have.

20
More **raccoons** live in **cities** than live in the **country.**

21
Every day at dusk between July and November, **1.5 million free-tailed bats fly out** from **under a bridge** in downtown Austin, Texas, U.S.A.

22
A video of a **New York City rat** went viral when the rat was filmed carrying a slice of **pizza** into a **subway station.**

23
A **man** dressed in a **rat costume** re-enacted the scene as **performance art.**

24
In 2017, more than a **third of U.S. homeowners** reported seeing a **rodent** in their **house**, according to a survey.

25
Cockroaches are found in **New Orleans** more often than in any other U.S. city.

26
In the Japanese city of **Nara, sika deer wander the streets** untouched because they are considered sacred.

27
Not seen in **San Francisco Bay, California**, since World War II, **porpoises** returned in 2011, swimming under the Golden Gate Bridge.

28
An image of a **flying squirrel** was caught on a motion-triggered **camera** near a **cemetery** in **Chicago.**

29
A **mountain lion** was **photographed** in **downtown Los Angeles,** California, near the Hollywood sign.

30
Eagles, bobcats, and **ravens** have all been spotted near the Potomac River in **Washington, D.C., U.S.A.**

31
There are plans to build a **wildlife bridge** over a highway in **Los Angeles** to help wildlife safely cross.

32
Snowy owls have been spotted on **New York City's Governor's Island.**

33
Pigeons naturally make their homes on rocky cliffs, so they are **comfortable** with **concrete urban landscapes.**

34
You can watch a live **webcam** of **sea lions** lounging on San Francisco's Pier 39, a popular tourist spot.

35
Tampa, Florida; Scottsdale, Arizona; and Atlanta, Georgia, have been named the **most pet-friendly cities** in the U.S.A.

1. Squirrels run in a jagged, zigzag motion to escape predators such as hawks. 2. A ladybug can eat 5,000 insects during its life. 3. Copperhead snakes use their yellow-tipped tails to lure prey. 4. When white-headed woodpeckers, which live in the forests of the Pacific Northwest, eat pine seeds, they cling to the bottom or sides of the pine cones to avoid the sticky sap. 5. The largest brown bears live along the coast and on the islands of southern Alaska—males weigh about 850 pounds (380 kg), more than a large motorcycle. 6. A raccoon's ringed tail can be about half as long as its body. 7. Bald eagles are born with pink legs; they turn yellow when they are about three weeks old. 8. Raccoons use their front paws and long fingers to snag frogs and other animals from ponds and streams. 9. About half the eight-inch (20-cm) length of red tree voles comes from their tail. 10. Moose, the largest member of the deer family, can weigh more than half a ton (450 kg) and stand six feet (1.8 m) tall at their shoulders. 11. The long tail of Cooper's hawks helps them maneuver through the forest as they hunt birds. 12. The Cooper's hawk captures prey with its feet and squeezes it to death. 13. Mule deer get their name from their large ears, which can be almost as long as their heads. 14. The timber rattlesnake makes a buzzing sound with its rattle when threatened. 15. Each one of a rattlesnake's rattles is also called a "button," and a new button is added each time the snake sheds its skin. 16. Gray wolves are the most widespread land mammal after humans and livestock. 17. Some woodpeckers can "drum" on a tree with their beaks as fast as 22 times a second. 18. In the late 1800s, Americans introduced the eastern gray squirrel into newly developed city parks, such as Central Park in New York City, U.S.A., to bring "nature" to city dwellers. 19. In the 1980s, scientists discovered that people were handing out more than 75 pounds (34 kg) of peanuts each week in Lafayette Park in Washington, D.C., U.S.A., leading to the highest density of squirrels ever recorded. 20. Great gray owls are the largest owls in North America—some even have wingspans that stretch about five feet (1.5 m). 21. Great gray owls don't build nests but use abandoned ones from ravens, raptors, and even gray squirrels. 22. Chipmunks sleep for about 15 hours a day. 23. Ladybugs secrete a bad-smelling liquid from their legs when threatened. 24. Female hawks are slightly larger than male hawks, which scientists think may have to do with protecting their nest. 25. Binturongs, small mammals that live in the rainforests of Southeast Asia, are also called bear cats because of their catlike heads and bearlike bodies. 26. Common around human developments, red foxes can jump over barriers that are more than six feet (2 m) high. 27. Only the underside of the tail of a white-tailed deer is white, which it flashes as an alarm signal. 28. Timber rattlesnakes can climb more than 80 feet (24 m) up into trees. 29. Male eastern gray squirrels are generally more active during the winter, and females are more active during the summer. 30. Red foxes wrap their fluffy tails around their bodies to keep warm. 31. When looking for their next meal, ticks grab on to a blade of grass with four of their legs and extend the other two legs to hop onto a host, such as a deer or human. 32. The coat color of Eurasian red squirrels can vary from all black to all red, and they have long tufts on their ears. 33. By 1919 European bison were extinct in the wild, but today a few thousand live in European forests, descendants of a program that bred animals kept in zoos. 34. Related to deer, elk are also known as *wapiti,* a Native American word that means "light-colored deer." 35. Hazel dormice, small rodents that are only about five inches (13 cm) long (not including their tail), have double-jointed ankles on their hind feet that let them climb down trees headfirst. 36. Some scientists think that a raccoon's black eye "mask" reduces glare and helps it hunt at night. 37. Squirrels are most active a few hours after the sun rises and a few hours before it sets. 38. Moose shed their antlers every winter and grow a new pair in the spring. 39. A big moose's antlers can stretch six feet (1.8 m) across from tip to tip. 40. Brown bears have curved, four-inch (10-cm)-long claws for digging up roots to eat and scooping out dirt to make a den. 41. A ladybug's bright colors—pink, yellow, or red—serve as a warning to other animals to not eat them. 42. Eurasian red squirrels have been seen peeling bark off of trees to get to the tasty sap beneath. 43. Acorn woodpeckers stash acorns inside holes that they've drilled into trees. 44. Scientists have found as many as 50,000 acorns hidden in one tree. 45. Legend holds that if ravens stop living in the Tower of London in Great Britain, the British empire will fall. 46. A woodpecker's powerful neck muscles and thick skull protect its body when it drills into trees with its bill to find insects. 47. The black rat snake can be as long as a sofa. 48. The scientific genus for the white-headed woodpecker, *Dryobates,* means "tree walker."

»100 FANTASTIC FACTS ABOUT FOREST CREATURES

49. Male mule deer engage in epic battles—they lock antlers and fight until one deer becomes exhausted. 50. Half a raccoon's weight can be made up of fat. 51. Squirrels are important to the forests they live in because new trees sprout from some of the seeds the squirrels bury in the ground. 52. According to some Native American myths, the Raven made all living things. 53. Hazel dormice sleep at the bottom of trees underneath leaves or in logs, and they have even been heard snoring. 54. Wood frog tadpoles seem to be able to recognize one another, as they form groups in the ponds where they hatch. 55. The distinctive "hump" on a brown bear's back is a powerful muscle that helps it dig and strike with its paws. 56. Squirrels are so agile they can climb upside down along a wire. 57. When possible, raccoons examine their food—fruit, insects, plants, eggs, and even garbage—underwater because their sense of touch is even better in water. 58. Studies have shown that raccoons can remember how to solve tasks for up to three years. 59. Bald eagles can survive for days without eating. 60. The smallest chipmunk species in North America, the least chipmunk, weighs about the same as a chocolate bar. 61. Bull elk, with huge antlers that can be six feet (1.8 m) wide, are one of the most photographed animals in Yellowstone National Park, U.S.A. 62. Northern goshawks, raptors that live in the Northern Hemisphere, can capture snowshoe hares twice their weight. 63. In Roman mythology, twin boys Romulus and Remus founded the city of Rome, Italy, and were cared for by a she-wolf as infants. 64. Ravens have been known to follow an animal's tracks to steal what remains of their captured prey. 65. Chipmunks hibernate over the winter but waken every so often to eat from their stash of seeds and nuts. 66. Binturongs have glands that spread their scent—which is said to smell like buttered popcorn or corn chips—to mark their territory. 67. Red tree voles can eat conifer needles from evergreen trees because they strip away the resin ducts that make the needles taste bad. 68. Ravens are the largest perching bird in North America. 69. Some ticks produce a sticky substance that keeps their feeding tube attached to an animal as they suck its blood. 70. Ladybugs hibernate in rotting logs over the winter. 71. Created in the 1920s, "bear claw" pastries have two sets of "claws" that separate as the treat is baked. 72. Ravens have been seen unzipping zippers to get at food. 73. Gray wolves in Yellowstone National Park live in packs of about 10 animals led by an alpha male and alpha female. The pack patrols a home territory, hunts, and cares for young wolves together. 74. In Norse mythology, the lord of all the gods, Odin, has two ravens who sit on his shoulder and tell him what they see as they fly around the world each day. 75. The bushy tail of red foxes, which has either a white or a black tip, is called a brush. 76. The way ladybugs unfold their flight wings gives scientists ideas for improving the design of umbrellas. 77. Mac the Moose, a giant moose statue in Saskatchewan, Canada, towers 34 feet (10.4 m) over the landscape. 78. Mule deer jump off the ground with all four feet at once in a move known as "stotting." 79. Townsend chipmunks, which live in the northwest United States, can hold as many as 100 oats in their cheek pouches. 80. Male moose have antlers, female moose don't. 81. A red-bellied woodpecker's tongue can extend two inches (5 cm) past its beak. 82. Binturongs make snorting and chuckling sounds when they're happy. 83. A newborn elk calf can stand 20 minutes after birth. 84. Black bears have short claws that they use to climb trees. 85. Hazel dormice were popular pets in Victorian England and were traded by kids in the schoolyard. 86. Brown bears usually give birth to two cubs in the winter, each weighing only about two pounds (1 kg). 87. Red foxes hunt on their own, not in packs. 88. Male elk make a high-pitched whistle and a low bellow to attract females. 89. The word "raccoon" comes from a Native American word that means "an animal that scratches with its hands." 90. Flocks of broad-winged hawks migrate from the eastern United States every year to spend the winter in Central or South America, traveling on drafts of thermal air instead of actively flying. 91. These flocks, called kettles, can sometimes contain thousands of hawks. 92. The heaviest chipmunk, the eastern chipmunk, weighs only 4.4 ounces (125 g). 93. Red foxes communicate with one another using facial expressions. 94. In the United Kingdom, ladybugs are called ladybirds. 95. Squirrels were popular pets in the United States in the 19th century. 96. Very agile climbers, raccoons can drop from the height of a four-story building without injury. 97. The nests of red tree voles, more than 200 feet (60 m) up in evergreen trees, have a separate bathroom area and a "kitchen." 98. White-tailed deer stay in groves of evergreen trees to protect them from winter snows. 99. They grow thicker coats for the winter and also have special glands that produce an oil that makes the hair waterproof. 100. To attract a mate, broad-winged hawks fly high in circles and then drop headlong, stopping right before reaching the ground.

great gray owl

1

RHINOCEROSES have CUP-SHAPED EARS that they can MOVE INDEPENDENTLY.

2

WOLVES have SMALLER and more ROUNDED EARS compared to their coyote cousins.

3

AFRICAN ELEPHANTS have the LARGEST EARS on EARTH.

4

CHORUSES of COQUI FROGS can be as LOUD as a lawn mower.

5

BLUE WHALES make WHISTLING CALLS UNDERWATER TO COMMUNICATE with one another.

6

THESE CALLS are sometimes LOUDER THAN a JET ENGINE.

7

The LONGEST EARS on a dog belonged to Tigger, a BLOOD-HOUND whose ears were 13.75 INCHES (34.9 cm) LONG—longer than a TOASTER!

8

BUSH PIGS living in Africa have LONG TASSELS of hair on their ears.

9

To stay warm during the winter, EURASIAN RED SQUIRRELS grow THICK HAIR on their EARS.

10

The term "LOP" refers to any RABBIT breed with EARS that HANG DOWN beside its head.

11

SEA LIONS have SMALL FLAPS OF SKIN FOR OUTER EARS, while seals have small earholes.

12

The LAMANCHA GOAT breed is known for its VERY SMALL EARS: They're only about ONE INCH (2.5 cm) in size.

13

In VERTEBRATES, the ABILITY TO HEAR FIRST EVOLVED in FISH living hundreds of millions of years ago.

14

Like other birds, PENGUINS don't have external ears; the holes to their INNER EARS are covered by feathers.

15

Grasshoppers, locusts, and crickets have EARS on their KNEES.

16

HOMING PIGEONS can hear sounds at VERY LOW FREQUENCIES; scientists think they use these sounds to help them NAVIGATE.

17

A DONKEY'S LARGE EARS may help COOL the blood that flows through them.

18

TURTLES and TOR-TOISES LACK EAR OPENINGS, but they can still hear a limited range of sounds.

19

GREAT GRAY OWLS can hear SMALL MAMMALS MOVING under a FOOT (0.3 m) of SNOW, and they plunge their talons deep into the snow to snatch them.

20

Just like humans', BIRDS' HEARING can be DAM-AGED if they are around loud noises too much.

21

When upset, RABBITS PIN THEIR EARS DOWN to their heads or TURN THEM BACKWARD.

22

ELEPHANTS FLAP their EARS to MOVE AIR around their bodies like a FAN.

23

The GREATER BILBY, a small mammal from Australia, has poor eyesight, so it USES ITS LONG EARS to help FIND INSECTS TO EAT.

24

The EAR OPENINGS on a barn owl's head are at different levels and angles, which helps AMPLIFY SOUNDS.

25

Even when KING PENGUINS are ASLEEP, they can tell the differ-ence between a SOUND a predator like an orca makes and harmless sounds.

SAY WHAT?

50 FACTS ABOUT ANIMAL HEARING

26

Scientists think that the ability of the GREATER WAX MOTH to hear sounds at a HIGHER FREQUENCY helps them avoid being eaten by bats, which use similar high-frequency sounds.

27

MOSQUITOES hear with HAIRS on their ANTENNAE that sense VIBRATIONS in the air.

28

SQUID and OCTOPUSES can DETECT some SOUNDS with an organ that has sensitive hairs.

29

MALE COQUI FROGS in Puerto Rico CROAK to ATTRACT FEMALES.

30

CATS can HEAR a larger RANGE OF SOUNDS than dogs can.

31

Many FISH HEAR by listening to VIBRATIONS from their SWIM BLADDERS, which allow them to control how buoyant they are.

32

When LARGE GROUPS of HOWLER MONKEYS CALL TOGETHER, the SOUND can be HEARD up to THREE MILES (5 km) AWAY.

33

"ELEPHANT EARS" are made from dough that's rolled flat, fried, and powdered with sugar and cinnamon.

34

A NAKED MOLE RAT'S EARS are just a small BUMP on each side of its head.

35

A DEAF POLAR BEAR named Alaska lived at the MARYLAND ZOO in Baltimore, U.S.A. Keepers used HAND SIGNALS to communicate with her.

36

BOTTLENOSE DOLPHINS have EAR-HOLES that are only about one-tenth of an inch (2.5 mm) across.

37

CAPYBARAS have EYES, EARS, and NOSTRILS on the TOP of their HEADS so that they can stay alert for predators when submerged underwater.

38

SNAKES HEAR by sensing VIBRATIONS that travel through the air.

39

The FENNEC FOX's EARS ALLOW it to HEAR PREY moving UNDERGROUND.

40

Its GIANT EARS can be HALF A FOOT (15 cm) LONG.

41

LYNX have TUFTS of black hair above their ears, which some scientists think may help them HEAR better.

42

TOOTHED WHALES pick up sounds through FATTY TISSUES located in their JAWS.

43

MEERKATS can CLOSE their EARS to keep out sand when digging for insects to eat.

44

BLACK-TAILED JACKRABBITS can have EARS that are almost as LONG as an iPad.

45

BASSET HOUNDS have LONG EARS that flap around their face as they walk, MOVING SMELLS to the dog's sensitive NOSE.

46

When MALE KAKAPOS are LOOKING for a MATE, their CALLS can be HEARD for as long as EIGHT HOURS.

47

A MALE KAKAPO makes about twenty *boom* calls and a HIGH-PITCHED *CHING* call that helps the female bird find him.

48

CATS can MOVE each of their EARS SEPARATELY to pick up a wide range of sounds.

49

A LION'S EAR PLANT produces ORANGE FUZZY FLOWERS.

50

The SPOTTED BAT ROLLS UP ITS EARS around its head when RESTING.

Siamese kittens

5,000 AWESOME FACTS ABOUT ANIMALS

1 Oxpeckers, a type of bird, eat ticks that live on the backs of animals, like rhinos: The **oxpecker gets food** and the **rhino gets rid of parasites.**

2 Along the coast of the Black Sea, **frogs hop on water buffalo to eat flies** that land on their fur.

3 **Meat ants eat** a **sugary substance** made by **caterpillars,** and in return the **ants act as bodyguards,** protecting the caterpillars before they morph into butterflies.

4 **Oxpeckers warn rhinos** if **danger** is **approaching** by flying off and screeching.

5

When **different animals live together** for a long time and **help each other** it's called **mutualism;** when **one is helped** and the **other isn't** helped or harmed it's called **commensalism.**

25 HELPFUL FACTS ABOUT ANIMALS THAT WORK

6 **Zebras** and **wildebeests** are often found in the same area of the African savanna: **Zebras eat** the **harder parts** of the **plants** and the **wildebeests eat** the **softer parts.**

7

Pederson shrimps seek protection from **sea anemones** in exchange for cleaning debris caught in the anemones' mucus.

8 **Tiger groupers open their mouths wide** and let **cleaner gobies eat bits of food stuck there;** the groupers get clean and the gobies get fed.

9 **Scientists** think **remora fish evolved** to have **streamlined bodies** so they **don't slow down** the **manta rays** they latch on to.

10 When prey is hiding, **coral trout** move back and forth in front of **moray eels,** "asking" them to flush it out.

11 **Coral trout** remember which **moray eels** are **best** at the **job** and **return** to the **same ones** over and over.

12 Carrier crabs carry venomous sea urchins on their backs that poke predators that come near.

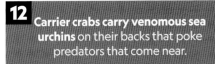

13 Coyotes and badgers are more successful hunting prairie dogs and ground squirrels when they work together than on their own.

14 Clownfish cover themselves in a sticky mucus to avoid getting stung by sea anemones.

15 In Uganda, warthogs seek out mongooses and lie down next to them so the mongooses will pick ticks off their backs.

16 Coyotes chase down the prey and badgers dig after them if they escape to an underground burrow.

17 Ostriches hang out near zebras because zebras stir up insects that the large birds like to eat.

18 Ostriches alert zebras, which don't have very good eyesight, when lions are approaching.

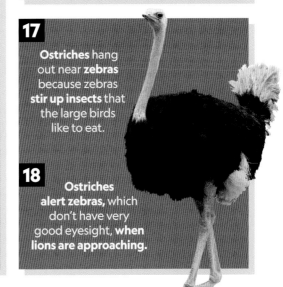

TOGETHER

19 Hawaiian monk seals turn over rocks to look for prey and other fish follow, hoping to steal some of the food.

20 Tiny frogs and giant tarantulas live side by side in Sri Lanka, Peru, and India, where the spiders offer the frogs some protection from predators, and the frogs eat small insects that try to steal the remains of the spider's prey.

21 Remora, aka suckerfish, catch a ride on lemon sharks—they latch on to clean parasites off the sharks' skin.

22 Drongos, an African bird, warn meerkats that danger is near by making loud calls.

23 Sometimes drongos trick meerkats with a false cry, which causes the meerkat to drop its food and run, providing the drongo a free meal.

24 In Israeli's Negev desert, gray wolves and striped hyenas hunt together in packs—the wolves are better hunters and the hyenas are better at smelling prey.

25 Suckerfish also snack on lemon sharks' leftovers after they've had a feeding frenzy.

15 SANDY FACTS ABOUT SEABIRDS

1
Seabirds that **fly long distances** over the **ocean** use their **sense of smell** to find **prey** far below.

2
The **wandering albatross** can fly more than **500 miles** (805 km) in a single day **without flapping its wings.**

3
The **calls** from a colony of **sooty terns** are **so loud** that the bird is **nicknamed** the **"wide-awake" tern.**

4. **The pelican** uses its **large throat pouch** like a **fishing net,** catching **prey** and then **draining the water** before it **swallows** it.

5
Every year during **breeding season**, the **American white pelican** grows a **horn** on its **beak** that later **falls off**.

6. The **ashy storm-petrel** weighs just about **1.3 ounces** (37 g), less than a golf ball.

7. Unlike other seabirds, **frigatebirds** don't have waterproof feathers. Instead of floating, they stay **airborne** for up to **six weeks** at a time.

8. Tens of millions of **seabirds** nest on the coasts of **Alaska** each summer.

10
In **China**, fishermen have used **trained cormorants** to **catch fish** for more than 1,300 years.

9. Cormorants can **dive 150 feet** (46 m) below the water's surface for food.

11. Short-tailed shearwaters migrate from **Australia** to **Alaska**, U.S.A.

12. The **little penguin** is the **smallest species** of penguin, weighing just **two pounds** (1 kg).

13
Seabirds have **glands** near their bills that **get rid of extra salt** from their blood. This allows them to **drink seawater**.

14
Penguins have **short feathers** similar to fish scales, which help them **swim**.

15
In 2017, the **world's oldest bird**, an **albatross**, had a **baby** at **age 66**.

1. Capable of **sprinting** more than **40 miles an hour** (64 km/h), **ostriches** are the **fastest two-legged land animals.**

2. **Fox cubs** use a **tug-of-war method** to **break open** a prey's **carcass.**

3. **Golden eagles,** one of the fastest flying birds, **sometimes play with sticks,** dropping them from high in the sky and then swooping down to retrieve them.

4. **Sailfish** have been clocked **leaping out of the water** at speeds of **68 miles an hour** (109 km/h)—as fast as a cheetah!

5. The **Anna's hummingbird** can **travel 385 body lengths** in **one second.**

6. **Cheetahs, the** world's **fastest land animal, can go from** zero to 60 miles an hour (97 km/h) in three seconds—that's **faster acceleration than most cars!**

7. **Nectar bats** can **twist their wings** and **hover** over a flower, much like a hummingbird.

8. Pound for pound, **chimpanzees** are one and a half times **stronger** than **humans** when it comes to **pulling** and **jumping.**

9. **A rabbit jumps to show it's excited, a behavior called binking.**

10. **Harpy eagles,** which live in rainforests from Mexico to Argentina, have **strong talons** capable of **snatching** and **flying off with prey** like monkeys and sloths.

11. **Amazon river dolphins' flexible necks** help them **navigate** around **trees** in flooded rainforests.

12. The word **"jaguar"** comes from an Indigenous word *yaguar,* which means **"He who kills with one leap."**

13. **Greyhounds** have **extra thick pads** on their **feet** that help absorb shock when they're **running.**

14. **Cows** sometimes **leap** when **given a change of scenery,** like when they're let out of their barn and onto the grass.

15. The **horned dung beetle** can **pull 1,141 times its weight**—the equivalent of a 150-pound (70-kg) person pulling six double-decker buses.

16. **Sharks** are covered in **V-shaped denticles**—tiny scales that **reduce drag** and let them **move** through the water quickly.

17. **Springbok,** a type of antelope, are known for **"pronking"—jumping straight up** with a rounded back and their heads bowed down.

18. **Impalas** can **jump** up to **9 feet 10 inches** (3 m) over an obstacle ahead of them.

19. A **white-tailed jackrabbit** that is being chased **can jump 15 feet** (4.6 m) in a **single bound**—that's the **length** of a **small car!**

20. **Red kangaroos** use their **long tails** as a counterweight when they hop, which **propels** them **forward.**

21. **With** one leap out of the water, spinner dolphins can spin multiple times.

22. Researchers think **spinner dolphins** sometimes **spin to get rid of fish** that latch onto their skin.

23. When **cats** and **dogs suddenly zip around the house,** it's called the **zoomies**—also known as Frenetic Random Activity Periods—which are caused by **pent-up energy** that they need to release.

24. To gain speed to **leap** out of the water onto ice, **emperor penguins release bubbles from their feathers,** allowing them to **swim three times faster** than normal.

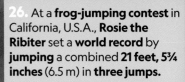

25. At a "goat yoga" studio **in** Oregon, U.S.A., goats wander around classes, sometimes lying next to participants **or** even climbing on their backs.

26. At a **frog-jumping contest** in California, U.S.A., **Rosie the Ribiter** set a **world record** by **jumping** a combined **21 feet, 5¾ inches** (6.5 m) in **three jumps.**

27. **Greyhounds,** the **fastest-running dog,** are sight dogs—they **chase game using their eyes** instead of following a scent.

28. In 2012, a **goat** named Happie set a **world record** by traveling **118 feet** (36 m) on a **skateboard.**

29. In the Bahamas, **pigs swim** in the **water** off tropical beaches.

30. If a **sailfish** and **23-time gold medal Olympian Michael Phelps** were to **compete** in a 200-meter race, the **sailfish** would **finish** in about **10 seconds** and **Phelps** in **1 minute 42 seconds.**

31. A **cheetah** can run **16 body lengths** in **one second;** a **mite** can run **322.**

75 FACTS ABOUT ATHLETIC ANIMALS THAT WILL MAKE YOU FLIP

32. Sea lions are so **flexible** their **heads** can **almost touch** their **backs.**

33. Snow leopards can **leap up to 50 feet** (15 m) in **one bound**— the **longest leap** of all the **big cats.**

34. The world record for high jump is 8 feet .45 inch (2.45 m); a **serval cat** can **leap more than nine feet** (2.7 m) **straight up.**

35. Grasshoppers **use muscles in their** knee **joints to catapult themselves** forward.

36. A **whippet dog** set a **world record** by **jumping 36 feet 2 inches** (11 m) off of a dock into water.

37. The **Amazing Acro-Cats,** a traveling group of rescued cats, perform **tricks like tightrope-walking** and **hoop-jumping.**

38. They may be **slow on land,** but **sloths** are **strong swimmers,** dropping from branches into rivers for a dip.

39. Brazilian free-tailed bats have been clocked at **99 miles an hour** (160 km/h) in level flight.

40. A **leopard** can **carry prey heavier** than **itself up a tree.**

41. In the **Iditarod,** an **8-to-15-day sled dog race** held annually in Alaska, **12 to 16 dogs pull a sled almost 1,000 miles** (1,609 km).

42. **Sifakas**—a type of primate— **move quickly** on the ground using a **two-legged side hop,** with their arms above their head to balance.

43. When threatened, **green basilisk lizards can run across the water** for up to **15 feet** (4.6 m).

44. **Flying snakes glide** from tree branch to tree branch, **fanning their ribs** to improve aerodynamics.

45. **The car company Jaguar** chose **its name** to reflect the **grace, agility, and power** of the **largest big cat in the Western Hemisphere.**

46. **Black-tailed prairie dogs** in Texas dug an extensive series of **tunnels**—called a town—that covered **25,000 square miles** (65,000 sq km).

47. An **elephant can lift 700 pounds** (318 kg) with its **trunk.**

48. In Southern California, **U.S.A., there is an** annual surfing competition **for dogs.**

49. **Spider monkeys** don't have thumbs, but their **tails** can **grip** on to **branches** when they swing from tree to tree.

50. **Leaf-cutter ants** use their jaws to **carry vegetation 20 times heavier** than **themselves.**

51. **Silverback gorillas** have **larger muscles** in their **arms** than in their legs, which is the opposite of humans.

52. Pound for pound, king snakes are the world's strongest constrictors, capable of killing other snakes 20 percent larger than they are.

53. **Guinea pigs hop straight up in the air** when they get **excited,** a movement called **popcorning.**

54. **Llamas,** which are sometimes used as pack animals, can **carry a load as heavy as 75 pounds** (34 kg).

55. **Pharaohs** in **ancient Egypt** used **greyhounds,** which can run faster than 35 miles an hour (56 km/h), to **help hunt small desert animals.**

56. **Male lizards** sometimes do **"push-ups"** to **warn** other lizards to stay out of their territory.

57. **Newfoundlands,** which have **partially webbed feet,** are sometimes used as **water rescue dogs.**

58. **Bini the bunny** holds a world record of **slam-dunking seven toy basketballs** on a **small hoop** in **one minute.**

59. **Boxers sometimes stand on their hind feet** and **"box"** with their **paws.**

60. While other **big cats** have **retractable claws, cheetahs'** are only **semi-retractable,** which helps them get a better grip when they sprint.

61. **Herding dogs,** such as collies, help farmers by **herding sheep** and **cows** into **pens.**

62. **Cheetahs** can **speed up** or **slow down** by **nine miles an hour** (14 km/h) in **one stride.**

63. **Labrador retrievers** have **tapered tails,** which help them **steer** in the **water.**

64. Researchers studied the **aerodynamic shape** of **king-fisher birds' heads** to improve the speed of Japanese bullet trains.

65. **Young chimpanzees** like to **play-wrestle** with each other.

66. **Marsh rabbits** can **swim underwater** to escape predators.

67. From a sitting position, **cats** can **spring up to nine times their height.**

68. **Grizzly bears** can **run** almost **twice as fast** as **polar bears.**

69. Some **goats** have **learned** how to **surf.**

70. **Japanese macaques** can **swim** the **equivalent of 10 laps** in an **Olympic-size pool.**

71. **Draco lizards** can **glide** through the air with **special flaps** of skin on their sides.

72. **Flying fish** can **glide** out of the water for up to **650 feet** (200 m)—the length of two football fields.

73. Flatfish use their fins to walk on the ocean floor.

74. A **great white shark** that researchers named Nicole **swam** from **South Africa** to **western Australia** and back—**12,427 miles** (20,000 km) **round-trip**— in less than nine months.

75. As the fastest-swimming shark, **shortfin makos** have earned the nickname **"blue dynamites."**

1

Animals that spend time **underground** and have **body parts adapted to digging** are known as **fossorial.**

2

Animals that **dig underground** often have **small eyes** and **ears** to help keep soil and sand from getting in them.

3

Termites build **cone-shaped mounds aboveground,** but the **colony lives** below the structure, **underground.**

4

In just one night, **aardwolves** can **slurp up 300,000 termites** using their **sticky tongues.**

5

Burrows not only **protect** the **animals** that live in them, but they can also help **prevent soil erosion.**

6

Tiny but tough mammals called **American pikas** build underground colonies in **harsh, rocky, treeless terrain.**

7

Honey badgers can **dig a burrow** in hard ground in just **10 minutes** with their sharp claws and strong legs.

8

But honey badgers have nothing on **aardvarks**—they can **dig a burrow** in **half that time.**

9

Male mole crickets dig **funnel-shaped tunnels** that act like **megaphones**—the crickets use them to call to females.

10

Millipedes lay between **20 and 300 eggs** in **loose soil.**

35 FACTS TO REALLY DIG INTO

11
Gophers can **move 2,000 pounds** (900 kg) of **dirt** in just **one year.**

12
Voles (also called meadow mice) create a **maze of aboveground "runways"** that **connect** their **underground nests.**

13
Voles, which come aboveground to eat plants, **stamp their hind feet** when **scared.**

14
Gray squirrels lick acorns before burying them in separate holes so that they can sniff out their food stashes again.

15
A **gopher's lips** are **behind its teeth** so the mammal **doesn't get dirt in its mouth** when digging.

16
As many as **50 mongooses** live in **underground colonies** and the group moves locations every few days.

17
Some **aardvark burrows** are **so large** that an **adult human** could **walk right in.**

18
Termites "farm" **fungus** that grows underground in their colonies. They use it to help **digest** the **tough wood** they eat.

19
Warthogs, which are active during the day, sleep at night in underground burrows.

20
Bilbys, rabbit-size marsupials that live in Australia, build **burrows** that can be **six feet** (1.8 m) **deep.**

21
In the winter, **black-footed ferrets** might **stay in their burrows for a week** before venturing outside.

22
Burrowing owls stash **food** in their **burrows;** in 1997 more than **200 dead rodents** were found in a single burrow.

23
Millipedes burrow through **soil** to **eat vegetation,** and if threatened they use their front legs to bury themselves.

24
In the 1800s, it was reported that a **prairie dog town** in Texas held **millions** of the **animals.**

25
Earthworms, also known as night crawlers, **feed aboveground** at night but **live underground** during the day.

26
Warthogs back into their **burrows** so their **sharp tusks** point outside and **scare away** potential **predators.**

27
Prairie dogs live in underground colonies called **"towns."** They use squeaky calls to alert colony members of danger.

28
After **cicadas** hatch from eggs, the **nymphs burrow underground,** where they live on the sap from tree roots.

29
Moles spend their **entire lives underground.**

30
Some **cicada species** can **live for 17 years,** but they spend most of that time **underground.**

31
Burrowing owls move into the **previous homes** of skunks or prairie dogs, digging to enlarge these underground dens.

32
Cathedral termites build **supertall mounds** aboveground, but these homes can also extend **several acres** (ha) underground.

33
When eating ants, the **giant anteater flicks its tongue** in and out as many as **150 times a minute.**

34
The **Botta's pocket gopher** pulls **plants** down by their **roots** to **eat** in its underground burrow.

35
Able to dig **6.5 feet** (1.9 m) **below** the **surface, earthworms** help **move nutrients** and **minerals** in the soil.

1. Octopuses, squid, cuttlefish, and nautiluses are cephalopods.
2. Most cephalopods have three hearts. 3. Octopuses have blue blood. 4. Cephalopods have doughnut-shaped brains.
5. Cephalopods have beaks similar to a parrot's. 6. Octopuses can remember humans. In captivity, they will crawl toward caretakers they like and squirt water at those they don't. 7. Nautiluses have up to 90 tentacles, the most of any cephalopod. 8. Octopuses can smell and taste with their suckers. 9. Nautiluses don't have suckers; their tentacles are covered with a sticky goo that helps them hold on to things. 10. The giant squid has eyes the size of basketballs.
11. Nautiluses are sometimes called "living fossils" because today's species look almost the same as extinct nautiluses from 500 million years ago. 12. The nautilus *Allonautilus scrobiculatus,* one of the rarest ocean animals, has only been spotted three times.
13. Cephalopods use jet propulsion to move through the water—the same force that launches rockets into space. 14. Cephalopods have soft bodies with no bones. (But nautiluses have shells.) 15. Squid and cuttlefish have eight arms plus two tentacles that they shoot out to grab prey. 16. Cephalopods are mollusks, the group of animals that also includes snails and slugs. 17. Some species of squid can swim as fast as 25 miles an hour (40 km/h)—that's as fast as some sharks!

octopus

18. Giant squid swim in all the world's oceans, but the first video of one in its natural habitat wasn't recorded until 2012. 19. Giant squid and sperm whales fight each other in the ocean's depths.
20. Vampire squid are named for their dark coloring and the webbing between their arms, which looks a bit like a vampire's cloak.
21. The deep-sea squid *Heteroteuthis dispar* has glow-in-the-dark ink. 22. The largest giant squid recorded was almost 43 feet (13 m) long. 23. Instead of a tongue, cephalopods have a radula, an organ covered with tiny toothlike projections. 24. If an octopus loses an arm, it can regrow it. 25. The 10-foot (3-m)-long tentacles of the colossal squid have swiveling hooks that help it grab hold of prey.
26. A 600-pound (272-kg) octopus can squeeze through a hole the size of a quarter. 27. Octopuses toss shells left over from their meals into trash heaps called middens outside their dens. 28. Two-thirds of an octopus's brain cells are in its arms, not its head. 29. Even if they're cut off, an octopus's arms will try to pick up food and feed the octopus. 30. The blue-ringed octopus has enough venom to kill 26 humans within minutes. It's the only octopus species that is dangerous to people. 31. Like chimpanzees and crows, octopuses are one of the few animals known to use tools. 32. Veined octopuses carry coconut shells to use as shelter. 33. Some cephalopods use their arms to "walk" along the seafloor. 34. Most squid are solitary, but bigfin reef squid come together and form a long line to scare off predators. 35. Captive octopuses can figure out how to open childproof pill bottles. 36. The flamboyant cuttlefish is just three inches (8 cm) long.
37. Nautiluses float by pumping gas and fluid in and out of their

»**100**
SLIPPERY FACTS ABOUT
OCTOPUSES AND THEIR RELATIVES

shell chambers—much the same way that a submarine moves. 38. Squids, octopuses, and cuttlefish can change their skin color to match their surroundings. 39. The mimic octopus can change its body shape to look like other animals, from a lionfish to a shrimp to a sea snake. 40. Cuttlefish have W-shaped pupils. 41. Octopuses can change their skin texture to match rocks, corals, or other surfaces nearby. 42. Octopuses can briefly come out of the water to hunt on land. 43. There are about 800 known species of cephalopod. 44. Cuttlefish can change to almost any color—but they're color-blind. 45. Squid use their color-changing skin to send messages to each other. 46. Cephalopods move by shooting water out of an organ called a siphon. 47. A giant octopus mother guards her eggs carefully: She blows oxygen-rich water over them, fends off predators, and never leaves them, not even to eat. 48. Cuttlefish sometimes flash colors and light at their prey, appearing to hypnotize it so they can move in for the kill. 49. Some scientists think cephalopods release clouds of ink the same shape and size as their body to confuse predators. 50. Most cephalopods live only a year or two. 51. The giant Pacific octopus hatches from an egg the size of a grain of rice, but can grow to be 16 feet (4.8 m) wide. 52. The deep-sea octopus *Graneledone boreopacifica* has been clocked taking care of its eggs for more than four years—the longest of any mother. 53. The nautilus lives in the largest of the chambers that make up its shell. 54. When the nautilus becomes too large for its chamber, it grows a new one and moves in. 55. An octopus can fit through any space larger than its beak. 56. The octopus *Haliphron atlanticus* catches jellyfish and uses their tentacles to entangle more prey. 57. The dumbo octopus has fins that resemble an elephant's ears. 58. Octopus suckers are strong: A large one can lift 35 pounds (16 kg). 59. Cuttlefish can see polarized light—like that reflected by glass and still water—better than any other known animal. 60. Octopus suckers can fold in half to pinch and pick up tiny bits of food. 61. Giant Pacific octopuses have about 280 suckers on each arm. 62. An octopus can change color in just three-tenths of a second. 63. An octopus can "see" (or detect light) with its skin. 64. Scientists invented a soft-bodied, squishable robot inspired by an octopus. 65. All octopuses have venom, which they use to paralyze prey. 66. Cuttlefish can change color to match their surroundings even in complete darkness. 67. While humans have iron in their blood to carry oxygen throughout their bodies, octopuses have copper. 68. Female blanket octopuses can grow

nautilus

to be six feet (1.8 m) long, but full-size males are less than an inch (2.5 cm) long. 69. Sperm whales are often found with circular scars from giant squid suckers. 70. Scientists believe all living squid may be members of the same species. 71. Smaller cuttlefish males change colors to disguise themselves as females to sneak past larger, rival males. 72. Cuttlefish can see in front of and behind themselves at the same time. 73. During the 19th century, cephalopod ink was used for writing, drawing, and painting. 74. One study found that cuttlefish can count at least to five. 75. The giant Pacific octopus can lay up to 100,000 eggs. 76. When scientists put cuttlefish in front of a checkerboard pattern, they were able to mimic it. 77. Octopuses change color while sleeping. Scientists think they might be dreaming. 78. The piglet squid is named for its large siphon that looks like a pig's snout. 79. Cephalopod means "head-foot" in Greek. 80. The smallest known octopus is *Octopus wolfi*—it's less than an inch (2.5 cm) long. 81. Cephalopod ink gets its color from melanin, the same pigment that colors human skin. 82. The giant Pacific octopus can move more than 700 pounds (318 kg). 83. Octopuses can solve mazes. 84. The striped pyjama squid (actually a species of cuttlefish) is named for the black-and-white stripes that cover its body. 85. A new robotic arm inspired by an octopus tentacle could help surgeons get to hard-to-reach parts of the human body. 86. The blanket octopus collects the stinging tentacles of Portuguese man-of-wars and holds them like weapons. 87. The southern pygmy squid has special glue glands on its back that it uses to stick to seagrass leaves so it can rest. 88. Sightings of giant squid may have inspired the legend of the kraken. 89. The Atlantic pygmy octopus uses its rasplike radula to drill a hole in crustacean shells, secretes poisonous saliva inside, and then eats its prey. 90. Giant Humboldt squid communicate by changing their color back and forth from red to white. 91. Octopuses can learn to complete a task by watching each other. 92. The larger Pacific striped octopus sneakily taps a shrimp on the back to scare it into the octopus's tentacles. 93. One species of deep-sea squid can detach its arms to distract predators. (They regrow them.) 94. Japanese flying squid can shoot themselves out of the water. 95. The word "octopus" means "eight foot." 96. About 17,000 species of extinct cephalopods have been discovered so far. 97. The sand octopus shoots jets of water into the seafloor to create quicksand, then buries itself to hide from predators. 98. Male and female larger Pacific striped octopuses "kiss" their beaks together. 99. Octopuses are known to be solitary, so it surprised scientists when they discovered an octopus "city" off the coast of Australia in 2017. 100. Scientists invented a shape-shifting material inspired by cephalopod skin.

1

There are more than 1,400 SPECIES OF BATS, and about one-fifth of them make their HOMES in AFRICA or on the island of MADAGASCAR.

2

BABY BATS are called PUPS.

3

FLYING FOXES, a type of bat, have some 20 DIFFERENT CALLS to COMMUNICATE with other BATS.

4

Most bats are ACTIVE at NIGHT and SLEEP during the DAY.

5

Mother bats GROOM THEIR BABIES to keep them CLEAN.

6

BATS have been on EARTH for some 50 MILLION YEARS.

7

BATS are the world's SECOND LARGEST GROUP OF MAMMALS— rodents are first.

8

To TAKE FLIGHT, bats have to FALL FROM A HIGH LOCATION; they can't take off from the ground like birds can.

9

BATS that HIBERNATE LIVE SIX YEARS LONGER, on average, than bats that don't hibernate.

10

The saying "blind as a bat" isn't true—many have GOOD EYESIGHT, and flying foxes can see 20 times better than humans.

11

A male BRANDT'S MYOTIS in Siberia LIVED to be at least 41 YEARS OLD, about twice as long as most bats live.

12

In European folklore, VAMPIRES were PEOPLE—NOT BATS— who came alive to feed on human blood.

13

In just ONE HOUR, a BROWN BAT can EAT 1,200 MOSQUITOES.

14

FLYING FOXES can BEAT their WINGS 120 TIMES per MINUTE.

15

STRAW-COLORED FRUIT BATS leave their roosts at night to FIND FRUIT to eat, mainly sucking up the sweet juices.

16

GHOST-FACED BATS get their name from their GHOULISH LOOK— their LARGE EARS meet across their forehead, making it look as if their eyes are inside their ears.

17

Some BATS live in CAVES, but they can also live in the HOL-LOWS of TREES, TELE-PHONE BOXES, and even ROLLED-UP BEACH UMBRELLAS.

18

HONDURAN WHITE BATS, which live in tropical rainforests in Central America, MAKE "TENTS" OUT OF LEAVES to keep dry in the rain.

19

BATS can EAT THEIR BODY WEIGHT in INSECTS in ONE NIGHT.

20

BATS have a great SENSE OF HEARING— they can HEAR a BEETLE WALKING on a LEAF.

21

Some 15 million MEXICAN FREE-TAILED BATS live in Bracken Cave near San Antonio, Texas, U.S.A.

22

The bats leave about 50 TONS (45 t) of guano, or BAT POOP, on the CAVE FLOOR EVERY YEAR, which beetles, flies, and mites use as food.

23

The KITTI'S HOG-NOSED, or bumblebee, BAT only weighs about as much as a dime—it's the WORLD'S SMALLEST MAMMAL.

24

Some MALE BATS SING like songbirds to ATTRACT MATES.

25

During the SUMMER, bats live under the concrete Yolo Causeway in DAVIS, CALIFORNIA, U.S.A., and form "BAT-NADOES" when they take to the skies to hunt insects.

26

The PALLID BAT, which lives in western North America, EATS SCORPI-ONS and is unaffected by their toxic stings.

27

Most BATS eat INSECTS, but some chase down MICE, BIRDS, and FROGS.

28

Some bats EAT SO MANY INSECTS their POOP CAN SPARKLE from bits of shiny wings and other body parts that reflect light.

50 HIGH-FLYING FACTS ABOUT *BATS*

29

BATS are the only MAMMAL SPECIES on Earth that can FLY.

36

BATS help plant NEW FRUIT TREES when they poop out THE SEEDS.

43

MOTHER BATS give BIRTH to ONE BABY A YEAR.

37

SCIENTISTS use WEATHER RADAR to TRACK BATS IN FLIGHT.

44

VAMPIRE BATS that have had enough to eat SPIT UP BLOOD TO SHARE with less well-fed bats in EXCHANGE for GROOMING.

30

The TONGUE of the tube-lipped nectar bat can be more than ONE AND A HALF TIMES AS LONG as its BODY.

38

There are 44 DIFFERENT ROOST SITES in Cairns, Australia, for SPECTA-CLED FLYING FOXES, including one at the city library.

45

Each bat's "WING PRINT" is as UNIQUE as your fingerprint.

31

VAMPIRE BATS can DRINK an ANIMAL'S BLOOD for more than 30 MINUTES without waking it up.

39

The WINGSPAN of the MALAYSIAN FLYING FOX can stretch SIX FEET (1.8 m).

46

More than 300 SPECIES of FRUIT—including mangoes and bananas—DEPEND on BATS to POLLINATE them.

32

BAT WINGS can FEEL SIMILAR to the FEEL of SKIN on HUMAN EYELIDS.

47

The WORLD'S LARGEST NURSERY FOR NEWBORN BATS is Bracken Cave, where CAVE TEMPERATURES above 100°F (38°C) help keep them warm.

33

Some bats can SQUEEZE through a SPACE that is about as WIDE as a QUARTER.

40

FLYING FOXES in Australia can TRAVEL 30 MILES (50 km) in ONE NIGHT, looking for food.

48

BATS belong to an order called CHIROPTERA, which means "hand wing" in Greek.

34

The LESSER LONG-NOSED BAT WEIGHS about AS MUCH AS FIVE GRAPES.

41

The LESSER LONG-NOSED BAT can REMEMBER when PLANTS are about to FLOWER so that it can visit them for their pollen.

49

VAMPIRE BATS can WALK and HOP on all FOUR LEGS.

35

Similar to a human hand, BAT WINGS have FOUR FINGERS and a TINY THUMB.

42

BATS have BELLY BUTTONS, just like humans.

50

BRAZILIAN FREE-TAILED BATS can reach SPEEDS of about 100 MILES AN HOUR (160 km/h).

1 Naked mole rats have **hair between their toes,** which they use to **sweep away dirt** as they dig tunnels underground to find food.

2 A **flounder** fish is **born with eyes on either side of its body,** but **as it grows, one eye moves to the top** of its head so both eyes are next to each other.

3

Unlike most monkeys, the **bald uakari** has a **short tail,** which it **wags when excited.**

4 **Skinny guinea pigs** are almost completely hairless, except for **some fuzz** on their **muzzles, feet,** and **legs.**

5 An **okapi** is striped on its hindquarters and **legs like a zebra,** but it has a **face that resembles a giraffe.**

25 FACTS ABOUT ANIMAL HEAD-

6 The shoebill has a **long bill** that resembles a wooden **Dutch clog.**

7

The **axolotl,** a type of salamander, has **pinkish red feathery gills** on the sides of its face that **wave in the water.**

8 To help **direct sounds** that they emit, **beluga whales change** the **shape** of their **forehead** and **lips** to make different **facial expressions,** appearing to **smile** and **frown.**

9 Patagonian maras, **long-legged rodents,** can walk, gallop, and hop on all fours.

10 **Dugongs,** relatives of manatees, sometimes can be seen **"standing" on their tails** in the water with their heads above water.

11 A **beluga whale's** neck bones aren't fused together, so it can **turn its head up and down** and **side to side.**

12

The **transparent, needlelike teeth** of a **viperfish** are so big that they don't fit inside its mouth when it's closed.

13

Male **proboscis monkeys** use their **extra-large noses** to make **honking calls** to impress females and intimidate their male rivals.

14

The **Komondor**, a type of Hungarian dog, has **long white cords of fur** that make it **look like a mop**, which **helps it blend in with the sheep** that it protects in pastures.

15

The **pink fairy armadillo** gets its distinctive color from its blood vessels, which are close to the surface of its armored shell.

16

Sunda colugos, a small mammal from Southeast Asia, **glide** the **length of a football field** using flaps of skin on the sides of their bodies.

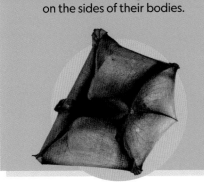

17

The blobfish, a pink fish found in the deep ocean off of Australia and New Zealand, gets its name from its soft bones and few muscles, which give it a **squishy blob appearance.**

18

The **Dumbo octopus's** earlike fins help it move and steer through water currents.

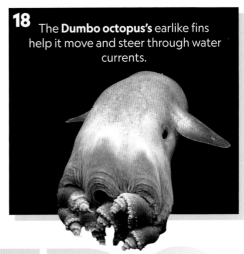

TURNERS

19

A **gerenuk,** whose name means "giraffe-necked" in Somali, is a type of antelope that lives up to its name with its **extra-long neck.**

22

A **white grizzly bear** was spotted in Canada's Banff National Park in 2020; the coloring is due to a **gene mutation.**

20

Namib desert beetles do a **handstand** in the sand to **capture moisture** from the air.

23

Tawny frogmouths are birds whose beaks are shaped like a frog's mouth.

24

The **male fiddler crab** waves its giant claw to attract females.

21

A **male turkey** has a **snood,** an up to five-inch (13-cm)-long fleshy bit of skin that hangs over its beak, which helps **attract females.**

25

Puss caterpillars were likely named because they resemble a **cat's soft fur.**

»15 FACTS ABOUT ANIMAL MASCOTS TO CHEER FOR

1

On the trading card of Screech, the eagle mascot for Major League Baseball's **Washington Nationals,** his favorite food is listed as gummy worms.

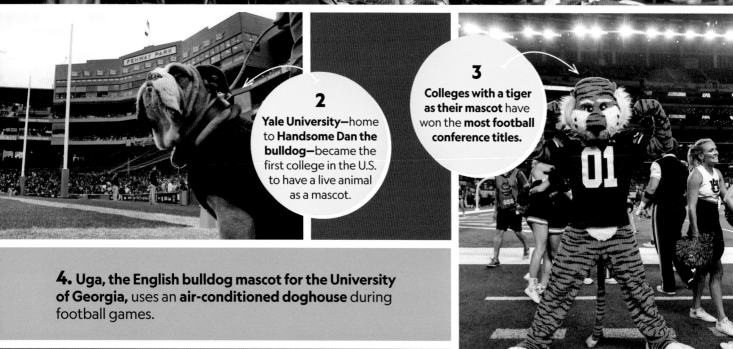

2

Yale University—home to **Handsome Dan the bulldog**—became the first college in the U.S. to have a live animal as a mascot.

3

Colleges with a tiger as their mascot have won the **most football conference titles.**

4. Uga, the English bulldog mascot for the University of Georgia, uses an **air-conditioned doghouse** during football games.

5

The **University of Arkansas at Monticello's mascot is a boll weevil,** a beetle that is a pest to cotton growers.

6. The **mascot** of the **Pittsburgh Penguins National Hockey League team** is named **Iceburgh.**

7. Tuffy the wolf, the mascot of North Carolina State's athletic teams, isn't a wolf—it's a mix of **German shepherd, Alaskan malamute, and Siberian husky.**

8. SuperFrog, the Texas Christian University horned frog mascot, wears a costume covered in **horns and bulging muscles.**

9. Rubbing the nose of a bronze statue of **Testudo, the University of Maryland terrapin mascot,** is said to bring you **good luck.**

10

The **Philadelphia Flyers hockey team mascot, Gritty,** has been known to eat ice that the Zamboni leaves behind on the rink.

11. The **Colorado Rockies Major League Baseball team made a dinosaur their mascot** after a *Triceratops* skull was found during construction of their stadium.

12. Wally the Green Monster, the mascot for the Boston Red Sox, is named after "The Green Monster," the nickname for the 37-foot (11.3-m)-tall wall in left field at Fenway Park.

13

In 1986, **students persuaded officials at the University of California, Santa Cruz, to change the school mascot from the sea lions to the banana slugs,** a bright yellow, slimy, shell-less mollusk commonly found on the redwood forest floor.

15

The **Milwaukee Brewers baseball team took in a stray dog** that stopped by their spring training camp in 2014, named it **Hank,** and kept it as a **mascot.**

14. Fang T. Rattler, the **mascot** of a **minor league baseball** team in Wisconsin, U.S.A., uses a **"bratzooka" cannon** to **shoot hot dogs to fans** in the stands.

1. **Mammals** that live in **cold climates** have **special adaptations** to reduce how much of their body heat is lost to the cold air.

2. Arctic foxes have **fur** that covers the **bottom** of their **feet** to help keep them **warm.**

3. There are **no land mammals native** to **Antarctica,** but **some** mammals such as whales and seals **visit** the **waters** offshore.

4. Emperor penguins have **four layers** of **overlapping feathers** that help **insulate** them against strong winds and bitter cold.

5. Snowy owls have long feathers that extend over their beaks.

6. Arctic wolves grow a **second layer of fur** to keep them warm during the winter.

7. Ribbon seals pull themselves across the ice by alternating strokes of their **front flippers.**

8. Some **fish** living around Antarctica have **colorless blood**—it lacks the red, oxygen-carrying pigment called hemoglobin. They get oxygen from the water instead.

9. The layer of **blubber** on a **bowhead whale** can be as thick as **12 inches** (30 cm).

10. A puffin has a special gland that produces oil to make its feathers waterproof.

11. Snow voles, rodents that look similar to mice, **build small walls** to **protect** their underground burrows from **melting snow.**

12. Every year, **arctic terns travel** some **25,000 miles** (40,200 km) from **Antarctica** to breeding colonies in the **Arctic** and **back again.**

13. A **reindeer's fur insulates** the animal's body so well against the cold that **falling snow won't melt** when it **lands** on the **reindeer's back.**

14. Bearded seals "talk" to one another using **trills** and **moans,** and some sounds can be heard underwater for 12 miles (19 km).

15. To get ready for winter, **arctic foxes change color** from brown or gray to white, which helps keep them **camouflaged** in their snowy home.

16. Musk oxen's shaggy, insulating coats include an **undercoat** that falls out when temperatures warm up in the spring.

17. Four species of penguin—**Adélie, chinstrap, gentoo, and emperor**—breed on Antarctica or its surrounding islands.

18. There are **more species** of **insects** in **Antarctica** than any other animal group.

19. Thick fur on the **paws** of Amur, or Siberian, **tigers** helps keep them **warm.**

20. A **snowy owl** is **strong** enough to **knock down** a **grown man.**

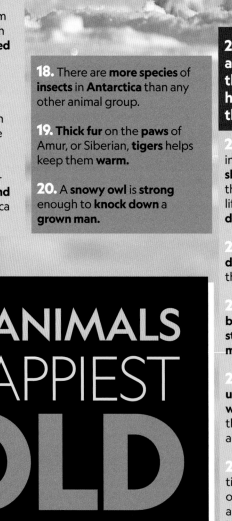

21. Arctic foxes' small ears and short legs help keep them warm by reducing how much heat is lost to the cold air.

22. Just as rings on a tree indicate its age, a Greenland **shark's eyes have tissue layers** that are added throughout its lifetime, allowing scientists to **determine** the **animal's age.**

23. In France, a cave contains **drawings of woolly mammoths** that date back **13,000 years.**

24. Common lizards in Siberia **bury themselves in soil** and **can stay frozen** for more than **two months.**

25. Snow voles live in burrows **underneath** the **snow** all **winter**—the snow helps keep the ground warmer than the air above.

26. Rock ptarmigans sometimes follow herds of caribou or musk ox, **nibbling** on **plants** and **insects** uncovered as the herds cross the snow.

75 POLAR ANIMALS THAT ARE HAPPIEST IN THE COLD

27. Chamois, goatlike animals that live in the European Alps, **travel to protected areas** on mountainsides to keep **out of the wind.**

28. Snowy owls are able to tolerate **temperatures** as low as **minus 40°F** (-40°C) on the frozen Arctic tundra.

29. Woolly mammoths, which lived in Siberia and went **extinct** a few thousand years ago, had **tusks** as long as **13 feet** (4 m).

30. Bearded seals, the largest seals in the Arctic, can grow to be **eight feet** (2.4 m) **long** and weigh some **800 pounds** (360 kg).

31. **Scientists** have recorded **201 bird species** in the **Arctic National Wildlife Refuge** in Alaska, U.S.A.—including snow geese, snowy owls, and snow buntings.

32. So that it can swim smoothly underneath the ice, a **beluga whale** doesn't have a dorsal fin on its back.

33. Bearded seals use their heads or claws to open up breathing holes in the sea ice.

34. An adult **snowy owl** can **eat** more than **1,600 lemmings** in a **year.**

35. Reindeer, which are native to Europe and Asia, and **caribou** that live in North America belong to the **same species.**

36. When **Arctic terns molt their wing feathers,** they rarely fly, instead **resting** on **packs** of **ice.**

37. Canada lynx are known as the **"gray ghosts of the North"** because of their stealth during nighttime hunts.

38. Glacier fleas make their **homes inside glaciers** and use an oily substance to protect themselves from melting ice.

39. Hoary redpolls, a small finch, might **pluck out** some of their **feathers** if the weather gets too **warm.**

40. Some scientists think that **wolverines store food** in **snow "refrigerators"** to keep it fresh.

41. Ermines, a type of weasel, pile up food for the winter; scientists found one hoard that had 150 lemmings in it.

42. In the winter, **moose** use their **hooves** to scrape away snow to **eat** the **mosses underneath.**

43. Wolverines have **short legs** and **wide feet** to help them **navigate** through **snow-covered mountains** and **valleys.**

44. The **veins** and **arteries** in **emperor penguin** bodies are close together, which helps them **recycle** their own **body heat.**

45. Ringed seal moms nurse their **pups in snow caves,** which they build to **protect** the pups from predators and to help **keep them warm.**

46. The **Antarctic toothfish** has **special proteins** in its **blood** that act like an **antifreeze** so it can live in supercold seawater.

47. Reindeer hooves have **fur** on the **bottom** to help **keep the animals from slipping** when traveling over ice.

48. The male emperor penguin keeps its **eggs** in a **special pouch** that maintains a **temperature** of about **100°F** (38°C), while winter air temperatures can drop to below minus 31°F (-35°C).

49. Yakutian horses quickly evolved characteristics like **bushy tails, shawl-like manes,** and **long shaggy hair** to survive Siberia's extreme cold.

50. As good swimmers, **moose** will **munch** on **aquatic plants** at and below the surface of a lake after the ice melts.

51. Beluga whales' thick layer of **blubber** can be as much as **40 percent** of their total body weight.

52. When they sense danger, **snowshoe hares** can stand completely still to **blend** in to their **surroundings.**

53. The **wood frog freezes solid** and its **heart stops** to **survive** the **winter.**

54. Leopard seals typically **hunt** prey when in the **water** but **come ashore** to **care** for their **young** on the Antarctic ice.

55. To escape the winter cold, **yellow-bellied marmots** spend more than half their lives **hibernating.**

56. When snow is especially deep, **moose conserve energy** by staying around **areas** that **humans have cleared.**

57. Caribou's special hair-covered noses warm up the cold air before it enters their lungs.

58. When hibernating, the **yellow-bellied marmot** can **slow down** its **heartbeat** from 180 times a minute to just 30.

59. Puffin chicks have a **thick layer** of **downy feathers** that helps keep them **warm** when their parents leave the nest to catch food.

60. Wolverines have **super-sharp claws** that let them **climb** sheer walls of **ice** in minutes.

61. Some **owls** that live in cold climates **thaw a stashed rodent carcass** by sitting on it as if it were an **egg.**

62. Unlike other tigers, **Amur tigers** have **fat** around their **bellies** and **legs** to help them stay **warm** in their environments, where temperatures can drop to minus 40°F (-40°C).

63. Reindeer can see ultraviolet light, which makes lichens, their major food source in the winter, look black against the snow.

64. **Adult Siberian newts** hibernate in "cushions" made of moss.

65. Walruses use their **tusks** to help them **climb out of frigid waters** onto land or ice.

66. Invertebrates known as **tardigrades** call Antarctica home—their **remains** have even been **found** more than **half a mile** (1 km) beneath the **ice.**

67. Canada lynx use their large, furry paws like snowshoes.

68. The **Antarctic tern's head** is **black** during the **summer,** but **white streaks** appear on it in the **winter.**

69. When members of the **British Antarctic Expedition** brought the **first dogs** to Antarctica in 1899, their landing was followed by a **four-day blizzard.** They **survived** by **sleeping** alongside the **dogs.**

70. Wind blew one of the **dogs** out to **sea** on **drifting ice**—it was found **healthy** and **safe** 10 weeks later.

71. To help conserve energy, **arctic foxes** and **wolves** can keep their **toe pads within one degree of freezing** even when standing on much colder ground.

72. Emperor penguins huddle in groups, **taking turns** standing on the cold outside, to **protect each other** from wind chills that can reach minus 76°F (-60°C).

73. South polar **skuas** spend much of the winter at sea, but when on land in Antarctica, they are **fierce protectors** of their **nests,** using their **wings** to **whack intruders.**

74. A **legend** from Slovenia held that a chamois or **ibex with golden horns** could **unlock** a treasure guarded by a dragon.

75. Fish called **arctic graylings** feast on insects during the winter, so that they can get fat enough to **survive** under **ice-covered rivers** for eight months of the year.

1
At least **40 percent** of the **world's** birds migrate.

2
Over its 30-year lifetime, the **arctic tern's** yearly flights can **add up** to the equivalent of **three trips** to the **moon** and **back.**

3
Usually, only **female walruses** and their **young migrate.**

4
The **great snipe** is the **fastest migratory bird,** reaching speeds of **60 miles an hour** (97 km/h).

5
Every year, **European** and **American eels** leave freshwater rivers and **travel** to the Sargasso Sea in the **North Atlantic.**

6
In 2019, **weather radar detected** a **cloud** of **migrating ladybugs 80 miles** (129 km) **across.**

7
During their migration, **humpback whales** stop at Raoul Island off the coast of New Zealand to **sing to each other.**

8
Many animals, including **salmon,** sense the **Earth's magnetic field** to **navigate** their **migration.**

9
Chinook salmon leap upstream, climbing more than **6,500 feet** (1,980 m) in **total elevation.**

10
Migrating **European white storks** join white pelicans and raptors to **form groups** that can stretch **125 miles** (200 km).

11
Bornean bearded pigs migrate, probably to find fruit. They're the **only pig species** to do so.

12
Every year, about **10 million fruit bats** migrate to a small patch of forest in **Kasanka National Park** in Zambia, Africa.

13
Emperor penguins walk about **125 miles** (200 km) over the **ice** to reach their **nesting grounds.**

14
Caribou migrate the **farthest** of any **land animal,** with some populations that **travel more than 745 miles** (1,200 km) **round-trip.**

15
Leatherback sea turtles can **swim 10,000 miles** (16,100 km) each year **in search of jellyfish,** their main food.

16
Semipalmated sandpiper birds gather in flocks of up to 300,000 individuals to prepare for migration.

17
It can take as many as **five generations** of **monarch butterflies** to **migrate north** from Mexico.

18
The **bar-tailed godwit bird** flies for **eight days** straight **without stopping.**

35 FACTS ABOUT MIGRATION

19
As many as **300 million monarch butterflies migrate** each **year.**

20
Each measuring more than six feet (1.8 m) wide, up to 10,000 **cownose rays migrate in groups** across the Gulf of Mexico **twice a year.**

21
Humpback whales can **travel** between Alaska and Hawaii, U.S.A., in as few as **36 days.**

22
Atlantic sturgeon have been **migrating** from rivers in North America to the ocean **every year since** the **time** of the **dinosaurs.**

23
Ruby-throated hummingbirds weigh as much as a nickel—but they **travel across** the **Gulf of Mexico** twice a year.

24
Bar-headed geese can reach **altitudes of 5.5 miles** (8.9 km) when **migrating.**

25
Globe skimmer dragonflies follow seasonal rains **11,000 miles** (17,700 km) to **lay** their **eggs** in temporary pools.

26
Millions of **golden jellyfish** follow the sun's path across a lake in Palau—the sunlight feeds organisms that live inside the jellyfish.

27
Sperm whales can be **30 or 40 years old** before they migrate on their own.

28
Megamouth sharks migrate daily: They leave shallow water to follow plankton, their prey, to the deep sea at sunset.

29
Even **plankton** migrate—they travel from the **deep sea** to the **ocean's surface** to eat during the cover of **night.**

30
Migrating **Canada geese take turns leading** the group.

31
When **gray whales** reach their feeding grounds in the Arctic, they spend **20 hours** a day **eating.**

32
In the summer, little **brown bats** sleep in trees. In the winter, they **migrate** to **warmer caves** or **mines** to **hibernate.**

33
Scientists think that **instinct** likely **drives birds and insects to migrate,** but large mammals such as moose have to learn how.

34
Adélie penguins migrate in an **8,000-mile** (12,875-km) **circle** to stay in Antarctica's sunlight.

35
Sea turtles migrate to the **same beach where they were born** to lay their eggs.

1. Apex predators are adult animals at the top of the food chain in their ecosystem—they aren't naturally preyed upon by other animals.   2. Orcas, or killer whales—the largest member of the dolphin family—are considered the top predator in the ocean.   3. Orcas hunt in groups using echolocation: They make sounds that travel underwater until they hit an object and bounce back, providing information about the object's location and size.   4. In Brazil, giant otters are known as "aquatic jaguars" for their fierce hunting instincts in rivers.   5. Spotted hyenas will consume all of a kill, including the bones.   6. Tigers, which hunt alone and mostly at night, rely on their stripes as camouflage in order to ambush their prey.   7. Gray wolves aren't the largest predators in their habitats, but as pack animals they can collectively take down animals much larger than themselves.   8. Filmmakers caught a group of territorial giant river otters scaring away two jaguars that had been stalking them from a riverbank.   9. Electric eels generate an electric field that is five times as strong as the voltage of a household wall electric socket.   10. Sperm whales can hold their breath for up to 90 minutes while they search deep underwater for squid to eat.   11. Greenland sharks live the longest of any vertebrate—up to at least 272 years.   12. Female Greenland sharks don't have babies until they are about 150 years old.   13. Jaguar attack and kill caiman, a relative of the alligator, instantly paralyzing it by biting down on the back of its neck.   14. Jaguars have the strongest bite, relative to their size, of all the big cats.   15. Saltwater crocodiles are the largest of all crocodilians.   16. Male saltwater crocodiles can reach up to 23 feet (7 m) long and weigh 2,200 pounds (998 kg).   17. Leopard seals get their name from their black spotted coat as well as from their fierce nature, which is similar to their big cat namesake.   18. Leopard seals are the only seal that feeds on warm-blooded prey, including other seals.   19. Leopard seals often wait underwater by ice shelves and snatch penguins as they hop in the water.   20. Tasmanian devils, which live only on the island of Tasmania, are the world's largest meat-eating marsupial.   21. Pound for pound, Tasmanian devils have one of the most powerful bites of any animal.   22. It is estimated that about 200 people are killed by a Nile crocodile every year.   23. A Nile crocodile, which weighs up to 500 pounds (227 kg), can eat half of its body weight in one meal.   24. The deep-sea-dwelling giant squid is the largest invertebrate on Earth, measuring up to 59 feet (18 m).   25. Giant squid, which have eight arms and two longer tentacles, eat fish, shrimp, and possibly small whales.   26. In the deserts of the American Southwest, mountain lions, bobcats, coyotes, and golden eagles are at the top of the food chain.   27. Coyotes often travel in packs, and the echoes of their howls sound like there are more of them than there actually are.   28. Coyotes run with their tails down; wolves run with their tails straight out.   29. The maned wolf, which lives in South America, looks like a fox and is named after a wolf, but it isn't closely related to either—it is a distinct species.   30. The world's population of spiders eats up to 882 million tons (800 million t) of insects every year.   31. The giant Pacific octopus, the largest of all octopus species, can grow to 30 feet (9 m) across and weigh more than 600 pounds (272 kg).   32. The giant Pacific octopus hunts at night, eating shrimp, lobsters, fish, and even sharks.   33. The giant Pacific octopus can use tools and recognize faces.   34. Polar bears can punch through several feet of ice in order to grab a seal from the water.   35. When polar bears have plenty of food to eat, they sometimes eat only a seal's blubber and skin and leave the rest.   36. When polar bears don't have other food options, they'll resort to eating bird eggs and small land mammals.   37. Australians call saltwater crocodiles "salties."   38. Saltwater crocodiles wait beneath the water's surface for prey to come near, then ambush it, pulling it underwater to drown it.   39. Saltwater crocodiles have a valve in their throat that keeps them from drowning when they open their mouth underwater.   40. Leopard seals, which are up to 12 feet (3.7 m) long and weigh up to 1,000 pounds (454 kg), have a powerful call, the vibrations of which can be felt aboveground on ice.   41. In Argentina, orcas swim in shallow water to grab sea lion pups on the water's edge.   42. In Antarctica, orcas work together to make waves splash over ice floes to knock seals into the water.   43. Tasmanian devils hunt everything from frogs to birds to insects at night, using their long whiskers to feel around small dark spaces.   44. While they eat, Tasmanian devils sometimes make shrieks that can be heard more than a mile (1.6 km) away.   45. Greenland sharks are slow swimmers—moving at about .75 mile an hour (1.2 km/h)—but sometimes have short bursts of speed.   46. Sperm whales have the biggest brain of any creature on Earth.   47. The famous white whale in Herman Melville's book *Moby-Dick* was a sperm whale.   48. Greenland sharks eat just about anything—from fish to seals to polar bears.   49. Greenland sharks sometimes eat land animals that wade on the shoreline or that have fallen into the ocean, including moose and reindeer.   50. Swordfish can reach speeds of up to 62 miles an hour (100 km/h).   51. Swordfish produce an oil that covers their snouts, helping them move through the water faster.   52. Swordfish capture their prey by thrashing their bills, or "swords," back and forth, stunning or injuring it.   53. Nile crocodiles use their strong tails to propel their

Komodo dragon

100 FEARSOME FACTS ABOUT TOP PREDATORS

entire bodies straight up out of the water.   54. American alligators, which live in freshwater rivers, lakes, swamps, and marshes of the U.S. Southeast, eat mostly fish, turtles, snakes, and small mammals. 55. Giant squid can catch prey 33 feet (10 m) away by shooting out two tentacles that have hundreds of sharp-toothed suckers on the end of them.   56. Giant squids' enormous eyes allow them to see in the darkness of the deep sea where most other animals can't see anything.   57. Bald eagles use their strong talons to fish, but they get most of their food from scavenging dead animals or stealing food from other animals.   58. In Alaska, U.S.A., some 4,000 bald eagles gather on riverbanks to snatch spawning salmon in the fall. 59. A giant squid has a doughnut-shaped brain, and its esophagus runs through the hole in the middle!   60. To turn in the water, alliga- tors fill up their lungs with air.   61. After baby alligators are born, their mother carries them in her mouth to the water and protects them from predators for up to two years.   62. Golden eagles are the largest and fastest birds of prey in North America.   63. Although they are capable of killing deer and small livestock, golden eagles mostly hunt rabbits, ground squirrels, marmots, and prairie dogs. 64. Great white sharks are the largest predatory fish in the ocean. 65. Most great white shark attacks on humans are "sample bites"— they usually release people rather than preying on them.   66. Sea otters are apex predators of the Pacific Ocean's nearshore environ- ment in North America.   67. Sea otters eat sea urchins, which can take over kelp beds—an important food source and habitat for many sea animals—if not kept in check.   68. Blue whales in the Antarctic eat several million krill, a type of small shrimp, in a single day.   69. African lions usually work together to hunt prey, but they often squabble over sharing their kill.   70. Blue whales are too big for most predatory animals to bother with, but there are a few records of a pod of orcas making attempts.   71. The maned wolf has exceptional hearing, which it uses to locate small animals scurry- ing in thick grass.   72. Jaguars, caiman, and piranhas avoid hunting electric eels for fear of an electric shock.   73. The alli- gator snapping turtle has a tongue that resembles a worm, which lures in prey so the turtle can attack at close range. 74. Whale sharks, the world's largest shark, only prey on small fish, but their size means they have no natural preda- tors.   75. Whale sharks can be as long as a school bus.   76. Whale sharks have unique spot patterns, just like a tiger's stripes or a human's fingerprints.   77. Even though grizzly bears are at the top of the food chain, much of their diet includes berries, nuts, fruit, and roots.   78. Grizzly bears love to eat moths. They can eat as many as 40,000 in one day.   79. The world's largest bird's nest was built by a pair of bald eagles. It measured 9.5 feet (2.9 m) wide and was 20 feet (6 m) deep.   80. False water cobras attack prey, like frogs and fish, then partly coil their body around it to keep a grip; then they swal- low it alive.   81. Golden eagles can dive at speeds up to 150 miles an hour (241 km/h).   82. The golden eagle is the most common official national animal in the world, and is the emblem of Albania, Austria, Germany, Kazakhstan, and Mexico.   83. Great white sharks can leap completely out of the water when attacking prey, breaching like a whale.   84. Great white sharks have 300 serrated teeth. When they lose a tooth, they grow another.   85. African lions live in groups,

called prides, of up to 40 lions.   86. A group of tigers—though rarely seen among these solitary cats—is called a streak.   87. Alligators are dark gray or black; crocodiles are olive green or tan.   88. A crocodile's bite force is about as strong as a great white shark's. 89. Bengal tigers make a successful kill in only one out of every 20 attempts.   90. African wild dogs hunt in packs of up to 20 and can take down animals more than twice their size.   91. Dragonflies are considered the most successful hunter on Earth. They capture 95 percent of the prey that they attack.   92. African lions, which hunt speedy prey like gazelles, have about a 25 percent hunting success rate.   93. Dragonflies have strong mandibles, chewing mouthparts with sharp, toothlike points.   94. Komodo dragons are found only on five islands of southeastern Indonesia, giving them the smallest range of any large apex predator species in the world.   95. A Komodo dragon uses its long tongue to sense prey up to a mile (1.6 km) away.   96. Snow leopards, apex predators of the Himalaya, have powerful legs capable of leaping 50 feet (15 m) in one jump. 97. Snow leopards use their long tails—up to three feet (0.9 m) long— for balance, and also as a blanket when they curl up to rest.   98. King cobras, the world's longest venomous snake, prey mostly on other snakes.   99. A king cobra can lift its body up so that it's tall enough to look a grown person in the eye.   100. The emerald tree boa isn't venomous, but it has a fast enough strike to snatch a bird mid-flight, then coil its body around it.

grizzly bear

7

The GIRAFFE WEEVIL gets its name from its very LONG NECK.

13

In 2015, SCIENTISTS found FOSSILS of giant EXTINCT LEMURS in an underwater cave. Some were as big as gorillas.

17

Some people believe the AYE-AYE is an omen of BAD LUCK.

21

The TENREC, which looks like a hedgehog, was PROBABLY the FIRST MAMMAL to arrive on Madagascar.

1

About 95 PERCENT of Madagascar's REPTILES and 92 percent of its MAMMALS live nowhere else on Earth.

8

The PANTHER CHAMELEON can be the SIZE of a HOUSE CAT.

22

The MADAGASCAN MOON MOTH can have an EIGHT-INCH (20-cm) WINGSPAN.

2

The MALAGASY GIANT JUMPING RAT can LEAP about THREE FEET (1 m) into the air.

9

The TOMATO FROG is named for its BRIGHT RED-ORANGE SKIN.

14

LEAF-TAILED GECKOS are named for their tails, which LOOK exactly like DEAD LEAVES, even missing pieces like you would see on a rotted leaf.

18

LEMURS are the MOST ENDANGERED GROUP of animals in the world.

10

The CALLS of an INDRI, a woolly lemur, can be HEARD from 1.2 miles (2 km) away.

19

AYE-AYES have an EXTRA, MINIATURE THUMB, giving them SIX FINGERS on each hand.

23

Other than humans, BLUE-EYED BLACK LEMURS are the ONLY PRIMATE to have BLUE EYES.

3

More than 100 SPECIES of LEMUR live on MADAGASCAR.

11

The FOSSA, Madagascar's largest carnivore, can be nearly six feet (1.8 m) long.

15

SCIENTISTS believe that AYE-AYES are the only primates to USE ECHOLOCATION to find prey.

20

EXPERTS think that mammals got to MADAGASCAR 50 million years ago by "RAFTING" across the OCEAN on large logs or clumps of vegetation.

16

CHAMELEONS range in length from the SIZE OF A FINGERNAIL to that of a LARGE HOUSE CAT.

24

A PANTHER CHAMELEON'S TONGUE can be one and a half times its body length.

4

"DANCING" LEMURS, also called Verreaux's sifakas, MOVE along the ground by HOPPING SIDEWAYS.

5

FEMALES are IN CHARGE of lemur groups.

12

The AYE-AYE uses its EXTRA-LONG MIDDLE FINGER to tap on trees, listening for the sounds of insect larvae moving inside.

25

Each RING-TAILED LEMUR has about 13 BLACK-AND-WHITE STRIPES on its TAIL.

6

LEMURS like to SUNBATHE in a "yoga" position with their BELLIES facing the SUN.

50

WILD FACTS
ABOUT *ANIMALS*
OF *MADAGASCAR*

ruffed lemur

32
The LOWLAND STREAKED TENREC can rub its QUILLS together to produce a HIGH-PITCHED CALL.

33
The EXTINCT ELEPHANT BIRD stood nearly 10 feet (3 m) tall and weighed up to 1,000 pounds.

34

Madagascar HISSING COCKROACHES can be THREE INCHES (7.6 cm) LONG.

37
TOMATO FROGS ooze TOXIC MUCUS through their skin.

38
About HALF the world's CHAMELEON SPECIES live in MADAGASCAR.

39
The FOSSA is a COUSIN of the MONGOOSE.

40
COMET MOTH COCOONS have HOLES in them so that rainwater can DRAIN out.

41
Of the 25 most ENDANGERED primates, SIX live in MADAGASCAR.

42
Madagascar has NO SNAKES that are DEADLY to humans.

43
Darwin's bark spider WEBS can SPAN up to 82 FEET (25 m) across streams, lakes, and rivers.

44
DWARF LEMURS store FAT in their TAILS for extra ENERGY.

45
CRESTED COUA CHICKS have red-and-white MARKINGS inside their MOUTHS that may act like a TARGET to show their parents where to feed them.

46
The MADAGASCAR DAY GECKO is called this because it is ACTIVE during the DAY, unlike most geckos, which are NOCTURNAL.

47
A RING-TAILED LEMUR'S TAIL is LONGER than its BODY.

48
The SILKY SIFAKA'S white fur and way of leaping through the trees gives it the nickname "GHOST OF THE FOREST."

49
The CHAMELEON *BROOKESIA MICRA* is so SMALL it could PERCH on a MATCH HEAD.

50
MADAGASCAR does not have monkeys, zebras, giraffes, lions, or rhinos like the nearby AFRICAN continent does.

29
The RADIATED TORTOISE can LIVE to be 100 YEARS OLD.

26
MANTELLA FROGS collect the POISONS in their SKIN from the insects they eat.

30
MALE PANTHER CHAMELEONS change their COLORS to bright yellow, red, or white to INTIMIDATE other males.

35
The WEB of the DARWIN'S BARK SPIDER is 10 times STRONGER THAN KEVLAR, the material used to make bulletproof vests.

27
Madagascar's FLYING FOXES are actually LARGE BATS.

31
LEMURS have "STINK FIGHTS." They run their tails along odor glands on their wrists and shoulders, then waft them at each other.

28
The world's SMALLEST PRIMATE is MADAME BERTHE'S MOUSE LEMUR. It's about 3.5 inches (9 cm) long.

36
RING-TAILED LEMURS live in GROUPS called TROOPS with up to 30 MEMBERS.

1

Common cuckoo birds lay their eggs in the nests of common redstarts, which then raise the young cuckoos.

2

The African double-banded courser bird places its egg next to antelope poop. The egg's color and pattern resembles the droppings, which keeps it hidden from predators.

3

When dark soot covered trees in England during the industrial revolution, an all-black form of the black-and-white peppered moth evolved to blend into the trees' dark bark.

4

Cells in a special layer underneath a chameleon's see-through skin become bigger or smaller, changing the reptile's colors.

5

Some stick insects have bumps that look like flower buds on twigs to help camouflage them.

6

In the winter, the coats of small mammals called ermines change from brown to white to blend into their snowy homes.

25 FACTS ABOUT TRICKSTER

7

When threatened, western hognose snakes hiss loudly and spread their necks to imitate cobras.

8

Owl butterflies sport large black spots with yellow rings on their wings that can look like owl eyes, keeping would-be predators away.

9

Hoverflies feed on flower nectar and look like stinging bees to keep threats away.

10

The green algae that grows on the fur of slow-moving sloths helps camouflage the animals in their rainforest home.

11

A kind of worm takes over a snail's eyestalks so that they look like caterpillars to birds; when birds eat the worm, it reproduces in the bird's guts.

12

Chameleons can move their eyes in different directions at once.

13

Sabre-toothed blenny fish look like helpful cleaner fish, which lets them swim up to unsuspecting fishes and take a bite out of their fins.

14

Leaf-tailed geckos flatten themselves against trees so well that even their shadows disappear.

15

Viceroy butterflies evolved to mimic the colors of monarch butterflies, whose bright coloration tells other animals that they taste bad.

16

Some hawk moths can puff up so that they appear to be a venomous pit viper.

17

A giant stick insect that lives on the Southeast Asian island of Borneo can grow to more than a foot (30 cm) long.

18

Bolas spiders release chemicals that mimic those released by female moths looking for a mate. Male moths then approach and the spiders eat them.

19

Mimic octopuses hide in rocks and dangle two of their arms outside their hideout to look like poisonous black-banded sea snakes.

20

Mimic octopuses hide at night but feed during the day, changing into the shape of different sea creatures to stay safe.

ANIMALS

21

If a chameleon lives in a desert it is often brown, but if it lives in a forest it is often green.

22

So-called stick insects blend into the forests and grasslands where they live by looking like brown or green twigs.

23

Snowshoe hares, whose white coats blend into their winter surroundings, have larger back feet than front feet, which act like snowshoes to support them in deep snow.

24

Soil and dust particles stick to the bodies of spiders in the Paratropididae family, camouflaging them.

25

The striped patterns on the wings of great horned owls help the birds blend into tree bark.

1. Some birds became **flightless** because they **lived in habitats** where they **didn't need to fly away** from **predators.**

2. Some **flightless birds evolved** other ways to **escape** predators, like **running at fast speeds.**

3. Flying birds have a keel, a ridge on their breastbone where flight muscles attach; most **flightless birds don't have a keel.**

4. Even though a **penguin can't fly,** it has a keel, which helps it **swim.**

5. Penguins' wings work like paddles in the water.

6. **Penguins walk** on the **soles** of their **feet,** rather than on their toes like most flying birds do.

7. **Penguins swim** underwater at speeds of up to **25 miles an hour** (40 km/h).

8. **Some species of penguins** spend up to **75 percent** of their **lives** in the **water.**

9. Flying birds have lightweight skeletons with hollow bones; **flightless birds** have **heavy leg bones.**

10. **Flightless birds live on the ground** and don't need to grab on to trees with their feet, so they **don't have an opposable first toe**—most flying birds do have one.

11. The egg of the extinct flightless elephant bird was the size of 150 chicken eggs.

12. The **dodo,** a 22-pound (10-kg) flightless bird, **lived** only on the island of **Mauritius** until it went **extinct** in the late **17th century.**

13. The **dodo** went extinct because pigs and rats introduced by Portuguese sailors **overhunted its eggs.**

14. **Moa,** ostrichlike flightless birds that lived in New Zealand until the 19th century, **weighed** as much as **550 pounds** (250 kg) and **laid one large egg.**

15. It could take as long as **10 years** for **moas** to reach their full size; **modern birds** are **full-grown** within **12 months.**

16. The **largest penguin species** ever discovered **lived 37 million years ago in Antarctica** and was 5 feet 3 inches (1.6 m) tall—18 inches (46 cm) taller than today's emperor penguins.

17. Scientists who discovered the **fossils of penguins** that lived in New Zealand **25 million years ago** gave them the name *Kairuku,* which means "diver who returns with food" in the Indigenous Maori language.

18. **Steamer ducks,** which live in South America and don't have to migrate to look for food, **use** their **strong beaks** to **open mussels.**

19. **Steamer ducks** use **hard orange knobs** on their **wings** as a **weapon** to attack other birds in fights over territory.

20. **Ostriches,** which today live only in Africa, are the **largest living birds.**

21. **Ostriches** grow up to **nine feet** (2.7 m) **tall** and **weigh** more than **300 pounds** (136 kg).

22. **One ostrich egg** is the **equivalent** of **two dozen chicken eggs.**

23. Steamer ducks got their name from the way they run across water, thrashing their wings like wheels on a steamboat.

24. The **ostrich** is the only bird with **two toes on each foot.**

25. The **ostrich** uses its **long toe** to **carry its weight** and its **short toe** for **balance.**

TAKE OFF WITH 75 FACTS ABOUT FLIGHTLESS BIRDS

26. Ostriches **have the largest eyes of any** land animal.

27. Ostriches can **spot** a **predator** on the horizon almost **two miles** (3 km) **away.**

28. Ostriches use their **wings** as **rudders** to steer while running.

29. An **ostrich** can cover up to **16 feet** (5 m) in a **single stride.**

30. Egyptian vultures toss stones on ostrich eggs to **crack** them open and **eat** them.

31. Ostriches blink once every minute.

32. Adult **male ostriches** have **black feathers;** adult **female ostriches** have **brown feathers.**

33. Emus stand up to **six feet tall** (1.8 m) and weigh up to **100 pounds** (45 kg).

34. Emus are strong swimmers.

35. Emus can **run** as fast as **30 miles an hour** (48 km/h).

36. Emus have a **powerful kick,** which they use to ward off predators.

37. One emu egg can make an **omelet** that can **feed** up to **six people.**

38. Emus are the only birds that have **calf muscles.**

39. Male emus—not females—incubate eggs.

40. Male emus go **seven weeks without eating** or **drinking** while they **sit** on the **nest.**

41. Cassowaries are the **third tallest flightless bird** and the second heaviest after the ostrich.

42. A **cassowary** has a **casque,** or **hard helmet,** on its head that is made of spongy material and covered in keratin, the same material as fingernails.

43. Scientists think the **cassowary's casque shows dominance** or helps the bird **push through the rainforest underbrush** to look for food.

44. Penguins often "porpoise," or leap out of the water when they swim.

45. The **southern cassowary** is sometimes called the **rainforest gardener** because it helps keep Australia's Daintree Rainforest healthy.

46. The **southern cassowary eats** more than **230 types** of **fruit.**

47. Cassowaries poop seeds larger than **avocado stones.**

48. The **southern cassowary** makes a **booming sound,** but humans can barely hear it.

49. Cassowaries are covered in **dense feathers** that, from a distance, look like fur.

50. A cassowary's feathers help keep the bird dry in the rainforest.

51. Cassowaries have **wattles**— fleshy red pouches of skin that hang from their necks.

52. Scientists think **cassowaries' wattles** might indicate **mood** because they change intensity in **color.**

53. Cassowaries can jump **seven feet** (2.1 m) straight up in the air.

54. None of the 18 species of **penguins** can fly; their **wings** are often referred to as **flippers.**

55. Cassowaries sometimes **spread their feathers like a net** to catch fish.

56. Ostriches have an **extra-long claw on each foot** that they use for **traction** when **running.**

57. Rheas, which stand four feet (1.2 m) tall, are the **largest birds** in **South America.**

58. Rheas' wings help the birds **balance** when they **run.**

59. Male rheas incubate the **eggs** and charge any animal that comes close to them—including female rheas.

60. Male rheas are **social** animals and are often seen **flocking** with deer and guanacos.

61. While **rheas** naturally eat fruit, lizards, and insects, they also eat agricultural crops, which makes them a **nuisance** to **farmers.**

62. Because of its unbirdlike appearance, the kiwi has been called an "honorary mammal."

63. Smithsonian's National Zoo in Washington, D.C., had a **contest** to name a **new kiwi chick,** and the winning name was **Whetu,** which means **"star"** in the Indigenous Maori language.

64. The **North Island brown kiwi** lays the **largest egg** compared to its body size of any bird.

65. A **North Island brown kiwi's egg** is up to **22 percent** of its body weight; an **ostrich's egg** is **2 percent** of its body weight.

66. A **kiwi's nostrils** are **uniquely located** near the tip of its long, curved bill.

67. Kiwis snuffle along the ground using their **sense of smell** to **locate prey.**

68. A **kiwi breaks** through its **shell** by **kicking** with its **feet.**

69. Kiwis are **nocturnal**—they forage for food at dawn and dusk.

70. Kiwis' wings are only an **inch** (2.5 cm) **long.**

71. Kiwis' wings have a **catlike claw** on the tip, but scientists don't know what it is used for.

72. Kiwis sleep and **nest** underground in **burrows.**

73. Kiwis have **modified feathers** on their **faces** that help them **feel their way** through dark burrows.

74. The flightless **Galápagos cormorant's wingspan is one-third** the **size needed to fly.**

75. Galápagos cormorants don't use their **wings to swim** in the water; they **kick their legs** instead.

1
The **pain** from the **sting** of a **bullet ant** can last longer than **12 hours.**

2
Assassin bugs, which are no more than an inch (2.5 cm) long, **pierce prey** with their beak and then **suck out** their **body fluids.**

3
Irukandji jellyfish are only one inch (2.5 cm) wide, but their **venom** is **more potent** than a **cobra's.**

4
A **golden poison frog** is the **size** of a **large paper clip** but has enough **poison** to **kill 10 people.**

5
Harvester ants find **seeds, plant them** in dirt, **wait for them to sprout,** and eat them.

6
Trap-jaw spiders snap their jaws on prey in just .00012 second— one of the fastest movements in the animal kingdom.

7
Although they are plant-eaters, **white-tailed prairie dogs** hunt ground squirrels, which are the same size and their competition for food.

8
The *Lonomia obliqua* caterpillar is covered in **tiny spines** that can puncture human skin and **release** a **deadly venom.**

9
When a **fire ant** mound is disturbed, the ants **swarm** as a group to **bite** and **sting** the attacker.

10
The **world's smallest frog** is almost impossible to see, but its **high-pitched call** is easily heard.

11
Deathstalker scorpions use the **tips** of their **legs** to **feel** for their **prey's vibrations** in the **sand.**

12
The **hooded pitohui** is one of the only poisonous birds in the world—its **feathers are toxic.**

35 FACTS ABOUT TINY BUT MIGHTY CREATURES

13
The **flamboyant cuttlefish** uses its **two tentacles** to **snag prey** and bring it to its beak to eat.

14
Red lionfish spread their fins, **herd prey** into a small space, and then **eat them.**

15
Assassin bugs pierce **prey** with their beak and then **suck out** their **body fluids.**

19
Blue-ringed octopuses, one of the **most venomous octopuses**, are the size of a pea when they're born and grow to the size of a golf ball.

16
The **tardigrade**, a **microscopic animal**, lives at the bottom of the ocean, inside hot springs, and at the top of Mount Everest.

17
Dung beetles grow to only one inch (2.5 cm) long, but they can **pull balls of poop** 1,141 times their own body weight.

18
Scientists taught **a goldfish** to "drive," or navigate, a tank toward a **visual target.**

20
Venomous pygmy rattlesnakes are less than two feet (0.6 m) long, and they **don't have a rattle.**

21
A palm-size **lowland streaked tenrec** has black and yellow **quills**, which it uses to **poke** its **enemies.**

22
The two-inch (5-cm)-long **hummingbird hawk-moth** flaps its wings 70 beats per second.

23
Female fairy wasps, which can be **smaller** than a **pinhead**, sometimes lay their eggs inside other insects' eggs.

24
Hydra, a half-inch (1.25-cm)-long tubelike aquatic creature, can **open its mouth wider than its body.**

25
Desert locusts swarm in groups of up to 70 billion, covering an area 1.5 times the size of New York City, U.S.A.

26
Pupfish, which are about one inch long (2.5 cm), **can live in any kind of water—** from fresh to salt and freezing to warm.

27
Lobster larvae sometimes **ride** on moon jellyfish, **eating** the **jellyfish** as they **travel.**

28
The **geography cone snail**, found in the Indian and Pacific Oceans, contains enough **venom** to kill several people.

29
The **venom** from an **immortal jellyfish** can **cause severe pain, heart failure,** and even **death** if left untreated.

30
The **carrier crab** has **modified back legs** that let it carry large objects, like dead coral and seaweed.

31
Pufferfish contain a **toxin** that makes them **taste bad**—and even **deadly**—to the fish that attack them.

32
Turritopsis dohrnii, also known as the **immortal jellyfish**, is as **small** as the **fingernail** on your **pinky finger.**

33
Brazilian wandering spiders belong to the genus *Phoneutria*, which means "murderess" in Greek.

34
Mosquitoes, which can **transmit diseases** like malaria, are **responsible** for **several million human deaths** every year.

35
The **panda ant** isn't a panda or an ant but a one-third-inch (8-mm)-long **black-and-white wasp** that **stings.**

1 Animals hibernate in different ways, but in all animals, **body temperature decreases, breathing slows,** and **metabolic rate**—the amount of energy used—**drops.**

2

Before an animal hibernates, it usually has to **increase its body fat,** which means it needs to eat more than usual.

3 Cold-climate garter snakes hibernate in dens, sometimes **gathering in groups of thousands.**

4 **Queen bumblebees** hibernate in **dirt** or in **tree stumps.**

WAKE UP
TO THESE

25

FACTS ABOUT

5 Some **bats** that live in **colder areas** where insects are scarce in winter **hibernate** in **caves, trees,** or **even attics.**

HIBERNATING ANIMALS

6 **Female bears** give birth to **cubs** during **hibernation.**

7 **Gila monsters,** a type of desert reptile, **hibernate in burrows for three months** of the year, **living off fat stored in their tails.**

8 **Common poorwills** are the only bird known to stay in a **dormant state** for an **extended period of time.**

9 Researchers are studying **wood frogs** to discover better **ways to store human organs** used for **transplants.**

10 Snakes and lizards sometimes **take over** an **unused burrow**—created by squirrels, mice, or other small animals—to wait out the **cold season.**

11 Dormice hibernate together as a **family.**

12 The **gray tree frog** produces a **special coating** on its skin to **keep from freezing** during **hibernation.**

13 **Hibernating bats** go into a deep sleep, and **may not** take a **breath** for an **hour.**

14 **Fire-bellied toads** hibernate **under logs for eight months** of the year. When hunting the rest of the year, this toad can't extend its tongue to catch insects like other toads, so it leaps toward them instead.

15 Before they hibernate, **American black bears** gain up to **29 pounds (13 kg) a week,** bulking up on berries and other food.

16 American black bears **stay in their den** for as long as **100 days, without eating, drinking, urinating,** or **pooping.**

17 Hibernating black bears take only **one** or **two breaths per minute.**

18 **Groundhogs** are known as true hibernators, their **body temperature** dropping from 99°F (37°C) to as low as **37°F** (3°C).

19 **Hibernating** can **keep animals safe.** One study found that small mammals are five times more likely to die when they're active than when they're hibernating.

20 The Hopi people's name for the **common poorwill,** *holchoko,* means **"the sleeping one."**

21 During dry conditions, **African lungfish dig a hole in mud to hibernate,** and can remain there for up to **four years.**

22 The **fat-tailed dwarf lemur,** which lives on Madagascar, **hibernates** during the long dry season, when food and water are scarce, often **curling up into a ball in a hollow tree.**

23 The **Arctic ground squirrel** hibernates for **up to seven months,** its **body temperature** dropping to 27°F (-3°C), but its **blood doesn't freeze.**

24 **Dormice,** which **double their size** before hibernation, can stay **dormant** for **11 months.**

25 When **snails** hibernate, they cover their shells in **slime** and **stay inside them** for the winter **months.**

1

SIXTY-SEVEN MAMMAL SPECIES LIVE in YELLOWSTONE National Park, making it one of the HIGHEST CONCENTRATIONS of mammals in the U.S.

2

GRIZZLY BEAR CLAWS are each up to FOUR INCHES (10 cm) LONG—about the length of two house keys.

3

MALE ELK are the MOST PHOTOGRAPHED animals in Yellowstone.

4

HIBERNATING GRIZZLY BEARS aren't deep sleepers—they WAKE EASILY if disturbed.

5

A SNOWSHOE HARE'S white winter coat turns BROWN in the SPRING to better BLEND in with the landscape.

6

Male bighorn sheep—called RAMS—have two layers of BONE above their brain that help ABSORB SHOCK during head-to-head fighting.

7

MOUNTAIN GOATS aren't goats. They are in the BOVIDAE FAMILY, which includes antelope and gazelles.

8

BOBCATS—which are twice as big as a house cat—are NAMED for their TAILS, which look as if they have been cut short, or bobbed.

9

When HIBERNATING, the TOWNSEND'S BIG-EARED BAT curls its long ears to look like a ram's horns.

10

During the SUMMER, as many as 20,000 ELK call YELLOWSTONE home.

11

The NUMBER of RINGS on a BIGHORN SHEEP'S HORNS reveal the animal's AGE—just like the rings on a tree.

12

A LYNX can SPOT a mouse 250 FEET (76 m) AWAY—almost the length of a soccer field.

13

BABY MOUNTAIN GOATS are called KIDS, males are called BILLIES, and females are called NANNIES.

14

Weighing up to 2,200 pounds (1,000 kg), BISON are the HEAVIEST LAND ANIMALS in NORTH AMERICA.

15

About HALF of AMERICAN BLACK BEARS in Yellowstone are BLACK. The others are brown, blond, or cinnamon colored.

16

COYOTES are nicknamed "SONG DOGS" because of the way they communicate with various long-range HOWLS.

17

A RED FOX'S BIG EARS allow it to hear LOW-FREQUENCY SOUNDS, including rodents digging underground.

18

BEAVERS sometimes SMACK their long flat TAILS to warn other beavers that a predator is near.

19

BISON have LIVED continuously in YELLOWSTONE since PREHISTORIC times.

20

In 2016, the BISON became the NATIONAL MAMMAL of the UNITED STATES.

21

A pair of ANTLERS on a typical ELK weighs about 30 POUNDS (14 kg).

22

WOLVES AREN'T WILD DOGS—they are classified as two different animals. Wolves are *Canis lupus* and dogs are *Canis lupus familiaris*.

23

A CANADA LYNX's PAWS SPREAD out when they hit the ground, which allows them to RUN IN SNOW.

24

BALD EAGLES can DIVE up to 100 miles an hour (161 km/h) to SNATCH fish from the water.

50 WILD FACTS ABOUT YELLOWSTONE

25
The FLAP of SKIN that hangs beneath a MOOSE'S THROAT—which stores fat—is called a BELL.

26
A BISON'S THICK COAT is so well insulated that SNOW can fall on its BACK and it WON'T MELT.

27
After a MOUNTAIN LION hunts an elk or deer, it takes three or four days to eat it.

28
In Yellowstone, a "BEAR JAM" is when a lot of PEOPLE stop in the MIDDLE of the ROAD to see WILDLIFE.

29
BEAVERS have a set of see-through EYELIDS that they use as GOGGLES when they SWIM underwater.

30
Able to run up to 53 miles an hour (85 km/h), PRONGHORN are the world's SECOND FASTEST LAND ANIMAL, after the cheetah.

31
SNOWSHOE HARES can TRAVEL 10 FEET (3 m) in one HOP.

32
A BALD EAGLE REUSES its same NEST year after year; it can be as big as 10 feet (3 m) across and 20 feet (6 m) deep.

33
YELLOWSTONE CUT-THROAT TROUT get their name from the bright red SLASH below their MOUTHS that looks like a cut throat.

34
An ELK'S ANTLERS can GROW by as much as TWO-THIRDS of an INCH (1.7 cm) every DAY from April to August.

35
WOLVERINES look like bears, but they're actually the largest MEMBERS of the WEASEL FAMILY.

36
The greater YELLOWSTONE ecosystem is HOME to more than 700 GRIZZLY BEARS.

37
DAM-BUILDING BEAVERS are considered second only to humans in their ABILITY to CHANGE their ENVIRONMENT.

38
Some of the SMALLEST ANIMALS in Yellowstone are MICROSCOPIC ORGANISMS that live in the extreme environment of HOT SPRINGS and GEYSERS.

39
MOOSE can DIVE 16 feet (5 m) UNDERWATER to retrieve plants from the bottom of a lake.

40
RIVER OTTERS can survive Yellowstone's cold winters thanks to NATURAL THERMAL POOLS, which keep lakes and rivers from freezing over so that the otters can FISH.

41
BADGERS and COYOTES sometimes hunt alongside each other.

42
GRIZZLY BEARS can SMELL a bloody animal CARCASS a mile (1.6 km) away.

43
GRAY WOLVES were NEARLY EXTINCT in the lower 48 states, but after being REINTRO-DUCED to Yellowstone in 1995, about 100 LIVE in the PARK today.

44
WOLVES' sense of SMELL is 100 TIMES better than HUMANS'.

45
Yellowstone Park RULES say that VISITORS have to give animals their SPACE—at least 100 yards (91 m) for wolves and bears, which is about the length of two Olympic-size pools.

46
RED FOXES wrap their FLUFFY TAILS around themselves to STAY WARM in winter.

47
ANIMALS in Yellowstone National Park have 3,000 square miles (7,770 sq km) to ROAM—that's larger than the U.S. states of Delaware and Rhode Island combined.

48
BOREAL CHORUS FROGS make a CALL that sounds like a finger running across the TEETH of a COMB.

49
WILDLIFE WATCHERS sometimes MISTAKE COYOTES for WOLVES in Yellowstone, but coy-otes are actually one-third the size of wolves.

50
PEREGRINE FALCONS are the FASTEST-DIVING BIRDS, swooping down to snatch prey—often other birds—from the air.

NATIONAL PARK ANIMALS

1

Turtles bury their **eggs** in the **ground** and leave them to **hatch** on their **own.**

2

Female bonobos join together to **fight males** in disputes over **food**—and the females often win.

3

Male three-spined sticklebacks, small fish with spines along their back, **build nests** for their **eggs** and then **guard** the nests.

4

If a predator threatens an **elephant baby,** all the **elephants** in the herd **form a circle** around the calf to **protect it.**

5

Mother black bears give birth to **cubs** inside **cozy dens** during the **winter** and do all the work to raise their cubs.

6

An emperor penguin dad incubates a **single egg** in a special **pouch on his feet** while the mom forages for food at sea.

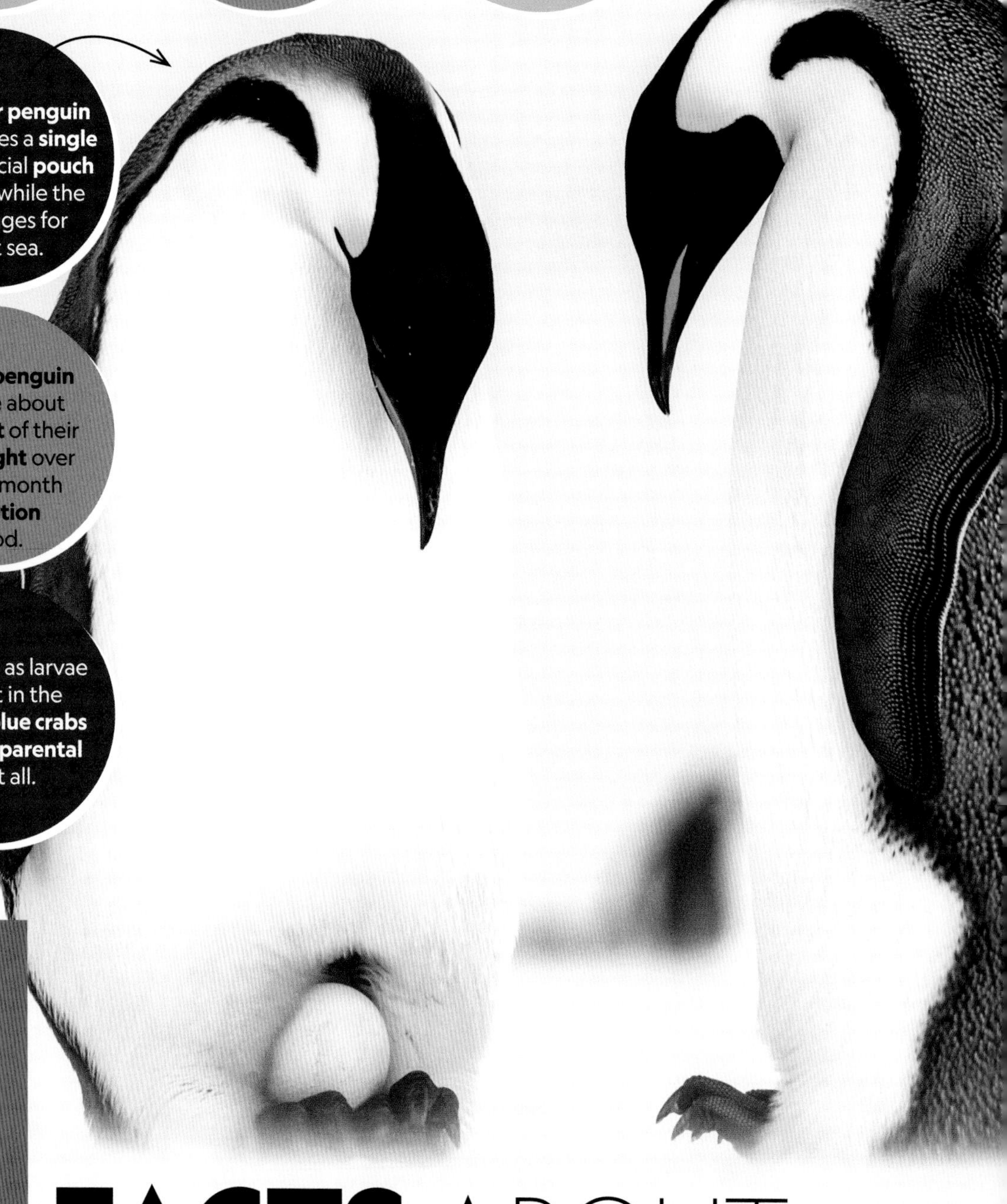

7

Emperor penguin dads lose about **40 percent** of their **body weight** over the four-month **incubation** period.

8

Weasels are born underdeveloped to keep their **mom's body small enough** during pregnancy so she can **catch prey in tight spaces.**

9

Starting life as larvae that float in the open sea, **blue crabs** receive **no parental care** at all.

35 FACTS ABOUT FAMILY LIFE
TO WRAP YOUR ARMS AROUND

10
A **male giant water bug** carries his **babies** (as eggs) on his **back** until they **hatch**.

11
Coarse-haired **wombat moms** have jelly-bean-size babies that can grow up to weigh more than 70 pounds (30 kg).

12
Discus fish secrete a **nutritious mucus** that their young eat until they are old enough to find food on their own.

13
Weddell seal moms raise their **pups** all by themselves, **teaching** them how to **hunt** and how to keep **breathing holes** open in the ice with their teeth.

14
A **strawberry poison dart frog** mom takes each of her **tadpoles** to a **separate location** to keep them from **eating each other**.

15
Female Komodo dragons in captivity have **reproduced without** a **male** around.

16
Birds called **megapodes** don't incubate their **eggs** but leave them in a **rotting pile** of plant matter to **hatch** by themselves.

17
Female great hornbills build **nests** in a **tree** or hollow log and use their own **poop** to **seal** themselves and their eggs **inside**.

18
When **red fox cubs** fight, they **stand up** on their **hind legs** and try to **push** each other over with their forelegs.

19
Belted kingfisher birds take turns incubating their eggs— **mom** sits on them at **night**, and **dad** in the **morning**.

20
Red panda moms eat their **cubs' poop** to keep their nest **clean**.

21
Butterflies lay their **eggs on leaves** using a **sticky, gluelike substance,** and then leave them to hatch.

22
Orcas live in **pods,** extended families that **remain together** throughout their lives.

23
Nile crocodile parents **guard** their **eggs together,** and males will help open the eggshells when the babies are ready to hatch.

24
To bond, male and female **western grebes run across** the **water's surface** and then **dive** into the **water together.**

25
Young female orcas "practice" by **babysitting** before having calves of their own.

26
Grunion fish bury their eggs in the sand during a **high tide;** the **eggs hatch** in two weeks **when another high tide** washes away the sand.

27
In about **80 percent** of **birds**, both **males** and **females share** at least some of the **duties** of **raising** their **young.**

28
Infant golden lion tamarins nurse from their mothers, but their **dads raise them.**

29
Male zebras snort to **warn** family members of **danger** so they can run away, usually in a zigzag.

30
Brazilian tapirs, donkeylike mammals, **carry** their babies for **more than a year** before giving birth.

31
Both male and female **blue-footed boobies** use their **large feet** to incubate their **eggs.**

32
After an **octopus mom** lays her **eggs** and **watches** over them until they **hatch,** she dies.

33
African bison don't form bonded pairs of males and females; they **live in mixed herds** or **all-male herds.**

34
The babies of some **caecilians,** which look like worms but are amphibians, **eat** part of their mother **before** they are **born.**

35
Male strawberry poison dart frogs repeatedly **pee on the eggs** of their young to keep them moist.

1 Animals whose **bodies drastically change structure** as they grow are said to undergo **metamorphosis.**

2 It takes about **two months** for **sea star larvae** to develop into adult sea stars.

3 So-called **tent caterpillars** live together in a **tent,** which they **build together.**

4 **Ant larvae lack legs** and **eyes.**

5 **Crawfish larvae travel hundreds of miles** (km) in the ocean as they develop, then they settle near the shore and **continue to molt until they reach adulthood** at about three years old.

6 **Caterpillars** are the **larval stage** of moths and **butterflies.**

7 The **first thing** a **caterpillar eats** is usually its **own eggshell.**

25 LIFE-CHANGING ANIMAL METAMORPHOSIS
ABOUT
FACTS

8 **Sea squirt larvae** begin life swimming in the ocean, but after about a day they **attach to a hard surface, absorb their backbone and tail,** and don't move again.

9 Instead of spinning a cocoon out of silk, **Hercules beetles create** a **chamber** out of their own **poop.**

10 **Ants** undergo **four stages** in their lives: **egg, larva, pupa,** and **adult ant.**

Adult

Eggs

Pupa

Ant Life Cycle

Larvae

11 Grasshoppers begin life by **hatching from eggs** and then become **nymphs**, which look like adult grasshoppers except they don't have wings.

14 As a grasshopper nymph grows, its **exoskeleton** becomes **too tight**, so it **molts** and **grows** a **new exoskeleton** in its place.

12

Scientists found a **10-inch** (25-cm)-**long bullfrog tadpole** in the **Chiricahua Mountains** in Arizona, U.S.A.

13 Frogs undergo **four stages** of life—from **eggs** to **tadpoles** to **froglets** to **frogs.**

15 Because **tadpoles** live in water, they have **gills** instead of **lungs** and don't have **legs.**

16 Most **caterpillars** are **eaten before** they become **adults.**

17

When threatened, **puss caterpillars spit burning acid** at their enemy's eyes.

18 As **caterpillars** turn into pupae, their **bodies break down** into a **soupy mixture** that will become an adult butterfly.

19 A **butterfly pupa** can be called a **chrysalis.**

20

When a **butterfly** emerges from the pupa, it takes a **few hours** for **blood** to **flow** into its veins, **stiffening the wings** so that it can **fly.**

21 **Queen ants** are **bigger** than other ants in their colony and **were fed more** when they were **larvae.**

22

Coast foam-nest tree frogs lay their **eggs** in a **foamy mass** on **branches** overlooking **streams,** and the **tadpoles drop** into the **water** below.

23 **Darwin's frogs** keep **tadpoles** in their **mouths** for about a **month** to let them grow, and then they **cough** to **release** them.

24 The **larva** of a **Hercules beetle** barely fits in a **human's open hand.**

25 A **froglet** has legs and lungs but also a **small tail** that **goes away** once it becomes **an adult** frog.

13. **Sixgill sharks** hunt near the water's surface at night, but can **dive 8,200 feet** (2,500 m) or more during the day.

14. Hatchetfish have eyes that point upward, allowing them to snag prey that falls from above.

15. Giant isopods are relatives of the pillbugs, or roly-polies, you might find in your back-yard—but they can be **16 inches** (41 cm) **long!**

16. It was thought that the **coelacanth** went **extinct** with the dinosaurs **65 million years ago,** but then in **1938,** a **fisher-man** caught **one.**

17. The megamouth shark has about **50 rows of teeth on each jaw.** It is a **filter-feeder**—it swims with its mouth wide open to gather **plankton.**

18. The **goblin shark's blood** can be seen through its skin, making it appear **pink** in color.

19. Coelacanths have been on Earth more than **360 million years.** That's more than 100 million years before the dino-saurs appeared.

20. Scientists discovered a species of **deep-sea comb jelly** that **moves** like a **hot air balloon.**

21. Most **anglerfish** are small, but **some can reach** more than **three feet** (1 m) in **length.**

22. When a **male anglerfish** finds a **mate,** he **attaches** himself to her **body** and becomes a **parasite,** living off her food supply.

23 A **female anglerfish** can have **six males hanging off her body** at once.

24. **Japanese spider crabs** can live **100 years.**

25. The **frilled shark** has **25 rows** of **backward-facing, three-pronged teeth.**

26. **Japanese spider crabs** will **eat** almost anything, including the **carcasses** of **dead animals.**

27. The deep-sea dragonfish's teeth are transparent, helping the animal sneak up on its prey.

28. **Japanese spider crabs decorate** their **shells** with sponges, anemones, and plants to **camouflage** themselves against the seafloor.

29. A **mated pair of shrimps** often takes **shelter inside** a type of sponge known as a **Venus's flower-basket.** Then the shrimps **grow too big to escape.**

30. Some **deep-sea fish** may be able to **detect color,** even in complete **darkness.**

31. Only **three humans** have ever **visited** the **deepest part** of the **ocean.**

32. **Hatchetfish** have **mirrorlike scales** that **deflect** and **scatter light,** helping them **hide** from **predators.**

33. Many **deep-sea animals** have **large eyes** that help **collect** as much of the **limited light** as possible.

34. The **fangtooth** has the **largest teeth** for its **body size** of any **fish** in the **world.**

35. Instead of squirting ink to avoid a **predator,** the **glass squid** pulls its **tentacles inside** its **body cavity** and then **fills itself** up with **nasty-tasting ink.**

1. The **deep sea** is the **largest habitat** on **Earth.**

2. Up to **two-thirds of ocean life** is still **undiscovered,** and many of these **species live** in the **deep sea.**

3. **Atlantic wolffish** have **blood** that works like **antifreeze**—it allows them to **survive** the **deep, cold waters** off New England's coast.

4. A blobfish's tissue is similar to the texture of Jell-O.

5. The **barreleye fish** has a **see-through head,** so it can look upward for food.

6. The **gulper eel,** or pelican eel, has a **pouchlike lower jaw** that can hold prey larger than its body.

7. Japanese spider crabs can survive even after losing up to three of their legs.

8. The **deep-sea worm** *Chaetopterus pugaporcinus* is **nicknamed** the **pig butt worm** because it **resembles** a **pig's rump.**

9. The **viperfish's fangs** are so **long** they **don't fit** in its **mouth.**

10. The **anglerfish** is named for the spine, tipped with a **glowing lure,** that **dangles** over its **mouth** like a fisherman's pole.

11. In 1977, scientists discovered **huge colonies of tube worms and bacteria** living near toxic, superhot water that billowed out through **hydrothermal vents** on the seafloor.

12. Below 3,280 feet (1,000 m), **animals survive with no sunlight** at all.

75 FACTS ABOUT ANIMALS OF THE ABYSS

36. The **fangtooth hunts** by **waiting to bump into something,** possibly because of its **poor eyesight.**

37. In the **1930s,** what **researchers** initially thought was the **seafloor on sonar** was a **huge mass of animals** traveling from the **depths** to the **surface** to **feed every night.**

38. Scientists discovered what may be the **longest animal ever recorded:** a **150-foot** (46-m)-**long siphonophore** in a deep-sea canyon, searching for prey in a galaxy-like spiral.

39. The **yeti crab** is named for the **hairlike structures** covering its **arms** that **resemble** the **yeti,** or abominable snowman.

40. **Ausubel's mighty claw lobster** was **named** for its **single barbed claw**—but the lobster itself is only about one inch (2.5 cm) long.

41. **Northern stargazer fish** stay **buried** in **sand** on the **seafloor** with just their **eyes exposed.** When prey swims by, the stargazer vacuums it up with its large mouth.

42. The **northern stargazer fish** has a **special organ** behind its eyes that can **deliver** an **electric shock.**

43. Most deep-sea animals **can't see the color red.**

44. Scientists think the **frilled shark** may **strike** at its **prey** by **launching** its body forward like a **land-living snake.**

45. The sea spider uses a huge proboscis, or mouthpart, to **suck up worms, jellyfish,** and sponges.

46. The **spiny deepsea king crab** is **covered** in **protective spikes.**

47. The **ghost shark** looks as if it's covered in **Frankenstein-like stitches.** They're actually **sensory organs** that help the shark hunt.

48. Bacteria live inside **giant tube worms** and provide nutrition for them.

49. The **black swallower** sometimes **eats fish so large** that its **body can't digest** them. The fish start to decompose inside its stomach and can even release gases that make the swallower float to the surface.

50. Fewer than **200 megamouth sharks** have ever been spotted.

51. Giant tube worms at the bottom of the ocean can be **eight feet** (2.4 m) **tall.** Their red tips, or plumes, get their bright red color from blood.

52. Anglerfish can **swallow prey twice** their **own size.**

53. The blobfish has no skeleton and hardly any muscles.

54. Nicknamed the **flying spaghetti monster,** *Bathyphysa conifera,* which is related to jellyfish, looks like an **upside-down bowl of noodles.**

55. A living **ghost fish,** named for its see-through skin and colorless eyes, wasn't **spotted** until **2016.**

56. The **width** of a **megamouth shark's mouth** is about **one-quarter** of its **body length.**

57. Giant tube worms, the **world's fastest-growing invertebrates,** shoot up at 33 inches (84 cm) a year.

58. The deeper the Pacific **warty octopus** lives, the **bumpier** its **skin.**

59. The **benthocodon jellyfish eats glowing animals.** Some scientists think its red color keeps its prey's light from shining through its stomach.

60. The telescope octopus has eyes on stalks, like a snail's.

61. **Zombie worms ooze acid** from their skin that **dissolves bone** so that the worms can eat the fat and protein inside.

62. Many underwater mountains called **seamounts** are **home to animals that live nowhere else.** There are an estimated 31,000 seamounts on Earth, but only a handful have been explored.

63. **Snailfish** can **withstand** an **underwater pressure** that **equals** approximately **1,600 elephants standing on a small car.**

64. The deepest a fish has ever been caught is almost five miles (8 km) below the surface.

65. The **viperfish swims at high speeds** and then **impales** its **victims** with its **sharp teeth.**

66. The **squidworm** uses its **10 tentacle-like head appendages,** which are each longer than its whole body, to **capture bits of food.**

67. **Pompeii worms** often sit so that their **tails rest** in **hydrothermal vent water** of up to **176°F** (80°C), while their **heads rest** in **water** at around **72°F** (22°C).

68. **Bacteria** live on the **hairlike structures** that cover the **yeti crab's claws,** which the crab waves over hydrothermal vents to help the bacteria grow. The **crab** then **scrapes** the **bacteria off** and **eats it.**

69. Glass sponges have **skeletons** made of **silica,** the same material used to make glass.

70. The **hydrothermal vent shrimp** *Rimicaris exoculata* **can't see.** Instead, its **eyes may be able to detect heat** given off by the vents around it.

71. Unlike their relatives the hermit crabs, **squat lobsters don't carry shells** to hide under. Instead, they **squeeze** into **crevices,** with only their sharp claws poking out to grab food.

72. The *Tomopteris* worm can **shoot out sparks** when it is **threatened.**

73. **Creatures** that **live** in the **deepest sea** experience **temperatures just above freezing** and **pressure more than 1,000 times stronger** than it is on the **water's surface.**

74. **Spotted ratfish** have **emerald-green eyes** that **reflect light,** like a cat's.

75. The fangtooth is so scary-looking it's nicknamed the ogrefish.

1
As many as 7,000 ELK MIGRATE from Grand Teton and Yellowstone National Parks to National Elk Refuge in WYOMING, U.S.A., EVERY WINTER.

2
You can take a HORSE-DRAWN SLEIGH RIDE past elk herds at the REFUGE.

3
WATER BUFFALO use their CURVED HORNS to DEFEND THEMSELVES against TIGERS and CROCODILES.

4
ANTLERS begin with a VELVET PHASE, during which they are COVERED in FINE HAIR.

5
ANTLER VELVET eventually DRIES UP and is RUBBED OFF on trees or other vegetation.

6
Some MALES carry VEGETATION in their ANTLERS to make themselves appear BIGGER and more IMPRESSIVE to mates.

7
ANTLERS grow from the TIP; HORNS grow from the BASE.

8
MALE IMPALAS have a SCENT GLAND on their FOREHEADS near their HORNS, which they rub on vegetation to show DOMINANCE.

9
At about three feet (1 m) wide, the LONGEST HORN on a living animal belongs to an ASIAN WATER BUFFALO—the longest recorded stretched 13 feet 10 inches (4.24 m).

10
MALE WATERBUCKS of Africa FIGHT by PUSHING each other with LOCKED HORNS and attempting to puncture the other in the side.

11
Even though NEW ANTLERS grow each year, GROWTH PATTERNS have a "MEMORY" and SIMILAR antlers grow OVER AND OVER.

12
INJURY to an ANTLER one year MAY CHANGE the antler PATTERN the following year.

13
MANX LOAGHTAN, a type of sheep, have up to SIX HORNS.

14
ELK ANTLERS GROW up to an INCH (2.5 cm) a DAY.

15
FEMALE HORNS are usually STRAIGHTER and THINNER for stabbing in self-defense.

16
SAIGA, a type of Central Asian horned antelope, have LARGE CHAMBERS inside their noses that help them BREATHE more EFFICIENTLY when TRAVELING in migrating herds.

17
RHINOCEROSES' HORNS continue to GROW their entire LIVES.

18
TRICERATOPS had THREE HORNS, two of which CHANGED SHAPE as they AGED.

19
ELAND, the largest African antelope, use their LONG HORNS to BREAK OFF BRANCHES that are too high for them to reach with their tongues and lips.

20
The word "ORYX" comes from the Greek word for "PICKAX."

21
Before they spar, ELK show off by MOVING their HEADS SLOWLY to show off their RACK.

50 POINTED FACTS ABOUT ANTLERS AND HORNS

22 MALE IMPALAS use their spiral HORNS to CHALLENGE each other's STRENGTH.

23 ANTLERS are used to show DOMINANCE, KNOCK FRUIT OFF TREES, and DIG HOLES in dirt or mud to rest or cool down in.

24 Both MALE and FEMALE REINDEER grow ANTLERS.

25 The TEXAS HORNED LIZARD has a PAIR OF HORNS on its head, which are covered with SPIKES that EXTEND when it is THREATENED.

26 MALE HORNS are usually THICKER at the BASE and can withstand more FORCE for FIGHTING.

27 MALE ELK can have up to EIGHT POINTS on their ANTLERS.

28 *TRICERATOPS* had small HORNLIKE PROJECTIONS on its CHEEKBONES.

29 The SAMI PEOPLE of Scandinavia use REINDEER ANTLERS for KNIFE HANDLES and TOOLS.

30 MOOSE DIG HOLES, URINATE in them, and then DIP their ANTLERS in—the smell ATTRACTS females.

31 RHINOCEROSES are BORN WITHOUT HORNS, but a STUB appears within a FEW MONTHS.

32 Generally, both MALES and FEMALES of LARGER ANIMALS, like RHINOS, have HORNS, but in smaller species, like the KUDU, FEMALES often DON'T HAVE HORNS.

33 ANCIENT GREEKS thought RHINO HORNS could CLEAN water.

34 The ASIAN LONG-HORNED BEETLE DOESN'T HAVE HORNS—it's named for its EXTRA-LONG ANTENNAE.

35 ANTLERS are bony structures that are SHED ANNUALLY.

36 SCIMITAR-HORNED ORYX are named for the way their HORNS are SHAPED: like Arabian swords called SCIMITARS.

37 Animals with the LARGEST set of ANTLERS typically SHED THEM EARLIEST in the season.

38 *KOSMOCERATOPS RICHARDSONI*, a relative of *Triceratops*, had 15 HORNS on its head.

39 What look like horns on the DESERT VIPER SNAKE are actually SCALES above each EYE.

40 A JACKALOPE is a MYTHICAL animal, described as a JACKRABBIT with ANTELOPE HORNS.

41 NEWBORN GIRAFFES are BORN with HORNS.

42 HORNS are PERMANENT and have a bony core covered in KERATIN—the same material as your fingernails.

43 DESERT BIGHORN SHEEP use their HORNS to BREAK OPEN and EAT cacti.

44 A MALE BIGHORN SHEEP'S HORNS can WEIGH MORE than ALL the other BONES in its BODY combined.

45 MALE JACKSON'S CHAMELEONS have THREE HORNS on top of their heads, giving them the LOOK of a *TRICERATOPS*.

46 MARKHOR, a type of wild goat, have CORK-SCREW-LIKE HORNS.

47 "MARKHOR," translated from a language of Afghanistan, means "SNAKE HORN."

48 The SOUTH AMERICAN HORNED SCREAMER, also known as the UNICORN BIRD, has a CURVED HORN, made of cartilage, that's SIX INCHES (15 cm) LONG.

49 SAIGA are POACHED for their TRANSLUCENT, AMBER-COLORED HORNS, which are SOLD on the BLACK MARKET as traditional Asian MEDICINE.

50 JACKSON'S CHAMELEONS LOCK HORNS and try to KNOCK EACH OTHER OFF narrow tree BRANCHES.

1 One out of **every four animal species** on Earth is a **beetle.**

2 All **beetles** have **two sets** of **wings.**

3 **Burying beetles bury carcasses** of small animals and lay their eggs nearby. When the **babies are born**, the **carcass** is their **first meal.**

4 **Ancient Greek coins** had **images** of **bees** on them.

5 Some plants grow **heated flowers** to encourage **beetles** to **visit** and spread their flowers' pollen.

6 The world's **longest** beetle is the **rhinoceros beetle.** Including its horns, it's about as long as a pencil.

7 In many cultures, **ladybugs** are considered **good luck.**

8 **Ancient Egyptians worshipped** the scarab beetle.

9 *Epomis* **beetles hunt** and eat frogs.

35
FACTS ABOUT
BEETLES
AND OTHER
BUGS

10
The **fogstand beetle** **leans into the wind** to **collect drops** of **water from fog** that roll into its mouth.

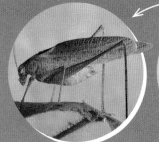

11
Katydids, a relative of crickets, have **ears** on their **knees.**

15
Leaf-cutter ants use their sharp **mandibles** to **tear off leaf pieces,** which they carry to their underground nests and use to grow a fungus they eat.

12
An **Argentine ant colony,** containing millions of workers and more than one queen, can **stretch** for **hundreds** of **miles** (km).

13
Trap-jaw ants can **close** their **mandibles** at speeds up to **145 miles an hour** (230 km/h).

14
Springtails use a special **forklike structure** under their abdomens to **jump** into the air.

16
Scientists estimate that of the **total weight** of all the **animals** in a Brazilian rainforest, more than a **quarter** is made up of **ants.**

17
The **snowflea** is a species of springtail, but their **small, dark bodies** look like **fleas** against the **snow** where they're found.

18
The Beatles got the idea to use a **bug-inspired name** from another band called the Crickets.

19
One fly species has a **proboscis** that is nearly **eight times its body length**—that's the equivalent of a 20-foot (6-m)-long human tongue!

20
Some species of **lacewing larvae camouflage** their bodies with the **dead bodies** of the **insects** they eat.

21
Green lacewings have **ears on their wings** to help hear bats that can eat them.

22
Houseflies taste with their **feet,** which are **10 million times** more **sensitive** than a **human tongue.**

23
Insects don't breathe through their mouths—they **inhale oxygen** through **holes** in the **sides** of their **bodies.**

24
When a **hawk moth caterpillar** is threatened, it raises its head and **inflates its body** to look like the head of a **snake.**

25
When **ticks** feast on **blood,** they can **grow** from the size of a **grain of rice** to the size of a **marble.**

26
Biting midges, also known as punkies and no-see-ums, are **small enough** to fit through the **holes** in a **screen door.**

27
Caterpillars have **12 eyes.**

28
Water-living **whirligig beetles** have **divided eyes.** The top half can see above the water's surface, and the bottom half can see underwater.

29
In Brazil, 4,000-year-old **termite mounds,** which termites still use today, dot an area the size of **Great Britain.**

30
An **estimated 10 quintillion** individual **insects live** on **Earth today.**

31
Flies are the **only insects** that **pollinate cacao trees**—where chocolate comes from.

32
A **midge beats** its **wings 1,000 times** per **second.**

33
A **termite queen** lays more than a **quarter billion eggs** in her **lifetime**—that's one egg every two seconds for 15 years!

34
Ants use chemical signals called **phero-mones** to **tell** other ants **where** to locate **food** sources and to **warn** of **danger.**

35
When the **Hercules beetle** is **dry,** it's **yellow** in color. When it gets **wet,** it turns **black.**

»15 FACTS ABOUT ANIMAL HOMES TO FIND SHELTER IN

1

Coral reefs are built from the **skeletons** of **coral animals**—each coral polyp creates a skeleton out of calcium carbonate that becomes part of the reef.

2

Thousands of **weaver ants** use **secretions** of **silk** from weaver ant **larvae** to **bind leaves together** for their **homes.**

3

Gila woodpeckers carve their **nests** out of **saguaro cacti,** with an **entrance** that is only about **two inches (5 cm) wide.**

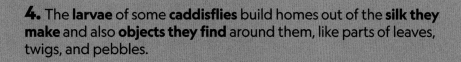

4. The **larvae** of some **caddisflies** build homes out of the **silk they make** and also **objects they find** around them, like parts of leaves, twigs, and pebbles.

5
When **hermit crabs** grow **too large** for their **shells,** they **search** for **new ones.**

6. Himalayan jumping spiders feed on insects that are blown into the **tall mountains** by wind.

7. Himalayan jumping spiders live at 22,000 feet (6,750 m) on **Mount Everest**—their species name means "standing above all."

8. For **wasps** that live in **colonies,** the **queen wasp** finds a good spot and uses **chewed-up wood pulp** to begin building the **nest.**

9. Red ovenbirds in South America build **nests of mud** that can weigh as much as **11 pounds** (5 kg).

10
The **largest coral reef** in the world, **Australia's Great Barrier Reef** stretches for some **1,400 miles** (2,300 km)—that's about the distance from New York City to Miami, U.S.A.

11. Beavers build dams out of **logs** and **stones,** and their **homes filter pollutants** from rivers, which helps **keep** the **water clean.**

12. A study found that **brown bears** choose **den sites** on **steep mountain slopes** that are situated to keep out water and to keep the bears **dry and warm.**

13
Nubian ibex spend their lives on **cliffs,** sheltering in **caves** in winter and returning to the **mountain slopes** in the summer.

14
Built with bits of **chewed-up wood, mud,** and **termite poop, termite mounds** in Australia's Northwest Territory can be **taller** than a **one-story house.**

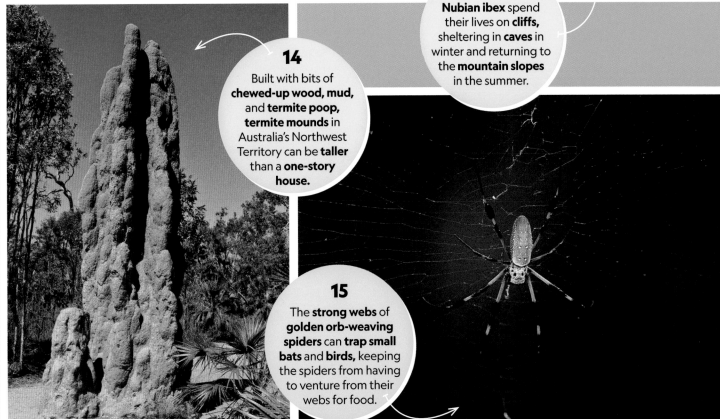

15
The **strong webs** of **golden orb-weaving spiders** can **trap small bats** and **birds,** keeping the spiders from having to venture from their webs for food.

A **GREAT WHITE SHARK'S** MOUTH HOLDS **300** SERRATED, TRIANGULAR TEETH.

»BEHIND THE 5,000 ANIMAL FACTS

Just how did we get 5,000 awesome facts about animals into this book? First, we came up with a list of all kinds of critters and their cool and crazy habits, habitats, and traits: from hovering humming-birds and precious pets to burying beetles and gigantic gorillas, from creatures that swim in the sea to those that fly high. Then we figured out how to fit all these facts about Earth's amazing animals on the pages. It was kind of like doing a jigsaw puzzle! Some topics have 15 facts. Some have 25. Some even have 100! We carefully researched each and every fact to make sure it's absolutely true. And we illustrated and designed the pages so well that you'll never want to stop looking at them. Then we added up all the facts to get to 5,000. It didn't take 5,000 people to make this awesome book—but it did take a colossal crew of writers, editors, photo editors, and designers—the most awesome book team around!

» CREDITS

AS: Adobe Stock; ASP: Alamy Stock Photo; BP: Biosphoto; DR: Dreamstime; GI: Getty Images; IS: iStockphoto; MP: Minden Pictures; NGIC: National Geographic Image Collection; NPL: Nature Picture Library; SS: Shutterstock

COVER (giraffe fur texture), Anna Timoshenko/SS; (halftone texture), Vyacheslav Kravtsov/AS; (zebra leopard fur pattern), Fidan Stock/SS; (puffin), Christoph Ruisz/imageBROKER RF/GI; (cheetah), Valentyna Chukhlyebova/SS; (fish), chonlasub woravichan/SS; (dragonfly), Cathy Keifer/SS; (chameleon), Eric Isselée/SS; (axolotl), Eric Isselée/SS; (tapir), Eric Isselée/SS; (blue-footed booby), Tui De Roy/NPL; (squirrel), panbazil/SS; (giant panda), Eric Isselée/SS; Spine (jaguar), Ana Vasileva/SS; Back cover (hummingbird), Chesampson/AS; (wombat), Dominik Rueß/AS; (grizzly bear), Sylvain Cordier/BP; (rhinoceros), Gualtiero Boffi/AS; 1, Rosa Jay/SS; 2-3, Visual and Written Photo Collection/BP; 4 (UP LE), mgkuijpers/AS; 4 (UP CTR), panor156/SS; 4 (UP RT), Sonsedska Yuliia/SS; 4-5 (CTR), thawats/AS; 4 (LO LE), Eric Isselée/DR; 4 (LO RT), Mikephotos2/DR; 5 (UP LE), kamnuan/SS; 5 (UP RT), Papik/SS; 5 (CTR), irin-k/SS; 5 (LO RT), Eric Isselée/SS; 6-7, Agora/SWNS; 8 (UP LE), Frank Hildebrand/IS/GI; 8 (LO LE), Tom Bird/AS; 8 (LO RT), Martin Maritz/DR; 9 (5), Jonas/AS; 9 (10), Alexander Machulskiy/SS; 9 (13), Eric Gevaert/AS; 9 (14), Albie Venter/SS; 9 (15), grandaded/AS; 10-11, whitcomberd/AS; 10 (4), kai egan/SS; 10 (20), Wet Lizard Photography/SS; 11 (34), Miroslav Halama/SS; 11 (57), Erika Kirkpatrick/SS; 12-13, Michel Bureau/BP; 12 (7), Eric Isselée/DR; 12 (18), Tobias Nowlan/IS/GI; 13 (21), Photoshot/AS; 13 (25), robertharding/ASP; 13 (27), Reinhard Mink/GI; 14 (UP), gopause/SS; 14 (LO), naturesauraphoto/AS; 15 (UP), Dorographie/AS; 15 (LO), PhotoBarmaley/SS; 16-17, ondrejprosicky/AS; 16 (LE), Uryadnikov Sergey/AS; 16 (RT), Vlad_Ghiea/AS; 17 (UP LE), volkova natalia/SS; 17 (CTR RT), AllCanadaPhotos/AS; 17 (LO RT), Dennis Minty/AS; 18 (1), Eric Isselée/AS; 18 (2), Dennis Donohue/AS; 18 (3), Eric Isselée/SS; 18 (4), chonlasub woravichan/SS; 18 (6), WaterFrame/Agence/Tom Stack/BP; 18 (7), Robert Eastman/SS; 18 (8), thawats/IS/GI; 18 (9), Tobias/AS; 19 (12), Subphoto/AS; 19 (13), Gallo Images/ASP; 19 (14), vladislav333222/AS; 19 (15), EtienneOutram/AS; 19 (16), olga demchishina/AS; 19 (17), G.J. Verspui/SS; 19 (18), kasira698/AS; 19 (19), Eric Isselée/SS; 19 (20), R. Maximiliane/SS; 19 (23), Iakov Filimonov/SS; 19 (24), Gerald C. Kelley/Science Source; 20 (UP), Luciano Candisani/MP; 20 (LO), Phil/AS; 21 (5), Cyril Ruoso/NPL; 21 (6), Paul D. Stewart/NPL; 21 (11), Tui De Roy/NPL; 21 (13), Yva Momatiuk and John Eastcott/MP/MP; 22-23, Irina/AS; 22 (8), Holger Kirk/SS; 22 (31), Ian Dyball/SS; 23 (43), Neal Cooper/DR; 23 (60), Uryadnikov Sergey/AS; 24-25, Luis Leamus/AS; 24 (2), Vadim/AS; 24 (8), Ian Beattie/ASP; 25 (9), Tony Heald/NPL; 25 (15), Paul E Tessier/AS; 25 (28), Paul Nicklen/NGIC; 25 (30), Aaron Amat/SS; 26-27, Stanislav Duben/AS; 26 (5), vaclav/AS; 27 (25), Heinrich van den Berg/GI; 28 (UP), Tsekhmister/SS; 28 (LO), Ami Vitale/NGIC; 29, Suzi Eszterhas/MP; 30 (1), Shpatak/SS; 30 (2), Ken Usami/GI; 30 (3), Patrick Moyer/AS; 30 (5), Scubasub/AS; 30 (7), cyb3rking/IS/GI; 30 (7), Liumangtiger/DR; 30 (8), Eric Isselée/AS; 30 (9), Baranov/AS; 30 (10), wanchai chaipanya/AS; 30 (12), Wil Meinderts/Buiten-beeld/MP; 31 (13), Ingo Arndt/NPL; 31 (14), Ekkapan Poddamrong/SS; 31 (16), mastersky/AS; 31 (17), svetlanistaya/AS; 31 (19), Rainervon Brandis/IS/GI; 31 (20), Yury Ivanov/AS; 31 (22), imageBROKER/SS; 31 (23), Andrea Izzotti/AS; 31 (24), craykeeper/IS/GI; 32-33, Konart/DR; 32 (2), havranka/AS; 32 (4), Richard Wright/Danita Delimont/AS; 32 (12), razihusin/AS; 32 (UP RT), John_Dakapu/SS; 32 (LO LE), mirecca/AS; 32 (LO RT), Valentin Valkov/SS; 33 (14), Juan Carlos Vindas/Moment RF/GI; 33 (16), Gerry Ellis/Digital Vision; 33 (18), hartmut nolte/EyeEm/AS; 33 (24), HeresTwoPhotography/AS; 33 (22), 1nana1/AS; 33 (22), Delphotostock/AS; 33 (25), Hendrata Yoga Surya/EyeEm/GI; 33 (27), Andrey Nekrasov/GI; 33 (30), Dmitrijs Bindemanis/SS; 33 (31), SS/Vitaly Ilyasov/SS; 34 (1), Olga Galushko/AS; 34 (2), Starover Sibiriak/SS; 34 (3), Erni/AS; 35 (5), arthorse/AS; 35 (10), bearacreative/SS; 35 (13), Shane P. White/MP; 35 (14), Matthijs Kuijpers/AS; 35 (15), Bence Mate/NPL; 36-37, Kelvin Aitken/Image Quest Marine; 36 (9), bennytrapp/AS; 36 (32), Chris Mattison/NPL; 37 (60), krisana/AS; 38-39, R. Jeff Huth/AS; 38 (7), Roberto Machado Noa/Moment RF/GI; 38 (8), drferry/IS/GI; 39 (26), PetrDolejsek/AS; 39 (28), Tom Kilroy/AS; 40 (UP), ArchMan/SS; 40 (LO), slowmotiongli/AS; 41 (UP), Paul Nicklin/NGIC; 41 (LO), Michael Smith ITWP/SS; 42-43, Evelyn/AS; 42 (3), Jim Cumming/SS; 42 (14), Jim Brandenburg/MP; 43 (46), kongsak sumano/SS; 44 (1), Kuttelvaserova Stuchelova/SS; 44 (2), blickwinkel/ASP; 44 (3), Sergey/AS; 44-45 (blue frog), Aleksey Stemmer/SS; 44 (6), Jirasak Chuangsen/SS; 44 (7), Tatiana Belova/AS; 44 (8), Roberto A Sanchez/E+/GI; 44 (9), Jeff Rotman/NPL; 45 (12), Doug Schnurr/AS; 45 (13), Piotr Krzeslak/AS; 45 (14), Shutter9Aum/AS; 45 (15), Odua Images/AS; 45(16), Aleksey Stemmer/SS; 45 (17), drew/AS; 45 (CTR LE), Peteri/SS; 45 (CTR RT), SS/panor156; 45 (19), johan63/IS/GI; 45 (20), chonlasub woravichan/SS; 45 (21), SailingAway/AS; 45 (25), Eduardo M. Rivero/DR; 46 (1), Simon Greig/SS; 46 (2), Hiroya Minakuchi/MP; 46 (3), Ondej/AS; 46 (4), Super Prin/SS; 47 (5), Vilainecrevette/SS; 47 (8), Jak Wonderly/NGP; 47 (10), Tomas/AS; 47 (13), Ann and Steve Toon/ASP; 47 (14), blickwinkel/ASP; 47 (15), Velvetfish/IS/GI; 48-49, Yoreh/SS; 48 (1), Elena799/SS; 49 (46 & 49), cameilia/SS; 50-51, Alex Snyder/NGP; 50 (7), Liz/AS; 51 (16), Caymia/IS/GI; 51 (27), Zoltan Bagosi/ASP; 51 (33), SCJohnG/AS; 52 (UP), Eric Isselée/DR; 52 (LO), Ondrej Prosicky/AS; 53 (UP), Milan/AS; 53 (LO), Danny/AS; 54-55, Muhammad Otib/SS; 54 (8), Deki/AS; 55 (20), Bruce Raynor/SS; 55 (35), Miroslav Liska/DR; 55 (40), imageBROKER/ASP; 55 (50), stasnds/AS; 56 (1), Wayne Morris/SS; 56 (2), wolfelarry/AS; 56 (3), MF Photo/AS; 56 (4), Eric Isselée/SS; 56 (5), Ernie Cooper/AS; 56 (6), Eric Isselée/AS; 56 (7), Jefunne/SS; 56 (8), billdayone/SS; 56 (9), Ivan Kuzmin/SS; 56 (10), beckystarsmore/AS; 57 (11 & 12), Rick & Nora Bowers/ASP; 57 (15), Mushy/AS; 57 (16), Narong Sangnak/EPA/SS; 57 (17), Protasov AN/SS; 57 (18), Dario Fogo/SS; 57 (18), Tartila/AS; 57 (19), AuntSpray/SS; 57 (21), Frog_Ground/AS; 57 (22), blickwinkel/ASP; 57 (23), Mirko Ivkovic/Moment RF/GI; 57 (25), tea maeklong/SS; 58 (1), cherylvb/AS; 58 (3), damedias/AS; 58 (4), cherylvb/AS; 59 (5), Bryan Toro/AS; 59 (7), David Fleetham/ASP; 59 (11), Nata-Lia/SS; 59 (12), Brent Durand/Moment RF/GI; 59 (14), H. Tanaka/SS; 60, Koilee/SS; 61, Anne B. Keiser/NGIC; 62-63, Juergen & Christine Sohns/MP; 62 (7), Album/ASP; 62 (11), Nejron Photo/SS; 62 (LO), Eric Isselée/SS; 63 (20), Album/ASP; 63 (26), Alexei Zavrachayev\TASS via GI; 63 (28), AF Archive/ASP; 63 (34), AF Archive/ASP; 64 (UP), dimj/AS; 64 (LO), endasiana29/AS; 65, Galyna/AS; 66-67, imageBROKER RF/GI; 66 (2), National Geographic Partners, LLC; 67 (24), Tom Walker/Photographer's Choice RF/GI; 67 (36), Svetlana Foote/SS; 67 (46), Gerald Marella/SS; 68 (1), Nantawat Chotsuwa/SS; 68 (3), Ferenc Cegledi/AS; 68 (4), cpisano/AS; 68 (6), haveseen/IS/GI; 68 (7), Mary Katherine Wynn/DR; 68 (8), blickwinkel/ASP; 68 (9), Darin Sakdatorn/AS; 68 (10), Hannalvanova/AS; 69 (12), Magnus/AS; 69 (13), JazzIRT/IS/GI; 69 (14), rockptarmigan/IS/GI; 69 (15), Andy Murch/Blue Planet Archive; 69 (16), Humberto Ramirez/Moment RF/GI; 69 (17), ralucacohn/AS; 69 (19), vladwel/SS; 69 (20), Sophie/AS; 69 (21), NickVeasey/GI/Science Photo Library RF/GI; 69 (22), frantisek hojdysz/AS; 69 (23), Ugurhan Betin/E+/GI; 69 (24), Charlieatyourservice/DR; 69 (25), Josh Forwood/IS/GI; 70 (1), Chris/AS; 70 (3), Wim Wyloeck/DR; 70 (4), Sunil Onamkulam/SS; 71 (6), Prasou/ASP; 71 (9), Binoy B Gogoi/SS; 71 (10), Agami/AS; 71 (12), kunanon/SS; 71 (13), sompreaw/SS; 72 (10), Heike Brauer/SS; 72 (27), panbazil/SS; 73 (34), Vladimir Wrangel/AS; 73 (42), chas53/AS; 73 (50), Alexander Potapov/AS; 73 (58), Joe Thongsan/SS; 73 (75), gallinago_media/SS; 74-75, Wild Carpathians/SS; 74 (7), Peter Hilger/AS; 74 (16), kuritafsheen/AS; 74 (UP), kamnuan/SS; 74 (LO), Eric Isselée/SS; 75 (18), damedias/AS; 75 (26), Yanukit/AS; 75 (27), JC Lobo/AS; 75 (32), kamnuan/SS; 76 (UP LE), Dorottya Mathe/SS; 76 (UP RT), ArtSilense/SS; 76 (LO), Fly_dragonfly/SS; 77, Odua Images/SS; 78-79, knelson20/AS; 78 (1), Eyal Bartov/ASP; 78 (4), Joao Virissimo/DR; 78 (7), Mark Thiessen/NGIC; 78 (15), ZSSD/MP; 79 (21), Doug Perrine/ASP; 79 (25), Eric Isselée/SS; 79 (29), Beverly Joubert/NGIC; 79 (36), Konrad Wothe/MP; 79 (38), Eric Isselée/SS; 79 (40), Tomasz/AS; 79 (45), jaroslava V/SS; 79 (48), fieldwork/AS; 80 (1), Nancy Elwood-Naturesportal/GI; 80 (2), WUT.ANUNA/SS; 80 (4), khlungcenter/SS; 80 (6), Solvin Zankl; 80 (7), Steve Downer/ARDEA; 80 (8), Leysanl/AS; 80 (10), JÈrÙme Mallefet - FNRS-UCL/BP; 81 (13), Raimundo Fernandez Diez/Moment RF/GI; 81 (14), Saraid/AS; 81 (15), Macrovector/SS; 81 (16), Paulo de Oliveira/BP; 81 (19), Robert Sisson/NGIC; 81 (20), Espen Rekdal/Blue Planet Archive; 81 (21), superjoseph/SS; 81 (22), pandemin/IS/GI; 81 (25), Solvin Zankl; 82 (1), Eric Risberg/AP Photo; 82 (2), Splash News and Pictures/Newscom; 82 (3), WENN Rights Ltd/ASP; 82 (4), topseller/SS; 82 (5), John Minchillo/AP Photo; 83 (6), Hintau Aliaksei/SS; 83 (8), Robyn Beck/AFP via GI; 83 (9), Reuters/ASP; 83 (10), frenta/AS; 83 (14), Magdalena Troendle/dpa/AFP via GI; 83 (15), Richard Richtmyer/AP Photo; 84 (4), Eric Isselée/SS; 84 (27), LifetimeStock/SS; 85 (63), Konrad Wothe/MP; 85 (68), dblumenberg/AS; 86-87, Krzysztof Wiktor/AS; 86 (1), Sylvain Cordier/BP; 86 (7), Simia Attentive/SS; 87 (12), Tsuguliev/SS; 87 (14), Stefan Scharf/AS; 87 (23), Dave Willman/AS; 87 (30), Timelynx/AS; 88 (UP), wacpan/SS; 88 (LO), The Ocean Agency/AS/AS; 89 (UP), Sergey Sivkov/AS; 89 (LO), suebg1 photography/Moment/GI; 90-91, Manok/AS; 90 (20), Timothy Craig Lubcke/SS; 91 (31), Wlad74/SS; 91 (36), titipong8176734/AS; 92 (1), Emanuele Biggi/NPL; 92 (3), Meepoohya/DR; 92 (5), Yuan Geng/AS; 92 (6), Sebastian Kaulitz/SS; 92 (7), Cosmin Manci/SS; 92 (8), hhelene/AS; 93 (12), fotoparus/AS; 93 (13), Melinda Fawver/SS; 93 (14), Metropolitan Museum of Art; 93 (17), Dariusz Majgier/SS; 93 (18), Ken Archer/Danita Delimont/AS; 93 (19), Michael S. Nolan/Blue Planet Archive; 93 (20), smuay/AS; 93 (25), Hussmann/AS; 94 (1), The Dog Agency; 94 (2), Bernard Weil/Toronto Star via GI; 94 (3), Astrid Stawiarz/GI; 95 (5), Ken McKay/ITV/SS; 95 (6), The Dog Agency; 95 (7), Vincent Sandoval/FilmMagic/GI; 95 (10), Harlso the Balancing Hound; 95 (11), Jeffrey Mayer/WireImage/GI; 96 (1), Four Oaks/SS; 96 (17), Alx/AS; 96 (40), Eric Isselée/SS; 96 (42), clarst5/SS; 97 (43), IrinaK/SS; 97 (55), madmonkey0328/SS; 97 (62), Catmando/SS; 97 (64), Gallinago_media/SS; 98-99, Marian/AS; 98 (2), gudkovandrey/AS; 98 (8), Romolo Tavani/AS; 99 (13), Copyright 2003 NBAE (Photo by: Barry Gossage/NBAE via GI); 99 (14), Brina Bunt/IS/GI; 99 (26), robertharding/ASP; 99 (28), Roman Samokhin/SS; 99 (34, both), Ronald H. Cohn/NGIC; 100 (UP), Eastman Arts/AS; 100 (LO), fivespots/SS; 101, Eric Isselée/SS; 102-103, Rita/SS; 102 (2), Nimit Virdi/SS; 102 (12), cynoclub/AS; 102 (17), Tsekhmister/SS; 102 (21), nataba/AS; 103 (36), Digital Vision; 103 (42), Picture Partners/AS; 104 (1), Harvey8/IS/GI; 104 (2), Ash/AS; 104 (5), Daniel Gale/SS; 104 (6), Rajo Mulia/SS; 104 (CTR), vnlit/SS; 104 (7), Michael Valos/AS; 104 (10), mania/SS; 104 (11), John Anderson/AS; 105 (12), Sabine/AS; 105 (13), Suzi Eszterhas/NPL; 105 (14), Reinhard Mink/Moment RF/GI; 105 (16), Eric Isselée/SS; 105 (18), Independent birds/SS; 105 (20), lunamarina/SS; 105 (22), Sekar Balasubramanian/AS; 105 (24), Shane Gross/NPL; 105 (25), phototrip/AS; 106-107, Aaron/AS; 106 (8), eye-blink/SS; 107 (10), PBorowka/AS; 107 (19), aquaey/AS; 107 (21), Aleksey Stemmer/AS; 107 (30), Tim Heusinger Von Waldegger/DR; 108 (1), Istvan Kovacs/SS; 108 (2), Friso Gentsch/picture-alliance/dpa/AP Images; 108 (3), Hiroya Minakuchi/MP; 109 (5), Roberto Michel/ASP; 109 (10), eqroy/AS; 109 (13), Miroslav Halama/SS; 109 (14), Eric Isselée/AS; 109 (15), Shaun Jeffers/SS; 110 (10), Svetlana Foote/SS; 110-111, Eric Isselée/SS; 111 (16), Ann & Steve Toon/NPL; 111 (18), Cherdchai Chaivimol/SS; 111 (26), Maximillian cabinet/SS; 111 (30), Chris Fourie/SS; 112-113, lightpoet/AS; 112 (1), Protasov AN/SS; 112 (6), Jamie Roach/AS; 112 (8), IFA-Bilderteam/Stone RF/GI; 112 (18), Igor Chus/SS; 112 (22), Rufous/SS; 112 (28), tr3gin/SS; 113 (40), Seregam/SS; 113 (48), Dan Kosmayer/SS; 113 (UP), irin-k/SS; 113 (LO), Protasov AN/SS; 114 (UP), nelik/SS; 114 (LO), Thorsten Nilson/EyeEm/GI; 115 (UP), Sarah Fields Photography/SS; 115 (LO), Picture Partners/ASP; 116 (3), picture.jacker/AS; 116 (5), Milous Chab/DR; 116 (7), Mikhail Melnikov/SS; 116 (8), Mark Mirror/SS; 116 (9), Svetlana Foote/SS; 116 (13), ducu59us/SS; 116 (15), Alicia Chelini/SS; 116 (18), Stephen Frink/The Image Bank RF/GI; 116 (21), Solvin Zankl; 116 (21), Shawn Jackson/DR; 117 (22), Eric Gevaert/SS; 117 (23), Tania Zbrodko/SS; 117 (24), steveball/SS; 117 (25), nmelnychuk/AS; 117 (25), EBFoto/AS; 117 (29), hriana/AS; 117 (30), nico99/SS; 117 (31), defun/AS; 117 (33), JethroT/AS; 117 (38), Kzmonrat/SS; 117 (39), dgwildlife/AS; 117 (40), imageBROKER RF/GI; 117 (42), Jan Martin Will/SS; 117 (43), Michael Nolan/Robert Harding/Collection Mix Subjects RF/GI; 117 (45), Funny Farm/Digital Vision; 117 (47), the Ocean Agency/AS; 117 (50), mgkuijpers/AS; 118 (2), robert_s/SS; 118 (3), Marie/AS; 118 (4), Jane Rix/AS; 118 (5), Malota/SS; 118 (8), Christian Musat/AS; 118 (11), PicturesWild/SS; 118 (11), Andrey Kuzmin/SS; 118 (12), Jak Wonderly/NGP; 118 (14), kenmc3/AS; 119 (15), Robert Muckley/Moment RF/GI; 119 (16), Wim Hoek/AS; 119 (17), mariait/SS; 119 (17), Eric Isselée/SS; 119 (20), Danny Ye/SS; 119 (21), Ariadne Van Zandbergen/ASP; 19 (22), jaroslava V/SS; 119 (23), Justin Ford/GI; 119 (24), gudkov andrey/AS; 119 (25), Tierfotoagentur/ASP; 120 (1), dotted zebra/ASP; 120 (2), Christophe Courteau/NPL; 120 (3), Cathy Keifer/SS; 121 (5), Frans Lanting/NGIC; 121 (10), Colin Marshall/Newscom; 121 (13), Steve Trewhella/FLPA/MP; 121 (14), Milena/SS; 121 (15), Heavitree City Vet/SWNS; 122-123, Yellow Cat/SS; 122 (5), Rene Martin/SS; 122 (19), Warpaint/SS; 123 (53), Papik/SS; 123 (69), Ultrashock/SS; 124-125, Ricky kuo/SS; 124 (8), bankrx/AS; 125 (16), jscalev/AS; 125 (27), Artush/SS; 126, Sascha Burkard/SS; 127, vnlit/AS; 128 (4), Kuznetsov Alexey/SS; 128 (13), Susan Schmitz/SS; 128 (18), Matt Jeppson/SS; 129 (22), mbrand85/SS; 129 (30), dwi putra stock/SS; 129 (32), Eric Isselée/SS; 129 (33), Lucas Bustamante/NPL; 129 (48), Grigor Atanasor/DR; 130 (1), marchello74/AS; 130 (2), All Canada Photos/ASP; 130 (3), marchello74/AS; 131 (5), Jonathan Ross/AS; 131 (10), ptashkan/AS; 131 (13), axily/IS/GI; 131 (14), adamkaz/E+/GI; 131 (15), suerob/AS; 132 (1), Eric Isselée/DR; 132 (5), Chaithanya/AS; 132 (6), JAG Images/AS; 132 (8), wacpan/SS; 132 (9), Eric Isselée/SS; 132 (9), Ariadne Van Zandbergen/ASP; 132 (10), Wlad74/SS; 132 (11), Erni/AS; 133 (12), Jesus/AS; 133 (13), Michael Bogner/AS; 133 (13), pixelrobot/AS; 133 (13), xpixel/SS; 133 (14), Eric Isselée/AS; 133 (16), dennisjacobsen/AS; 133 (18), Vladimir Wrangel/AS; 133 (19), Richard Seeley/SS; 133 (20), Eric Isselée/AS; 133 (24), Nerthuz/SS; 134-135, Westend61/GI; 135 (47), Grigorita Ko/SS; 135 (53), Valentina_S/SS; 135 (62), Eric Isselée/SS; 136-137, Phillip Colla/Blue Planet Archive; 136 (7), vaclav/AS; 136 (8), GlobalP/IS/GI; 136 (17), Papilio/ASP; 137 (26), agefotostock/ASP; 137 (31), Keith Szafranski/IS/GI; 138 (UP), Eric Isselée/SS; 138 (CTR), Chansom Pantip/SS; 138 (LO), Ana Vasileva/SS; 139, Natalia/AS; 140-141, Maggy Meyer/SS; 140 (1), Andre Anita/IS/SS; 140 (10), Eric Isselée/SS; 141 (15), Benjamin Robert Mitchell/SS; 141 (16), Maggy Meyer/IS/GI; 141 (24), Pete Walentin/imageBROKER RF/GI; 141 (26), East Village Images/SS; 141 (29), Papa Bravo/AS; 141 (34), buellom/AS; 142 (1), Ozja/SS; 142 (11), Digitalstormcinema/DR; 142 (12), Ozja/SS; 142 (14), Mark Carwardine/NPL; 143 (20), © National Geographic Partners, LLC; 143 (24), Eduard Kyslynskyy/SS; 143 (32), Dirk Wiersma/Science Source; 143 (34), Jaime Chirinos/Science Source; 143 (50), Ryan M. Bolton/ASP; 144 (1), BBC Natural History/GI; 144 (2), Grant Thomas/IS/GI; 144 (3), Sinhyu/IS/GI; 145 (5), R. Andrew Odum/Photodisc/GI; 145 (10), Wildestanimal/Moment RF/GI; 145 (13), Tomasz/AS; 145 (14), Tom McHugh/Science Source; 145 (15), Liquid Production/SS; 146 (2), Jared Lloyd Photography/Moment RF/GI; 146 (3), Jean Kobben/AS; 146 (4), David Kjaer/NPL; 146, Freder/IS/GI; 146 (5), Tom Pennington/GI; 146 (5), Chris & Monique Fallows/NPL; 146 (6), Konrad Wothe/NPL; 146 (7), DR; 147 (10), birdiegal/AS; 147 (11), Kandfoto/IS/GI; 147 (14), shocky/AS; 147 (15), Igor Stramyk/DR; 147 (16), Buddy/AS; 147 (19), Dieter Meyrl/IS/GI; 147 (21), ymgerman/AS; 147 (22), Anand Varma/NGIC; 147 (23), mgkuijpers/AS; 147 (25), Alan Murphy/BIA/MP; 148-149, Richard Whitcombe/AS; 149 (67), Svetlana Foote/SS; 149 (62), Steffen Foerster/SS; 150 (2), master1305/AS; 150 (7), Nick Upton/NPL; 150 (10), cynoclub/SS; 151 (18), Cyril Ruoso/NPL; 151 (24), Slobodan Kunevski/SS; 151 (27), lancesagar/AS; 151 (29), Alexander/AS; 151 (33), Eric Isselée/AS; 152, Eric Isselée/IS/GI; 153 (UP), mgkuijpers/AS; 153 (LO), Paul/AS; 154-155, Kertu/AS; 154 (2), Anolis01/IS/GI; 154 (19), Konart/DR; 154 (22), fruttipics/IS/GI; 154 (26), Eric Isselée/AS; 155 (35), Stefan Scharf/SS; 156 (2), Ed Reschke/Stone RF/GI; 156 (3), Eugene Sim/AS; 156 (4), Andrew Hutchings/SS; 156 (5), Joel Sartore/NGIC; 156 (6), Ivan Kmit/AS; 156 (7), Nick Caloyianis/NGIC; 156 (8), Eric Isselée/AS; 157 (12), Jeff Stamer/AS; 157 (13), Pefcon/SS; 157 (17), Yatra/SS; 157 (18), Laura/AS; 157 (20), reptiles4all/SS; 157 (24), M-Production/AS; 157 (22), Rich Carey/SS; 157 (25), Aleksandar Dickov/SS; 158 (1), Smith Collection/Gado/GI; 158 (2), Agami/AS; 158 (3), Photofest; 159 (5), Fine Art Images/Bridgeman Images; 159 (10), Mark Reinstein/Corbis via GI; 159 (13), Sovfoto/Universal Images Group/SS; 159 (14), Manchester Daily Express/SSPL/GI; 159 (15), The White House; 160, Eric Isselée/AS; 161, Philippe/AS; 162-163, Daniel Kloe/IS/GI; 162 (1), Jim Cumming/SS; 162 (10), LiskaM/SS; 163 (16), passion4nature/IS/GI; 163 (17), Eric Isselée/SS; 163 (29), Steve Winter/NGIC; 163 (35), Javier Brosch/SS; 164 (LE), Dionisvera/AS; 164 (CTR), Sonsedska Yuliia/SS; 164 (RT), Eric Isselée/DR; 165, Stephen Mcsweeny/SS; 166-167, dionoanomalia/AS; 166 (9), panbazil/SS; 166 (10), DoraZett/AS; 166 (11), Lloyd Luecke/DR; 166 (15), Leonardo Castro/AS; 166 (19), Rolf Kopfle/AS; 167 (32), Juan Carlos Munoz/AS; 167 (39), Oeyvind/AS; 167 (47), Naoki Nishio/SS; 168 (1), Hislightrq/AS; 168 (3), Peter/AS; 168 (5), crisod/AS; 168 (6), Patryk Kosmider/AS; 168 (6), anankkml/AS; 168 (7), John A. Anderson/SS; 168 (10), Alexey/AS; 168 (11), Richard Carey/AS; 169 (12), FishTales/IS/GI; 169 (13), Jim Cumming/SS; 169 (14), Oksana Golubeva/SS; 169 (15), Liz Leyden/GI; 169 (16), charlie davidson/SS; 169 (17), Aaron Amat/SS; 169 (20), Emanuele Biggi/NPL; 169 (21), Carlos Grillo/AS; 169 (22), Robbie Ross/AS; 170 (1), tilialucida/AS; 170 (2), Steve Oehlenschla/SS; 170 (3), Thomas P. Peschak/NGIC; 171 (5), Shattil & Rozinski/NPL; 171 (10), Sean Pavone/AS; 171 (13), Peter Scoones/NPL; 171, (14) jgolby/AS; 171 (15), L. Sullivan/USFWS; 172-173, KK Stock/SS; 172 (6), Valentyna Chukhlyebova/SS; 172 (25), Nynke/AS; 173 (52), morelia1983/AS; 174-175, Ignacio Yufera/BP; 174 (6), Ignacio Yufera/BP; 174 (9), kostiuchenko/AS; 175 (15), Daniel Heuclin/NPL; 175 (14), Jason Hahn/AS; 175 (25), Bernatskaya Oxana/SS; 175 (26), Bob Langrish/FLPA/MP; 175 (31), Mauricio/AS; 175 (33), esdeem/SS; 176-177, Mikephotos2/DR; 177, wildestanimal/SS; 178-179, Martin Pelanek/SS; 178 (2), Farinoza/AS; 178 (18), Milan/AS; 179 (29), Beth Ruggiero-York/SS; 179 (47), Karine Aigner/NPL; 180 (2), Jim Greenfield/Image Quest Marine; 180 (3), Imagebroker/ASP; 180 (4), Eric Isselée/AS; 180 (5), Eric Isselée/DR; 180 (6), Holger T.K./AS; 180 (6), Johan/AS; 180 (7), izanbar/IS/GI; 180 (8), Andrey Nekrasov/Image Quest Marine; 180 (9), Stephen Meese/AS; 181 (12), mauritius images GmbH/ASP; 181 (14), Lenkadan/SS; 181 (16), Oliver Thompson-Holmes/ASP; 181 (15), Science History Images/ASP; 181 (18), NOAA/ASP; 181, cynoclub/AS; 181 (19), kyslynskyy/AS; 181 (20), Michael and Patricia Fogden/MP; 181 (21), photomaster/SS; 181 (25), Brett/AS; 182 (1), John McDonnell/The Washington Post via GI; 182 (2), Charles Krupa/AP Photo; 182 (3), Albert Pena/CSM/SS; 183 (5), photoncatcher36/AS; 183 (10), Len Redkoles/NHLI via GI; 183 (13), Tyler/AS; 183 (15), Ross D. Franklin, File/AP Photo; 184-185, Natures Momentsuk/SS; 184, Diego Cottino/SS; 186-187, Fernando Frazão/AS; 186 (6), Lamzin Vladimir/AS; 186 (13), Igor Dmitriev/AS; 186 (14), longtaildog/IS/GI; 186 (butterflies), thawats/AS; 186 (CTR), irin-k/SS; 187 (butterflies), thawats/AS; 187 (24), Krish/AS; 187 (26), BlueOrange Studio/AS; 188, GlobalP/IS/GI; 189, Scott E Read/SS; 190-191, nattanan726/SS; 190 (2), dblumenberg/AS; 190 (11), aussieanouk/AS; 190 (14), Dmitry/AS; 190 (20), Eric Isselée/AS; 190 (22), FotoCorn/AS; 191 (34), Mickeyd600/DR; 191 (36), seewhatmitchsee/SS; 191 (37), asbtkb/AS; 191 (46), imagenavi/AS; 192 (4), byrdyak/AS; 192 (5), Morley Read/DR; 192 (6), Milan/AS; 192 (7), Michelle Gilders/ASP; 192 (8), Anneke/AS; 192 (10), ondrej prosicky/AS; 192 (12), Cathy Keifer/AS; 193 (14), ArtushFoto/AS; 193 (15), Jason Patrick Ross/SS; 193 (16), Mark Bowler/NPL; 193 (19), Trueog/IS/GI; 193, reptiles4all/SS; 193 (21), Mehmet Karaca/AS; 193 (21), Stu Porter/AS; 193 (22), Cheattha/AS; 193 (23), Jim Cumming/SS; 193 (25), Lee/AS; 194-195, Kevin Schafer/Moment Mobile RF/GI; 194, Anan Kaewkhammul/SS; 196, Dimijan/SS; 196-197, Inna/AS; 196 (2), Ra'id Khalil/SS; 196 (4), Farinoza/AS; 196 (12), Daniel Heuclin/BP; 197 (19), Yusran/IS/GI; 197 (20), Daniel Heuclin/BP; 197 (29), Steven Kovacs/Blue Planet Archive; 197 (30), Reinhard Dirscherl/The Image Bank RF/GI; 197 (31), Cigdem-Sean Cooper/ASP; 198 (2), Cavan Images/AS; 198 (3), dragon_fang/AS; 198 (4), Danut Vieru/SS; 198 (5), Michael Fiala Motor-Sports/AS; 198 (6), Rosa Jay/SS; 198 (7), vaclav/AS; 198 (8), All Canada Photos/ASP; 199 (9), ondreicka/AS; 199 (11), slowmotiongli/AS; 199 (15), KQ Ferris/AS; 199 (18), Poly Liss/SS; 199 (21), Michel Gunther/BP; 199 (23), PiLensPhoto/AS; 199 (25), Roberto Machado Noa/Moment RF/GI; 200-201, Jouko van der Kruijssen/Cultura RF/GI; 200 (3), Png Studio/ASP; 200 (11), DCrane Photography/AS; 200 (22), Doug Steakley/Photodisc/GI; 201 (36), Chase Dekker Wild-Life/Moment RF/GI; 201 (46), Olof Bergqvist/SS; 202-203, Stefan Christmann/NPL; 202 (5), Suzi Eszterhas/MP; 203 (13), Laurent Ballesta/NGIC; 203 (18), WildMedia/AS; 203 (24), Steve Gettle/MP; 203 (28), Kevin Schafer/MP; 203 (35), Dirk Ercken/SS; 204 (2), D.P. Wilson/FLPA/MP; 204 (3), Christin Lola/AS; 204 (4), Avalon/Picture Nature/ASP; 204 (6), Cathy Keifer/SS; 204 (butterflies), Lightspring/SS; 204 (caterpillar), Eric Isselée/SS; 204 (ant), Andrey Pavlov/SS; 204 (8), Gerald Robert Fischer/AS; 204 (8), ead72/AS; 204 (9), Eric Isselée/SS; 205 (12), Earyn McGee; 205 (13), GlobalP/IS/GI; 205 (13), Rudmer Zwerver/SS; 205 (14), zhang yongxin/AS; 205 (15), Eric Isselée/DR; 204 (10), aottorio/AS; 205 (17), lukjonis/AS; 205 (18), Steven Russell Smith Photos/DR; 205 (20), Kimpin/AS; 205 (22), David Shale/NPL; 205 (25), amit/AS; 206 (UP), besjunior/AS; 206 (LO), Solvin Zankl/NPL; 207, David Wrobel/Blue Planet Archive; 208 (4), eyeCatchLight/SS; 208 (18), 3Dalia/SS; 208 (3), Silvano Sarrocco/AS; 208 (16), rostovdriver/AS; 208 (7), ajakor/AS; 208-209, Johan Swanepoel/SS; 209 (27), David Osborn/SS; 209 (35), Eric Isselée/SS; 209 (36), anankkml/AS; 209 (41), Vahe/AS; 209 (45), Eric Isselée/SS; 209 (46), Sergiy Grek/IS/GI; 210-211, Christian Musat/SS; 210 (8), Theodore M. Davis Collection, Bequest of Theodore M. Davis, 1915/Metropolitan Museum of Art; 210 (beetles), irin-k/SS; 210 (ants), asharkyu/SS; 211 (11), Tammy Wolfe/ASP; 211 (15), vaclav/AS; 211 (18), Michael Webb/GI; 211 (28), Jan Hamrsky/NPL; 211 (27), Peeravit/SS; 211 (35), Eric Isselée/SS; 212 (1), John Anderson Photo/IS/GI; 212 (2), Nattawut/AS; 212 (3), heng huang/EyeEm/AS; 213 (5), NPD stock/AS; 213 (10), Felix Martinez/Moment RF/GI; 213 (13), Mike Potts/NPL; 213 (14), Enrico Della Pietra/SS; 213 (15), John Dorton/SS; 214, David Doubilet/NGIC; 215 (UP LE), Super Prin/SS; 215 (UP RT), krisana/AS; 215 (CTR LE), Miroslav Halama/SS; 215 (CTR), defun/AS; 215 (CTR RT), Anand Varma/NGIC; 215 (LO LE), Tsekhmister/SS; 215 (LO RT), Eric Isselée/SS; 217, sompreaw/SS; 218, Gudkov Andrey/AS; 219, Nancy Elwood-Naturesportal/Moment Open/GI; 220, Chase Dekker Wild-Life Images/Moment RF/GI; 221, Wlad74/SS; 222, Dorottya Mathe/SS; 223, slowmotiongli/AS; 224 (UP), Eric Isselée/SS; 224 (LO), Tsuguliev/SS

Boldface indicates illustrations.

221

»INDEX

Since 1888, the National Geographic Society has funded more than 14,000 research, conservation, education, and storytelling projects around the world. National Geographic Partners distributes a portion of the funds it receives from your purchase to National Geographic Society to support programs including the conservation of animals and their habitats. To learn more, visit natgeo.com/info.

For more information, visit nationalgeographic.com, call 1-877-873-6846, or write to the following address:

National Geographic Partners, LLC
1145 17th Street NW
Washington, DC 20036-4688 U.S.A.

For librarians and teachers: nationalgeographic.com/books/librarians-and-educators

More for kids from National Geographic: natgeokids.com

National Geographic Kids magazine inspires children to explore their world with fun yet educational articles on animals, science, nature, and more. Using fresh storytelling and amazing photography, *Nat Geo Kids* shows kids ages 6 to 14 the fascinating truth about the world—and why they should care. **natgeo.com/subscribe**

For rights or permissions inquiries, please contact National Geographic Books Subsidiary Rights: bookrights@natgeo.com

Designed by Amanda Larsen, Julide Dengel, Anne LeongSon, and Gus Tello

Library of Congress Cataloging-in-Publication Data

Title: 5,000 awesome facts about animals.
Other titles: Five thousand awesome facts about animals
Description: Washington, D.C. : National Geographic, 2022. I Series: 5,000 awesome facts I Includes index. I
   Audience: Ages 8-12 I Audience: Grades 4-6
Identifiers: LCCN 2021019634 I ISBN 9781426372612 (hardcover) I ISBN 9781426372629 (library binding)
Subjects: LCSH: Animals--Juvenile literature.
Classification: LCC QL49 .A1598 2022 I DDC 590--dc23
LC record available at https://lccn.loc.gov/2021019634

The publisher would like to thank Julie Beer, author and researcher; Stephanie Warren Drimmer, author and researcher; Michelle Harris, author and researcher; Ariane Szu-Tu, project editor; Grace Hill Smith, project manager; Lori Epstein, photo editor; Eva Absher-Schantz, director, art & design; Amanda Rock, fact-checker; Joan Gossett, senior manager, managing editorial; and Anne LeongSon and Gus Tello, associate designers.

Printed in the United States of America
23/VP-PCML/2